MISTI B.

Forgive Us Our Debts, Please!

*Daily Humor for Debtors,
Compulsive Spenders and Underearners*

For information about this title or to order additional books and/or electronic media, contact the publisher:

LightStepper
17403 Chase St.
Northridge, CA 91325
www.lightstepper.com
email: misti@lightstepper.com

Publisher's Cataloging-in-Publication data
B., Misti.

Forgive us our debts, please! Daily humor for debtors, compulsive spenders and underearners/ Misti B.

Print ISBN: 978-0-9903560-2-8
eBook ISBN: 978-0-9903560-2-7

Printed in the United States of America
Cover design by TSG

God, grant me the serenity
To accept the things I cannot change,
Courage to change the things I can,
And wisdom to know the difference.

ACKNOWLEDGMENTS

It's impossible to thank everyone who contributed to the evolution of this book. I've heard heartbreaking stories of people living in fear about money, and I've watched those same people become healthy, spiritually centered, and prosperous due to the program and fellowship of Debtors Anonymous.

This book is for the people who've inspired and continually offered me direction and kindness (thanks, Ben); for those who've taken my many phone calls, and given me hope. Thanks to my friends and family who have loved and cared for me on this journey. And thank you, God, for finally getting through to me. It's really not about the money.

Misti B.

INTRODUCTION:

I'd spent tens of thousands of dollars on seminars and financial planners, and read almost every book on the market about money. If a CD, manual, or guide had the word "secret," "millionaire," or "financial freedom" in the title, I'd buy it. I figured I'd Do What You Love and the Money Would Follow, and, with enough work, I could become *The Millionaire Down The Street*. I tried to *Get Rich Quickly*, and when that didn't work, I attempted to *Get Rich Slowly*. I focused on *Thinking and Growing Rich*, and studied *The Rich Dad & The Poor Dad*. I read everything written by that perky blond financial guru with the Midwestern accent, and anything else Oprah recommended.

None of them worked for me.

Like many debtors, no matter how much money or how many possessions I had, I lived with constant anxiety and the feeling that there "wasn't enough." I figured my problems would be gone if I could just land a chunk of cash, a higher-paying job, or a better investment strategy.

I went to my first Debtors Anonymous meeting in the late '90s. I was so freaked out, I never went back. I wanted to blame the situation on bad luck and a rotten economy. But when I found myself in 2009 in debt and broke again, sitting in a room with five other debtors – all strangers to me – I knew I was in the right place. After a few meetings, it became clear I had a problem no book, plan, or investment strategy would resolve.

I needed a spiritual solution.

I started working the Steps and the Tools of DA, because it wasn't enough for me to merely understand *why* I debted. I needed to learn *how* to handle *life* differently. While there are people for whom a management plan works, debtors like me require a spiritual approach to financial problems.

Several years into recovery, I noticed that while I was going to meetings, being of service, and working the Twelve Steps, something was missing: I hadn't been laughing very much. So, I started writing my humorous observations about my experiences in recovery.

I know, being in debt is not not funny, especially when you feel your only options are going to a DA meeting or offing yourself in a parking lot (see: January 11th entry). No matter how down and out you may be, I believe humor can help you recover from debt, compulsive spending and underearning.

Forgive Us Our Debts, Please! contains daily meditations based on my observations about life in recovery. I don't represent DA; I'm just a member who believes laughter helps people heal. No matter how bad your situation is, if you're struggling with money, you could probably use a few laughs.

I'll admit, I wonder: *will debtors buy a meditation book?* Can they even afford it? And, if they can, will they spend their money on a book as opposed to, say, a pair of designer shoes or a new BMW? I don't know. What I do know is that if you hate this book—I don't think you will—I'll refund your money. Or, perhaps instead of a refund, would you consider giving the book to someone who finds it useful? Frankly, I'm a debtor. It's not like I have stacks of cash lying around for book returns.

If, on the other hand, you find joy, inspiration or relief from these meditations, please feel free to let me know: misti@mistibwrites.com.

January 1

FANTASYLAND

Before I found Debtors Anonymous, my New Year's fantasy revolved around meeting a very, very rich widower in his nineties.

It's not like I wanted to do anything inappropriate. I was broke, not crazy.

My dream was that said generous widower, in exchange for my lively conversational skills, would offer relief from my mounting debts with a cash infusion. Or at least include me in his will.

I figured, *What the heck, I'm kind of fun and old people need company. Besides, I like some of the things old people like: playing bingo, watching* I Love Lucy *reruns, and visiting the gastroenterologist. I, too, have the tendency to be cranky, and I don't mind screaming at people to get off my lawn.*

My fellows in DA told me no one was going to rescue me from my money woes. They told me the solution to my money problems could, however, be resolved by trusting in a Higher Power, not some rich nonagenarian. I hated hearing the part about not being rescued, because finding a rich widower seemed much easier, but I kept going to meetings and eventually I began to understand. Hoping someone else would take care of me or solve my financial problems was selfish and irresponsible.

Part of my recovery from debting was coming to believe I wasn't inept. In truth, I was highly capable and able to take care of myself. I just didn't want to.

Slowly by slowly (my version of slowly but surely), I learned to take the next indicated Step–no matter how hard it was–and trust that a Power greater than myself was going to see me through things.

Letting go of my "rescue fantasies" of being saved by some rich, old widower was ultimately a relief, especially because I'm not really good at bingo and I don't like taking afternoon naps. And truth be told, I don't enjoy going to the gastroenterologist that much.

It's Not About The Money:

Today I'll trust my Higher Power for help. I don't need to be rescued.

January 2

WEALTHY RELATIONS

"The key indicator for wealth is relationships. Ask yourself: How many people do I know, and how much ransom money could I get for each one?"

– Jarod Kintz

This sums up most of my relationships before Debtors Anonymous. I know, I know, I sound like a total jerk, but it's the truth. Before I found DA, I had plenty of hidden agendas, especially when it came to my friends and career.

My first thought when meeting someone new was, *What can they do for me? Who do they know?* Are they well connected? I wasn't terribly obvious about my agenda, but beneath the surface was the subtext, *How can I benefit from this relationship?* As a result, many of my friends were a lot like me. So, when I lost everything and stopped being "fun" or able to help them in some way, many of my "friends" were gone. Vanished.

DA taught me the real values of relationships are kindness, consistency and loyalty, not what other people can do for me or my career.

Today, I try to love and be of service to my friends, and I no longer value them based upon what they can "do" for me. I have a Higher Power who takes care of me so I don't have to worry about connecting with the "right" people in order to gain success or fame, or ... whatever.

I know, I know, now I sound like a total saint, but I'm not. There are times when the whole ransom thing really appeals to me. But that's usually only when I consider my family members, because they can be pretty annoying. And sometimes I'd prefer to have the cash.

It's Not About The Money:

My value has nothing to do with a number.

January 3

SHORTCUTS

The first DA meeting I attended was a big disappointment. There wasn't much of a discussion going on, and there were no financial planners offering stock tips or advice on how to increase my credit scores.

I wasn't able to "cross talk," as they called it. I didn't get to jump in and ask questions or make comments, which I was dying to do, because I wanted to tell the woman crying about her fifty-thousand-dollar credit card debt that her watch alone was worth at least a good six months of my rent, and if she'd just sell that, she'd have half of her debt paid off. Duh!

I didn't really plan on going back to that meeting, because when it was my turn to share and I told everyone I'd been unemployed for a year, not one person offered me a job lead. I'd just wasted an hour and a half sitting in a folding chair in some cold church basement and I didn't even get one stock tip? Not even a latte or a croissant?

But I was desperate for answers so I kept going back. I finally began to understand why DA doesn't offer financial or real estate advice, or ideas on How to Make Money at Home in Three Easy Steps!

There are no shortcuts. DA is a spiritual program.

The answers come, sometimes quickly, sometimes slowly. Mostly slowly. But the results are rich: a connection to a loving Higher Power and a reprieve from the "dis-ease" of debting.

And while I'm fine with never having gotten a stock tip at a meeting, I'll admit, I wouldn't mind a free latte or a chocolate croissant.

It's Not About The Money:

No shortcuts, no lattes. Just a sweet connection with a Higher Power.

January 4

POINTS

I had few expectations when I came to Debtors Anonymous. All I really wanted from life was to be safe, rich, happy, and entertained twenty-four hours a day. And thin.

"Your comfort and security is not the point or the purpose of the DA Program," said my sponsor the other day.

"Umm, okay. Then what is the point?"

"The purpose of DA is to maintain solvency, and to find sanity and peace around money by practicing a spiritual Program and the Twelve Steps. And to be of service to others."

"Wow, that sounds like a boatload of fun," I barked, "but I'd rather have a house on the beach, a nice job, and money stockpiled in an IRA. If I had some financial security, I'd be of service to others."

"Oh, really? That's all it takes for you?"

"Yes. I'd even start my own charity. I'd travel the world, giving talksab-out clean water and stuff like that, or saving the huskies from being forced to run in those stupid sled races–"

"Keep coming back," he said as he hugged me and walked away.

I thought his response was a little curt, and it showed how much he needed to learn about me. I mean, I may be shallow but *I am* charitable. When was the last time you heard of anyone trying to save a husky from the freezing cold and demanding sled racers?

I'm sure my sponsor will come around, once he sees how deep my commitment to service really is.

It's Not About The Money:

Recovery has nothing to do with money or security.

January 5

PLANS

I'd never imagined myself living long enough to need a long-term life plan. It's not like I was really suicidal, I just never considered my future in a financial-ish way. I had a hard enough time handling the present. When you're in a lot of debt, and you're ordering from the dollar menu at Taco Bell for dinner every night, the future isn't tremendously exciting.

I'd gone through phases of earning and saving a lot of money but I just couldn't hold on to it for very long. Whenever I'd get a chunk of cash saved up, something would happen and I'd be forced to spend it. So, why bother planning?

When I got into DA and heard people talk about long-term savings, I would go dim. I couldn't even *contemplate* the future; it was enough for me to keep from debting and save a little –sometimes pennies –one day at a time.

Now that I look back on it, DA sort of tricked me into long-term planning by having me keep my focus on the short term. Because the short term eventually becomes the long term, and when you don't debt and you save, even if only a little, you end up having a financial plan for the future.

I still think about long-term planning and savings in that way–a little bit at a time, one day at a time. Because if I think too far ahead, I'll start freaking myself out.

I may start a mutual fund for debtors. If I do, I think I'll call it Short-Term Planning for the Long Term, although I'm not sure "long term" will appeal to debtors. Maybe I'll just start a mutual fund for debtors and not even tell them about it.

It's Not About The Money:

God, help me remember I don't have to scare myself about the future.

January 6

THROWING MONEY

I've always wanted to have enough money to throw at my problems. You know, that insane kind of money allows you to do whatever you want, whenever you want? Money that says, *Have my private jet ready in fifteen minutes, and tell William and Kate I'll be at the castle by sundown!*

I'd like to tell you I want that kind of crazy money so I can help save the polar ice caps, or start a group like the Concerned Citizens for Something or Other, but the truth is, I want the money for me, myself, and I. I'm a debtor, and my mind tells me that having more money will solve my problems and guarantees me a trouble-free life.

While there are many problems that money can solve, my reasons for debting have little to do with money. They come from a spiritual hunger that money can never fulfill. It's a craving for love and safety, which only come as a result of a relationship with a Higher Power.

DA has taught me to focus on a spiritual solution when it comes to my debting problems. And, while I don't (mostly) get what I want, I always get *exactly* what I need.

I'll admit, I wouldn't mind having a few problems to throw crazy money at, because it would be kind of fun. In the meantime, I'll keep handing my problems over to God, because the probability of them working out are *way* better than throwing imaginary money at them.

It's Not About The Money:

I don't have any problems that God can't solve.

January 7

BANK LOVE

Up until a few years ago, I despised banks. In fact, I'd routinely get into sparring matches with tellers when I had to go inside for any reason other than making a deposit or withdrawal.

I was so angry at them. Why did they think it was okay to charge me to hold my money–granted it was rarely more than a hundred dollars at any point in time–but that was beside the point. They were using my money and loaning it to other people and charging us both! They also had the audacity to charge me fees when my checks didn't clear!

When I worked the Twelve Steps in DA, I began to see that the banks weren't the problem. I was my problem. And I wasn't so angry with my bank as I was at myself, because I didn't know how to manage my money. I was resentful because I didn't have the life I wanted. That's a lot of baggage to dump on banks, even for one whose insignia is a stage

!

It's not like I love banks these days, but my perspective has changed.

Banks provide a service that I value–though I'd value it much more if the fees were lower. But when I'm keeping track of my spending and reconciling my accounts, I see the bank as a partner in my recovery. Okay, partner might be pushing it a bit, but at least I don't see banks as evil anymore.

The best part is that since I began working the Tools of DA, I no longer bounce checks, so aside from bad service or unnecessary rudeness, I rarely have reason to get into fights with tellers. You know what I love most about banks? I don't have to pay them overdraft fees anymore!

It's Not About The Money:

I'll do what I can to manage my accounts, so there's no need to yell at bank tellers.

January 8

WIMPY

"I will gladly pay you Tuesday for a hamburger today." – Wimpy

There are those who believe that Wimpy, the portly character from the Popeye cartoons, was just a manipulative crook who took advantage of his friends. They claim that Wimpy never planned on paying Popeye back when he borrowed money from him for a hamburger. And then there are those–most of whom happen to be debtors–who think Wimpy wanted to follow through on his promise to pay, but he just didn't get the how-to part.

The debate continues to rage on.

Was Wimpy being honest when he promised to pay Popeye back, or was he a lying cheat looking for a free lunch? Unfortunately we'll never know the truth, because rumor has it Wimpy died tragically in 2006 from injuries sustained in an accident.

According to the rumor, Wimpy approached a hot dog cart vendor on a crowded New York City street and said, "I'll gladly pay you Tuesday for a hot dog today."

"Whaddaya take me for, a stool pigeon or somethin'?" the vendor screamed before rolling the hot dog cart over Wimpy and flattening him like a pancake.

Wimpy never learned that chronic debting leads to a lot of pain and can have disastrous results. If only Wimpy had known how empowering it is to take care of yourself instead of leeching off other people.

Poor Wimpy didn't have the benefit of Debtors Anonymous. The irony is, police found a stack of five-dollar bills in Wimpy's wallet as they peeled him off the street and carried him away.

It's Not About The Money:

I will gladly pay today what needs to be paid today.

January 9

PRISONS

In Victorian England, debting was considered so bad it was worthy of jail time. In fact, debtors' prisons were created for people who simply owed a lot of money and the Brits often put hardened criminals and murderers in cells with debtors. Many Colonial American cities created debtors' prisons using the same model as those in Great Britain.

Luckily, in 1830, someone in the US government realized it might be hard to get money from a deadbeat if said deadbeat was rotting in jail, so the debtors' prisons were declared illegal. And, while I've never been to jail–though I did spend two hours in a holding tank for arguing with an LAPD officer over an old parking ticket I'd forgotten about–I do know what it feels like to be emotionally imprisoned because of debt. It's like having a pair of stainless steel handcuffs slapped on you and being tossed into a jail cell with a gaggle of death-row inmates. Minus the handcuffs, the inmates and the other stuff that go with jail time. So, in that sense, emotional imprisonment is totally and utterly unlike real prison, but that's not the point I'm making.

The point is: debting, compulsive spending, and underearning can bring a person down.

When I came into Debtors Anonymous, I was in bondage, certain I'd never see the light of day. All I could do was not debt, one day at a time. I couldn't even think about a future free from financial fear and anxiety. As I began to trust in a Higher Power and work the Twelve Steps, my outlook started to change. I learned that while I wasn't a bad person, my attitudes and behaviors would definitely require consistent, significant change.

I'm so happy that debtors' prisons no longer exist because, no doubt, I would've ended up in one, and I don't think I'd do well in prison. Especially if I was forced to share a cell with a serial killer, or someone with really bad hygiene.

It's Not About The Money:

Thanks, God, because I'm no longer imprisoned by debt.

January 10

BULLS 'N' BEARS

I woke suddenly at 3:30 this morning, panicked about my finances. I had enough cash saved to get me through a year, but for some reason, this morning, it just wasn't enough.

If I don't do something fast, I'll lose everything and end up on the streets. I'll be forced to forage for meals from the garbage can of that pizza joint down the street... and die from gluten poisoning.

So I powered up my computer and decided to become a day trader. Never mind that I can barely distinguish a bull from a bear and have no idea how the NASDAQ works.

In the predawn haze, I was certain I'd have to make money FAST, especially if I wanted to be able to buy a pound of bananas when they reach sixty bucks.

This is what happens when I'm consumed with fear. I forget I have a God and think I'm in charge of figuring everything out. Fear convinces me I must do something, NOW, like become a day trader (although I know nothing about stocks), or buy a coffee shop in Belize (even though I can't locate Central America on a map), or get an advanced degree (when I can't even afford dinner, much less pay off a fifty-thousand-dollar school loan).

After staring at stock charts until the sun came up, I turned off the computer and finally admitted I wasn't going to figure my life out at 6:30 in the morning. At least not this morning.

I got down on my knees and said the following prayer, "Hey God. it's me again. I keep thinking that money is the problem. Can you show me how to appreciate everything I have in this moment, and be okay with it?" I repeated that prayer over and over, throughout the day until I meant it. Which was, in my estimation, around 8:45 that evening.

It's Not About The Money:

I have all that I need, I want all that I have.

January 11

DREADS

"I only dread one day at a time." – Charlie Brown

For me, it was more like, "I only dread one second at a time," because when I hit bottom, I was in bad shape. I'd lost it all: my car, my job, my condo, my boyfriend. Some derelict had even stolen my bicycle! I had three part-time jobs, none of which paid enough for me to rent an apartment or a room in a house, so I couch-surfed for a year.

Desperation makes you willing to try something different, so when a friend suggested I go to ninety DA meetings in ninety days, I did it.

The first thirty days I could barely sit through an entire meeting without crying. I was in so much pain I wanted to throw myself off a ledge, and God did *not* seem to be the answer to my financial problems. After all, I was the one who'd ruined things, why would God bother to help *me?*

I know, this is starting to sound depressing, but stay with me. It gets better.

By day sixty I started feeling better, and by the time I made it to the ninetieth meeting, I started thinking I'd be okay. And while it was still a stretch for me to believe God was on my team, I no longer felt I was being punished. I began to discover a healthier, saner way to deal with my debt.

I no longer dreaded every second I was alive.

See? I didn't stick my head in an oven or kill myself, although I did plan on running a garden hose into the truck I'd borrowed from my cousin, but I didn't, because I didn't have a hose. And, when I got to the thrift store to buy a hose, I discovered a gorgeous, almost new Burberry coat! It was either the hose or the coat. No one in their right mind would pass up an almost new Burberry coat for ten dollars.

Because of DA, I no longer dread every moment of my life. In fact, I'm excited about the future. I've taken up scuba diving and golfing, and I've learned to fly a plane. I'm also two inches taller than I used to be. Just kidding. DA can't make you taller.

It's Not About The Money:

There's nothing to dread when I turn things over to God.

January 12

VOICES

"We admitted we were powerless over debt, that our lives had become unmanagable."
– DA Step #1

Early on in recovery–and later on as well–I thought my powerlessness would diminish in time. As in, after I'd done my "time" in DA, I'd be able to control my debting, overspending, and vagueness about money.

There's this voice in my head that whispers things like, *Someday, when you're recovered, you'll have it all figured out. You won't need meetings; you'll be able to manage your money without help from God or DA. You'll be rich without having to work for it, and you might be able to get out of paying taxes!*

Part of me wants that more than anything else–to avoid responsibility, and yet, still be in control. Of myself, other people, the nation, the industrial complex, and the European Union. Heck, I'd run the whole darn solar system if I could! In reality, I know zero about the world's economy, I barely passed astronomy in college, and when I look at the results of trying to manage life on my own, it's clear I shouldn't listen to that voice in my head.

Instead, I'll stop, pray, and remember that the voice is wrong about this particular issue. I might even say to the voice, *Hey, voice, thanks for sharing, but I don't agree with you.* I might have to tell the voice to shut the heck up! And I might have to use harsher language. With the voice, that is.

It's Not About The Money:

God, help me shut the front door on that voice.

January 13

REST OF YOUR LIFE

Despite what many people would like you to believe, today is not The First Day of the Rest of Your Life.

No, today is just One Day in the Entirety of Your Life, A Blip on the Radar of What Might Be a Very Long Life. So relax, everything's going to be okay. Your life is not predicated upon what you do, or don't do, today.

As a debtor, I relate to the anxiety around making each day "count." My hyperactive set-the-world-on-fire personality presupposes that doing everything in one day is the solution. I'm impatient, impulsive, and compulsive. I want to earn more, pay off my debts, improve myself, and reach for the stars. My natural disposition tells me it's important that I combine thinking with a lot of activity to achieve maximum results.

I *rarely* consider connecting to God as a way to get more accomplished, which is odd, because I've had days when I did nothing more than pray and wait, and I'll be darned if I didn't get exactly what I needed at that moment!

I can't do it all and shouldn't even try because there are times when my intensity repels the very thing I want. When I put God first and ask Him for guidance, life unfolds pretty nicely. And I get stuff done. Now, that's not to say I'm going to just sit around and wait for answers to show up on my doorstep, or anything. But, then again, I just might.

It's Not About The Money:

It's not The First Day of the Rest of Your Life. Easy does it.

January 14

QUASI-POWERLESS

"We admitted we were powerless over debt, that our lives had become unmanageable." – DA Step #1

I wouldn't call it complete powerlessness. It was what I would call "quasi-powerless." It's not like I had mountains of credit cards; I wasn't neck deep in debt with a loan shark. It wasn't anything a better job, a cash infusion, or a little financial planning wouldn't solve, or so I told myself.

When I came into DA, I wasn't willing to view my debting, underearning, and compulsive spending as a spiritual problem. Money was a problem. As in, the lack of it. Navel gazing and philosophizing about my "relationship with money" was not going to fix my busted bank account.

It took a while for it to sink in that debting wasn't just an "issue." It was a deep-rooted fear that I wasn't safe in the world, and despite my efforts to fix myself, the situation only got worse.

I had to admit I was totally powerless over my debting. There was nothing "quasi" about it. It was and is real. Until I began to turn my will over to a Higher Power, my life – when it came to debting – was unmanageable.

Today, I don't worry so much about knowing the outcome of the actions I take; I don't have to try to solve important financial problems with urgency, like I used to. I simply take the right actions, stay debt free one day at a time, and try to be of service to others ... and let God be in charge of the results. The best part is, when I do that, I feel utterly calm and totally in control. In the most non-controlling way possible, that is.

It's Not About The Money:

There is no such thing as "quasi-powerlessness."

January 15

I DUNNO

I'm not being arrogant when I say I'm an outstanding judge of what's best for me.

Knowing what's best for me is a skill that's served me well for most of my life–apart from the relationship with that dentist from Colorado, the one who stole millions from a Brite Smile office and asked me to marry him while he was engaged to someone else; or the realtor from Arizona with the house-flipping scheme who lied to me about his children, his ex-wife and his education. Those were definitely exceptions to the whole "I know what's best for me" rule. But aside from that, I had a pretty good grip on things.

Needless to say, I wasn't terribly open to other people's opinions about how I should fix my financial problems by the time I got into recovery. In fact, I recall saying to someone, "I've been running my life for some time. I don't need your input on how to screw things up further, thank you very much."

It took me a while in DA before I could see that I shouldn't always rely upon my own judgment. While I didn't quite "get it" that my problems were spiritual in nature, I did get that they were most likely the result of the stupid things I'd done.

So, maybe I don't know everything, I thought one night after months of going to DA meetings. *I know what movies I like, but maybe I don't know the big stuff, like what brings about long-lasting happiness or how to truly love other people. Maybe God has a better idea of what works. So, maybe I don't know everything, but I think I might be right about this whole DA thing working.*

While knowing what I like is nice, recovering from debting is much nicer. It's brought me deep contentment and joy, and that's something I thought would never happen. So, it could be that I really do know best. Or not. I'm willing to leave it at that for now.

It's Not About The Money:

I don't know what I don't know.

January 16

TIME BLUES

It can start out as benign as forgetting what I've had for dinner, or it can present itself as being consistently late for work or commitments. It can be as extreme and harmful as waking up one day, stuck in a dead-end job in a city I despise and having no idea where the past five years have gone.

While the last example sounds like a subtle form of dementia, it's not. It's time-debting and it's real. It's an active decision to deny the life I desire by ignoring, postponing, or not paying attention to time.

It's letting life go by without taking responsibility for the way I spend it. Time, like money, can be spent wisely, invested well, or frittered away.

I use a DA Tool called time recording to keep track of my hours throughout the day. I simply keep a notepad with me and at the top of each hour, I list what I'm doing or working on. It helps me get clarity about what I accomplish in a workday. Since I tend to have selective amnesia and rarely think I've done much, time recording allows me to see how I can redirect my efforts. Or give myself a break.

It sounds hard, and it is. But I do it anyway because it keeps me from going unconscious and wasting days away, or wanting to shoot myself for not achieving anything.

Why not give it a try yourself, today? At the top of each hour, jot down what you do on a piece of paper. Don't get all critical and judgy about it, just write down what you did, in a general sense. You might feel empowered and amazing. On the other hand, you might feel depressed. And that's okay, too, because at the very least you'll be aware and possibly enlightened about your behavior and where you might want to improve. C'mon, don'tcha wanna be enlightened? Yes, I thought you'd say that. Good job!

It's Not About The Money:

I'll keep track of my time today as best I can.

January 17

30 DAYS

"What if I do the Tools and the Twelve Steps and they don't work for me?" I asked my new DA sponsor at a meeting.

"Elaborate on that," he said.

"Well, what if this Steps-and-Tools stuff doesn't work, and I don't get a job and still end up alone and broke? What then?"

"Okay, I want you to start by calling me every day for thirty days and we'll see how it goes."

Wow, he's pretty dim, I thought. *Did this guy not hear anything I just said?*

I had nothing else to do so I called my new sponsor every day to check in. Each day it was the same thing.

"Nothing's happened. My life sucks," I'd say, before diving into a litany of complaints about how I would never get ahead or earn another dollar, and how I would rather be dead than broke and humiliated.

He'd listen patiently and say, "Why don't you ask your Higher Power for some help, then go to a meeting and call me again tomorrow?"

I did it, but it seemed pretty stupid and not at all what I wanted to do.

And then somehow, after about twenty-nine days, things started to change inside me. I was going to meetings, living out my miserable life, but I was feeling better. I was helping other people, volunteering, and taking commitments at the meetings I attended. I felt an – albeit small – glimmer of hope.

"So, is life a little better?" my sponsor asked me at the thirty-day mark.

"No. It still sucks," I lied. Life was better and I was even feeling connected to God, but I wasn't going to let my sponsor win.

"Okay, call me for another thirty days and we'll see how you feel then."

"You're on!" I said, thinking I still might be able to prove him wrong.

It's Not About The Money:

It's okay to admit things are getting better.

January 18

BEST LIFE

It was a new year and I was trying so hard. I'd just bought a book called *The Best Year of Your Life Ever* and I really wanted it to work.

I'd decided to give up my self-defeating behaviors, save money, and stop wasting my life in selfish, meaningless pursuits. I'd Live Today As If It Were My Last, and only Do Things That Mattered. I'd stop putting off for tomorrow what could be done today, and do it ASAP! I'd Stop Dreaming About the Future and Live the Life of My Dreams!

I read the first chapter of the book, along with the list of the things I was going to accomplish that year. Then I lost the book the next day. *Is this a sign that I'd never have the life of my dreams? That I'm destined to have the worst year of my life?*

When I came into DA, I put a moratorium on self-help books. What I discovered was that trying to control my year, my life, and my universe was a desire to control things over which I have no control. I can plan for the future but I can't know how things will turn out. I have to trust I can take the action and leave the results in God's hands.

I know how I'd like things to turn out. If I were in charge, I'd be living the it up in the Seachell Islands, while the rest of the world was, well, working for a living. See what I mean? I have a very immature idea about what the "life of my dreams" is and what's best for me, and it never includes heartbreak, loss, or pain.

Although I think I always know what's best for me, I don't. Which is why I'm glad I'm not God.

It's Not About The Money:
I'm glad God's in charge and not me.

January 19

PROTECTION

Debtors are sometimes like characters in those clichéd '80s TV cop shows. You know, the ones where a killer's on the loose and the police show up to offer extra protection to the person the serial killer might be targeting, but the person refuses their help?

"This is my home and I'm not running scared," the soon-to-be-victim stubbornly proclaims. *Yes, a serial killer's on the loose but I don't need any protection, thank you very much."*

Really? How about maybe letting the cops hang out until the killer passes through your neighborhood?

In the case of a debtor, the scene often goes something like this:

The debtor who's drowning in money and credit problems shows up at a DA meeting and a fellow DA member offers his or her phone number to the newcomer.

"I don't need the help of some group," the newcomer announces. "I can figure this money stuff out."

Really? How about telling someone–probably not a police officer but someone who cares about you–the truth about how your money worries keep you up at night? How about being willing to ask for some darned help?!

Like the know-it-all future victim in those cop shows, the debtor who refuses help is asking for trouble. The whole I-can-handle-things-by-myself attitude is what keeps us from getting better. Saying "no" to help from others is kind of dumb.

Now, you're reading this book, so you're probably willing to get help, which is a good thing. And you know what? It makes me feel better just knowing you're open to getting help!

You know what else makes me feel good? The fact that a police officer just moved into the condo next to mine. If he ever stops off at my door and wants to offer me protection, I'll take it. I'll take all the help I can get.

It's Not About The Money:

There's no crime in asking for help, especially if it's from God.

January 20

HOPE

"Where once we felt despair, we will experience a newfound hope."
– *DA Promise #1*

Hope is cool, I thought when I heard this promise in a meeting, *for some people.* But what *I need is an answer to my damn money problems, people, not a handful of hope!*

By the time I got to DA, the only thing I was hoping for was a roof over my head and groceries for the week. Hope, unless it came in the form of a voucher or a coupon that would cover my cell phone bill, was just some lofty ideal.

Hope is the expectation of something we desire, the belief in the possibility of it occurring. When I was at my financial bottom, hope was not an option. I was more comfortable riding the Dark Horse of Despair and I'd persuaded myself that hope wasn't an option for "people like me."

Because I was so broke I had nowhere else to go, I got involved in DA and did what the people I respected did. It took several years before I could even find enough faith to believe that God loved me and wanted to help me. And it took at least that long for me to feel truly hopeful about the future.

But when things started to shift, they really shifted. I came out of the haze of debting and had the desire to live again. Really live. I began to yearn for things I'd denied myself for a very long time. I began to write again. I began to dance and sing. I even began to speak fluently in languages I'd never even heard before.

That's not true. I don't speak in foreign languages, but I *will be soon,* because I'm planning a debt-free trip around the world next summer. This, my friends, is what hope can do for you.

It's Not About The Money:
Newfound hope is very cool.

January 21

PRG

I arrived at my first DA pressure relief group (PRG) with a huge stack of unpaid bills. I was in terror about what to do next. I had thirty dollars in my checking account and wasn't earning enough to cover my expenses, which were not extravagant.

"I've gone over the numbers again and again," I said, deflated. "Nothing you tell me is going to make it add up. I'm doomed."

Imagine my surprise when the man and woman I'd asked to do my PRG said, "Okay, let's pray."

Um, praying isn't going to help me at this point, folks, I thought, but I didn't say it because they were helping me for free. And they'd bought my coffee. I didn't want to talk about spiritual stuff, I didn't want to go over the thirty dollars in my account, I wanted answers!

They didn't give me answers. They helped me come up with a plan for paying off my debts, which, oddly enough, did not include eating cheese sandwiches so that I could pay my creditors back. It was a plan that began with putting self-care first. What I learned from that first PRG was that recovery from debting wasn't about paying off all my debts. It was about turning my will over to a Higher Power.

Little by little, things began to change. I put God first, did what was in front of me, and worked the Program of Debtors Anonymous. These days, my PRGs are not about just surviving but about pursuing new opportunities, and my dreams and visions. I no longer bristle when my PRG partners ask me to pray because I know prayer works. *How* it works, I haven't a clue, I just know that when I'm asked to do it, I do.

It's Not About The Money:

When I turn my will over to God, the numbers add up.

January 22

SERENE

I looked up the word "serene" today and it read: *clear and free of storms or unpleasant change. Marked by or suggestive of utter calm and unruffled repose of quietude.*

I would like to be serene. I would like to be calm and unruffled and I would love to be repose of quietude, although I'm not really sure what repose or quietude looks like.

I'm definitely calmer since I started working the Steps and Tools of the DA Program. All in all, I am much more serene than I have ever been. Is my life perfect? No. I still worry about my financial situation and struggle with feelings of "I'm not enough." But just because I struggle with doubt doesn't mean my life isn't good. Because of DA I'm able to handle whatever life presents without completely freaking out or running away. I don't attract–as many–crazy people or situations as I used to. For the most part, my life is free of storms and unpleasant change.

Today, when I start creating problems because it's familiar and comfortable, or when I start obsessing about money and all the things I'm missing out on, I stop, say a prayer and turn my worries over to my Higher Power. Then I reach out to people who can offer a spiritual perspective about my situation. A kind and gentle reminder that I am loved is often all I need.

I've discovered that, for the most part, I *am* calm and unruffled, and I *am* serene. So then, I guess I should get started on the repose and quietude stuff. If only I knew what they looked like.

It's Not About The Money:

What does serenity look like for you today?

January 23

ASSETS

In a 2013 survey, the New York Post reported that 42% of the millionaires interviewed said they didn't feel rich. Those interviewed said they would need liquid assets of at least seven million dollars to feel "truly wealthy."

Wow, what a bunch of greedy bastards, I thought. *If I had a million bucks, you wouldn't hear me complaining about anything ever again!*

I started to write down the costs of things I'd need in order to feel truly wealthy: a house on the upper east side of Manhattan, an Aston Martin, a closet filled with designer clothes and shoes, a second home–something unassuming–on Martha's Vineyard since being confined to the city would get to me after a while. A high-class gym and a private trainer, as well as membership at the country club, seemed pretty obvious.

A million dollars wasn't even close to enough.

What kind of a country do we live in, I thought, *when a girl can't even survive on a million bucks? When she can't dream of having a decent life because she doesn't have the requisite seven million in liquid assets? What is happening to this world? No wonder people are going crazy!*

As Sonny, one of the T-Birds in the movie Grease would say, "Somethin's gotta be wrong!"

I ran the numbers again. They didn't add up. There was no way on Earth I'd be able to have a decent life with a million dollars.

I called my sponsor. His response was, "There's never enough of *anything* when you're in a debting mindset."

"Well, I ran the numbers and I think I'm being fairly reasonable about my needs."

My sponsor suggested I go to a meeting and do something nice for someone else without telling anyone. I did both. Afterward I felt so genuinely happy and at peace, I practically forgot that a measly million dollars is nowhere close to being enough to live on these days.

It's Not About The Money:

Unless I bring God into it, the numbers never add up.

January 24

VAGUECATION

After I'd been earning consistently in DA for a while, I started to slack off. I stopped keeping track of my spending and started rounding things off. Tracking my numbers and reconciling my accounts went on the back burner.

I've been working my tuckus off, I thought. *I deserve a vaguecation!*

What began as a few days off from thinking about and keeping track of my finances turned into a few weeks, then…months. I couldn't figure out why, but I was experiencing a low-grade panic, and before long, I was living in a state of low-grade terror.

One morning I woke at four a.m. in a cold sweat. I had no clue how much money there was in my checking account, nor did I have any idea where I'd spent my money over the previous six months.

I decided right then and there that I simply could not afford to take another vaguecation.

When I take a break from my finances, I forget things, spend impulsively, and before you know it, I'm in overdraft land. The tension of not knowing where my money is going or how I'm handling it makes me irritable, restless, and discontent. And I feel completely disconnected from my Higher Power.

Even though it doesn't always feel that way, it's easier for me to consistently keep track of my numbers and my spending than it is to take a vaguecation. I am a high-strung, Type-A Personality and I've *never* been able to totally relax and have fun when I go on a long break.

I take that back. Vaguecations are great, but just like beating the neighborhood kids at Dodgeball and eating Almond Joys and pizza for breakfast, they can get old after a while.

It's Not About The Money:

Vaguecations aren't all they're cracked up to be.

January 25

REMARKABLE

Working a DA Program isn't stress free. It requires willingness and a commitment to rigorous honesty that many people don't have.

Really, who wants to admit to having screwed up their own life? Who wants to tell the truth about being a cheater and a manipulator, or to admit they're entitled, greedy, or that they loathe the government and banking institutions? See what I mean? Recovery requires us to be brutally honest and ask penetrating questions of ourselves.

And even after you've done the heavy lifting, worked the Twelve Steps, made your amends, and started to change your lying, cheating ways, there are new things to work on, like: paying bills on time, paying taxes, not incurring unsecured debt, and promising to doing things that don't include putting your own desires first.

Recovery is not cumulative. When I stop paying attention to details, when I start slacking off on the spiritual or the tangible aspects of my DA Program, I can feel a difference. My attitudes and actions around my earning, spending, and debting start to shift and I get slippery with my commitments.

The good news is that, even when I get behind on my numbers or miss a few meetings, I can begin again. It all starts with a prayer of surrender and an outreach call, or a meeting. If I seek it, serenity is never far away.

Yes, rigorous honesty is a lot of hard work but it's worth the effort.

So, give yourself a pat on the back right now and think about how utterly remarkable you are. At least, I think you are, and believe me, I don't toss that kind of praise around lightly!

It's Not About The Money:

Today, you're willing, and that's pretty remarkable.

January 26

SCARY

Sometimes I get scared I'll never have enough money. How much is enough? I don't know, and I probably never will.

When I get scared, I stop enjoying life. I get grumpy and stingy. I hoard money and kindness, and I withhold my love. I lose my zeal for life. I stomp around and demand things from people.

Fear makes me do stupid things.

The antidote is turning my fears and my will over to God and taking consistent actions that fly in the face of my uncertainty.

I know, that sounds tremendously unglamorous and not spectacular, but it's true. The only thing that works for me is to get up in the morning, turn my will over to God, and then take whatever action is required – which might just be making the bed or taking a shower. This is especially important when I'm certain life is pointless and I'll never accomplish anything or have enough money. So, I meditate and pray, keep my commitments, and try to be of service to others.

As a friend of mine likes to say, "Taking action is hard when you're in fear, but what else are you gonna do?"

Yes, there are still days when I'm scared, but if I take even the smallest step towards recovery, the fear eventually starts to pipe down. Which isn't to say I don't sometimes give fear a swift, gentle stomping. I guess that's why they call it a "practice."

It's Not About The Money:

The fear may or may not go away. God never leaves.

January 27

COLLECTOR

Today is Hug a Debt Collector Day. The objective is simple: Give a debt collector some positive attention within the next twenty-four hours.

You might consider taking a debt collector out to breakfast or, maybe for a cup of tea. If that's too much, perhaps you could just send an anonymous letter to the debt-collection department of some major bank and say, "I hope you debt collectors are having a lovely day!" It's not like you have to take them out to a movie, or go for a drive in the country together. Just be willing to offer an ounce or two of kindness.

Why, you ask?

Because debt collectors are human beings, and the fact you're behind on your credit card payments does not make them inherently bad. Sure, they badger you at all hours, day and night, and treat you as if you were the scourge of the earth, but let's face it, they're just doing their job and we debtors don't need to be so judgmental.

If you're feeling up to it and really want to celebrate your DA recovery, simply put your arms around the first debt collector you see and give them a big hug, or a firm handshake. You don't need to go crazy and promise to pay off all your debts at once. In fact, it's recommended that you refrain from touching *anyone* you're currently in negotiations with.

If all this is too much for you, you might consider hugging a lawyer instead. The important thing is that you practice giving kindness today in places and to people where no one else will. Or wants to.

As the DA slogan says: Let it begin with me.

It's Not About The Money:

Even debt collectors require a minimum of three hugs per day.

January 28

REMODEL

When I came into DA, I wanted to keep up appearances, to look like I had it "together," and that I was just checking things out. I made it clear that I wasn't planning on sticking around.

"You like those home makeover shows, don't you?" my new friend in DA asked me.

"Of course!" I said. "I love seeing those decrepit old houses turned into beautiful homes. My favorite part is when the TV crew shows up and there's a big red bow on the house. And I love it when the entire town gathers at the front door, and everyone's crying–"

"You're like one of those dilapidated houses," he said. "Your foundation is bad. You don't just need some fixing up, you need a complete rebuild."

"Uh, okay. Thanks, I guess?" I laughed, although I secretly wanted to kick him in the shins. I did not like hearing I needed any kind of fixing.

As time went on, I began to like the idea of equating my recovery to a home makeover. There's nothing more exciting than when the host shows up at the house and sends the family on a paid vacation while the construction crew does extensive repairs and renovations. It's thrilling to think about my life as an *Extreme Home Makeover* episode, because I imagine myself as a leaky, dilapidated bungalow no one wants and then, suddenly, I'm an eight-bedroom mansion–except in recovery, I'm the crew and I have to do most of the work. And I don't get sent away on a paid vacation.

There are times when I have to remind myself that ultimately, God is in charge of my reconstruction, and He can't renovate without moving a few things around. Sometimes from the ground up. Which is okay with me, because that simply means when things are finished, I'll might be getting a visit from my neighbors and a big red bow on my front door.

It's Not About The Money:

Things may have to be moved around a little today. It's okay.

January 29

MINTY

In a rare moment of hope, I decided to sign up for the free online personal finance services from that company with the icon shaped like a mint leaf. I was committed to getting my act together, putting my accounts in order, and tracking my budgeting goals.

For two years, I received the following updates:

Where your money went: Nowhere
What you saved: Nothing
Your budgets: You have none
Your goals: You have none
For your attention: Everything. Are you still there?

It got to the point where I'd get angry whenever I saw e-mails from that company, which only served to remind me what I wasn't doing, the trips I wouldn't be taking, and the goals I hadn't achieved. That fascist, know-it-all company was hell-bent on rubbing my lack of progress in my face.

I finally closed the account. It's one thing for a company to provide a free service, but it's another thing to taunt and humiliate customers. I can humiliate myself. I don't need anyone else's help.

It's Not About The Money:
Things are exactly as God would have them be today.

January 30

H.P. POWER

In Debtors Anonymous we are asked to be willing to turn our lives over to a Higher Power.

This throws a lot of people off, and for good reason. Many of us have had bad experiences with religion and feel disconnected from God. The beauty of the Program is that there's a place for anyone and everyone to believe what they want. We find our Higher Power in the right time.

In the beginning of recovery, I struggled with believing that God was looking out for me. I figured He was waiting for me to mess things up again so He could punish me. Ultimately, I came to believe in a God was there watching over me, wanting a relationship with me.

Today, my God and I are kind of tight, and I say that not in a braggadocios way. I say it because my journey from a Higher Power who was ready to pull the rug out from under me to a Higher Power who cares about me has taken a lot of time. But it's been worth it. Today God shows up for me in ways I would never have imagined, or recognized in the past.

The thing is, no one in DA cares what or who your Higher Power is. Some people consider their Higher Power the Program itself. Some people consider it the universe. You get to choose, although, if you're a debtor, I would caution you about making Santa Claus as your Higher Power, no matter how tempting it is.

Of course, I say that in jest. People don't confuse a Higher Power for some big white-haired guy whose only purpose is to reward them with nice, shiny things. Of course not.

It's Not About The Money:
I'm no longer playing God, and that's a good thing.

January 31

SELF-DEBTING

I showed up at the DA workshop on self-debting with a chip on my shoulder. I don't know what I was expecting, aside from a few hours of mystical gibberish about "loving the self," but I'd promised a friend I'd meet her there. She never showed.

I didn't like the looks of the people from the moment I entered the room. There were a lot of sequins combined with animal prints and crocheted sweaters. With sneakers. And that was just the men. I remember thinking, *No wonder these folks seem so depressed! Look at all the bad clothes and haircuts. If this is what self-debting looks like, I want out!*

I sat down anyway and quickly discovered that although I may have had enough sense to not combine feather earrings and clogs, I was *definitely* a self-debtor. A snotty, albeit well-dressed one.

As the workshop went on, I started to see my self-debting patterns: dismissing my own feelings, indecision, and a persistent fear of ending up homeless that was almost paralyzing. I didn't feel I deserved a good life, and so I didn't have one. I had no job, no savings, and no plan for my future. I didn't have a lot of debt, but I could only afford the basics. Self-debting runs deep, takes many forms, and isn't always obvious to outsiders.

"Self-debting is the inability to identify or fulfill our personal needs, and involves feelings of emotional indebtedness, stress, anxiety, and despair," the leader read aloud from a Debtors Anonymous pamphlet. "Self-debting can also mean taking drastic measures to hide evidence of problems with money or debt, including paying creditors to the detriment of one's own needs, or spending excessive amounts of time managing finances."

These were behaviors I'd struggled with my entire life, but never understood or had a vocabulary for. I always assumed I was a just little "off" when it came to money.

As I glanced around the workshop, I felt a little sad, but mostly humbled and truly hopeful. These were my people and I loved them. All of them. *Now, if I could just get my hands on their wardrobes,* I thought, *I'd be ecstatic.*

It's Not About The Money:

Taking care of myself frees me.

February 1

SAN-ISH?

"Came to believe that a power greater than themselves could and would restore us to sanity." – *DA Step #2*

Right, I thought to myself the first time I heard this at a DA meeting. *If I were insane (a word the teller at my bank once used when referring to me), then maybe this Step would be critical to recovery. In areas other than money, I tend to be reasonable and balanced. My debting never caused me to do anything majorly destructive so the whole "insanity" thing doesn't apply.*

It's not like a person can literally go insane over money.

Well, maybe some people do, but whatever. I mean, it's not like you can die from debting. Yes, people have killed other people because they owed money to the wrong people, but that's not relevant to this discussion.

I've never done anything illegal. Totally illegal.

And it isn't as if I can't stop spending or debting whenever I want to, on my own. I can. I'm sane enough to put that little black AmEx card back into my wallet. I could control my spending if I wanted to. I just don't want to. Yet.

If debting was affecting my job (what job?), or my quality of life (what quality?), then it would be different. But it's not.

Debting could be a problem, but it's nothing that paying the minimum on my Visa can't remedy. Once I get the minimum paid off, I'll feel much better. Then I can start looking for a great job doing what I love.

To say that debting is a "dis-ease" that requires the help of a Higher Power makes it sound so…out of control.

I'm not out of control.

I mean, it all depends on how you define the phrase "out of control."

It's Not About The Money:

At least *my* insanity is under control, *right?*

February 2

TRUST

In the 1990s, companies would send their employees off to corporate retreats. It was kind of like adult camp, where a group of employees would spend days trying to bond with their unlikable coworkers, or engage in pointless exercises like "trust falls," where one person falls into the arms of another who, hopefully, catch them. Then, they'd sit in circles and say nice things they didn't mean to colleagues they despised.

I've been to a few corporate retreats, and I never felt like I could suddenly trust my backstabbing coworkers just because we did a two-day scavenger hunt together. I've never been able to bond with anyone who works in human resources at *any* company, and I've always wondered what falling into the arms of a creepy systems engineer in an ice-cold hotel ballroom had to do with increasing trust or improving my job performance.

I love that Debtors Anonymous doesn't ask me to do meaningless exercises in order to force a false sense of intimacy with other people. No one expects me to trust them, the Program, or even a Higher Power until I'm ready.

Trust takes time.

I'm also glad that DA doesn't ask anyone to do trust falls, especially not at my home group meeting, because there are a few cranky old guys at that meeting. I'd bet dollars to donuts they wouldn't even try to catch me if I fell.

It's Not About The Money:

DA meetings are trust-fall-free zones.

February 3

BAFFLED

"Clarity will replace vagueness; we will intuitively know how to handle situations that used to baffle us." – *DA Promise #2*

Oh, how I used to love being vague about my numbers and my spending. I liken it to looking under the hood of my car–*why should I bother if no smoke was coming out?* This attitude, by the way, cost me two cars.

I alternated between believing there was some inexhaustible supply of money that had nothing to do with the results of working hard, and worrying I was a paycheck away from living on the streets.

Part of my vagueness came from not feeling I was competent enough to handle basic money skills. I was certain there was some financial handbook that had been distributed to everyone (e.g, *those damn rich people or those folks who had normal families*) except me. Things like taxes, insurance, savings, and planning for the future baffled me.

DA taught me the way out of vagueness starts with asking for help from my fellows when I felt it coming on. I continued to reach out for help until things made sense, or I feel clear about my spending, my earning and my numbers.

Know what continues to baffle me? Why I still refuse to look under the hood of my car, even when there's no smoke coming out.

It's Not About The Money:

What can I do to get out of vagueness today?

February 4

DIAGNOSIS

After I'd been in DA a while, I became more aware of my loved ones' spending habits. And because I had some recovery, I used that knowledge to judge–in a friendly way, of course–how they were handling their finances. Unfortunately, most of them were pretty dysfunctional when it came to money.

Because the principles of DA say debting is a self-diagnosed problem, I've decided against confronting anyone–so far. Instead, I'm passing on the list of questions for you to use for your own friends and family. Of course, DA would never approve of this list but as I like to say, "Judge away!"

1. Do your friends/loved ones give serious consideration to e-mails from Nigerian royalty that offer millions in exchange for their bank account information?
2. Do your friends/loved ones disappear for days at a time then reappear suddenly, showering you with lavish gifts, all paid for in cash?
3. Have your friends/loved ones ever threatened a bank executive?
4. Do your friends/loved ones take extra plates of food–and party favors–with them when they leave a party?

While answering yes to one of these questions *might* signal a problem, a yes to two or more of the above questions definitely points to a major problem. Of course, it is not advisable to announce your finding to said friends and family member. Just knowing you're right – as always – is enough, is it not?

It's Not About The Money:

I'm glad I no longer have to judge other people.

February 5

MIRACLES

Recently my sponsor suggested I keep a journal to keep track of all the miracles I've experienced since I started DA.

"I guess I'll need a few Post-its. I don't have much to write down."

He reminded me that when he first met me, I had sixty dollars in my bank account, no job, and no place to live. Within two years' time, I received a large inheritance I'd never seen coming. I'd gone from sixty bucks to a nest egg that I could survive on for years if necessary.

"Okay, so that's one," I relented. "One. Miracle." I jotted the number one on the palm of my hand. "But I don't want to rely on the inheritance because it'll be gone in a New York minute. And I still don't have a decent job."

He handed me the napkin from under his coffee cup. "What about your idea for the meditation book?"

"Yeah, but most debtors can't afford a meditation book!" I hissed. "I mean, sure, *you'll* buy one, but that will hardly pay my rent."

He reminded me that I'd recently landed several writing projects.

"Nothing full-time, though."

"You're right." He laughed. "There's no point in writing down the miracles. Nothing good ever happens to you. And I'm fairly sure nothing will work out.

"On second thought, don't even bother with Post-its. Save your money." He grabbed the napkin from my hand and shoved it in his pocket. "The inheritance is practically gone anyway." He paid his bill and left, shaking his head.

I don't know when he got to be so negative, my sponsor. Just to spite him, I decided to start keeping a journal with a list of all the miracles I've experienced since I started DA.

It's Not About The Money:

Today, I'll write down my miracles even if they only require a Post-it.

February 6

NIGHTMARES

I used to have a nightmare in which I had sixty jobs and was fired from half of them.

Actually, that wasn't a nightmare; it was my reality! I had a knack for landing what seemed like fantastic jobs that'd inevitably go bad. Or I'd take a job I wasn't interested in while waiting for something better to come along and voila! The boring job would fall apart for seemingly no reason at all.

Yes, there was the tyrannical boss who liked to drop Ecstasy at company parties, and the one who showed up late to meetings, drunk. There was the executive who carried his Emmy statuette around the office when he felt insecure, and the accountant who wouldn't give me final accounting records until I handed over a thousand dollars to help pay for her son's rehab.

Deep down I knew I'd played a part in these job disasters, and when I did my Fifth-Step inventory, I began to see what it was. Most of it stemmed from ego and arrogance. I'd alternate between thinking I was a genius who could and should be running the company, to believing I was a complete fraud who couldn't cross the street on my own. I created chaos, especially when things were going well. I'd miss deadlines, get into conflicts with colleagues, and be hostile toward the boss when things didn't go my way.

When I saw my part in these situations, I felt like a real jerk, until my sponsor explained that self-sabotage is common among chronic debtors.

Yes, it's kind of strange, but it's what we debtors do.

With the help of the Tools and Steps of DA, and a renewed connection to God, I'm learning to show up, do my best, and not create or participate in drama at work. Which isn't always easy to do because my colleagues can be irritating.

I take pride in my work now and most of my experiences are positive. In fact, it's been ages since I was last "let go," and I'm proud of that. Besides, getting fired *is* a nightmare, what, with all the crying and screaming. And it can be a real bummer when law enforcement gets called.

It's Not About The Money:

Thanks to DA, I no longer have to live out my nightmares.

February 7

STEPPING

Things had improved after my first year in DA but they weren't exactly great. I was underemployed, couch-surfing at friends' places, and I wasn't even making a dent in my credit card debt. I was going to meetings and keeping track of what I spent, but I was discouraged.

"I've decided to quit DA. I don't think it's working," I told my friend as we left the meeting.

"Are you working the Twelve Steps?" asked my know-it-all friend as he jumped into his new sports car while I prepared to wait for the bus. He obviously had no idea what it meant to suffer.

"Well..." I said, (Whenever someone answers a yes-or-no question with a "well," the answer is "no.") "I'm working the Steps in my other Program."

"There's no such thing as recovery by osmosis," he replied. "If you don't work the Steps in DA, you won't see the changes. The power of this Program is in the Steps."

Mr. Smarty Pants eventually became my sponsor, and as much as I hated admitting it, he was right. The work I had done in my other Twelve-Step Program didn't cross over. There's no such thing as osmosis when it comes to recovery from debt.

I started working the Steps in Debtors Anonymous and it was one of the hardest things I've ever done. Tracking my numbers, staying current on my bills, and dealing with money in a healthy way does not come naturally to me. It takes a ton of contrary action. But life is getting...good, thanks to the Steps and DA. And to my sponsor, who does know a lot. Although I would never tell him that.

It's Not About The Money:

When I do the work, I get results - peace, sanity, and serenity.

February 8

SHUSH!

"Shhh, shhh. No, no, don't speak. Don't speak,"
– Helen Sinclair, "Bullets Over Broadway"

There are times when I repeat this phrase to myself as a reminder to be still. It helps quiet the chatter in my head and allows me to hear what's going on around me. Some people use meditation to quiet their inner voices, but to each his own. I go for a more theatrical approach.

Shhh, shhh! Don't speak! I think when I want to calm myself down, or when I need to stop myself from saying something off the top of my head. Or when it's time to slow down and be in the moment.

When I take the time to be still, I always feel the peace and presence of my Higher Power, and a connection to my creativity. I gain perspective and the ability to discern between the things I can and cannot change.

I have an idea! I'll say to myself. *Why don't we take some time to sit still and be quiet? It's important for our mental health to do that. Like tonight; it's a beautiful, clear night. What do you say we sit out on the lawn and stare up at the stars? Or we could wake up at dawn and enjoy the sweet little hummingbirds that gather near the fountain by the back door?* And I'll respond to myself with, *That's a brilliant idea. Let's start tomorrow!*

And then there are the times when my mind gets so busy I forget about the date I've made with myself and things start to go sideways. But that's okay. I'll keep on trying.

It's Not About The Money:

If only for a moment today, I will wait and not speak.

February 9

SCORE

Some years ago, I was arguing with my sister about a financial situation. She screamed at me and called me "stingy" as she stormed out. For some reason that word hurt me more than anything she's ever called me, and believe me, she's called me plenty of names in our lifetime.

She knows nothing about me, I thought. *I am very generous with my friends. Just not with her!*

The truth is, when it came to members of my family, I was miserly and, well, stingy before I found DA. I felt justified because they had hurt me deeply and I refused to give them anything other than common decency. I made certain they'd never get away with anything, where I was concerned.

I was the ultimate scorekeeper.

DA showed me that if I wanted to experience serenity, I couldn't be emotionally withholding, resentful, and miserly with my family and then make up for it by being overly generous with my friends. Because of the work I've done in recovery, I'm able to let my family off the hook. I can't take back what happened in the past but I can live differently now. For me, that means being kind and giving them the respect that every person on this planet deserves. When I see my family as people who need love, I'm able to be there for them in the same way I would for a newcomer: without expectations or demands.

It's not like I throw gold coins at my relatives when I see them at family functions or anything, but my attitude has definitely changed. I no longer withhold kindness or keep score. I'm more open and generous. And they don't call me stingy anymore. At least not to my face, they don't.

It's Not About The Money:

When I'm part of the solution, I don't have to worry about the score.

February 10

FABULOUS

I was the kind of debtor who loved to "exult in my defects."

I enjoyed telling amusing stories about my adventures related to my irresponsibility: "geographics," moving to a new state without a plan or a job or connections, hoping things would just work out; losing money on dicey investments; taking trips alone to foreign countries with no cash or health insurance. I was the kooky, adorable "lost soul," the "wanderer," and I secretly gloried in my defects. I also got a lot of attention for it. People loved retelling the stories about my ill-fated escapades.

It was ruining my life.

In reality I wasn't lost or inept; I was a debtor. I debted for a myriad of reasons, including fear there wasn't enough, fear that God wouldn't take care of me, anxiety, greed, arrogance, pride and insecurity.

When I started to become conscious about what I was doing to myself, I was pretty surprised. I knew I'd have to change my ways, take responsibility for the results of my decisions and the way I presented myself to people. I had to stop playing the part of the "airhead" or the "irresponsible" one if I wanted to recover. I had to relate to people as a whole person, not a screwup.

My irresponsibility isn't totally gone but it doesn't run my life like it used to. I'm hopeful that with God's help, it will lessen. Which will make me very happy, because I don't want people to see me as irrresponsible or airheady. I would prefer that they see me as simply "fabulous."

It's Not About The Money:

Guess what? You're pretty darn fabulous, yourself!

February 11

SECRETS

"Why didn't you tell me about the gold coins?" my sponsor queried. There was no judgment in his voice, it was more like concern.

I'd received an inheritance, and my sponsor had suggested that I write down everything I had inherited and read it to him.

I didn't include the large bags of gold coins in my list.

"I told you about the coins. I just didn't write them down," I snapped. *What business was it of his?*

"Look, I don't care about the coins, but I don't think you didn't included them because you like keeping secrets about money."

I rolled my eyes internally. *Why is this important?*

"It's important," he responded, "And it might be something for you to write about. We're only as sick as our secrets."

"What a few canvas bags of coins has to do with my mental health, I do not know," I said as we ended our conversation.

But I did know. I wanted to keep the money a secret for no reason other than I wanted it all for myself. It was noone else's business. It was an old response to not getting my needs met as a kid, but my sponsor was right. I'm a debtor who doesn't want *anyone* to know the "whole story." *Some* people can know *some* parts, but one person knowing *everything* was just not my thing.

Secrets got me into massive debt and brought me to DA. I can't keep secrets and recover.

I called my sponsor back.

"You were right. I lied. I didn't want you to know about the coins and I don't want to do that anymore."

Sharing with someone who knows my secrets, yet loves me has been a huge part of my recovery from debt. And, it helps me avoid those awkward moments when I forget what I've lied about.

I still like keeping secrets. I also like fatty foods like fried chicken and okra, but I don't eat them because they're notoriously bad for your heart. That's sort of how I feel about money secrets.

It's Not About The Money:

God, show me how to let go of my secrets.

February 12

NOTHIN' IS NOTHIN'

Brad was a retired marine who managed the new home sales division where I was a realtor. He drove a crimson Corvette, and he was short on time and shorter on tolerance with people. Especially realtors.

Seemingly every day, fights would break out between realtors who'd accuse each other of stealing one another's clients. These fights would inevitably occur before the home had been sold.

I was sitting in Brad's office one morning arguing with another realtor about who should get the full commission on a house I'd worked hard on – until my colleague stepped in and tried to steal the client. She was demanding fifty percent of my commission. Things were getting pretty intense between us until Brad stepped in.

"Have you people got a contract in your hands? And by that I mean, a signed contract?" Brad demanded.

"No, sir," we confessed in unison.

"Not yet," I quantified.

"Then get outta my office! There's nothin' to talk about 'til you people have got a buyer and a signed contract," Brad said.

"Fifty percent of nothin' is nothin'," he said, pointing toward the door.

It took a while for me to comprehend Brad's math, but it finally clicked. Fifty percent of nothing is nothing. My colleague and I were fighting about things that hadn't happened and might not ever happen. The problem was all in our heads, because we didn't have a signed contract.

I often repeat that phrase to myself when I start worrying about things that just *might* happen. *Fifty percent of nothing is nothing.* Now even *I* can understand that kind of math.

It's Not About The Money:

Fifty percent of nothing means there's nothing to worry about.

February 13

ALMOST FAMOUS

Marco and I had been buddies since middle school. We'd seen each other through the trauma of musical auditions, horrible breakups, and even more painful breakouts.

Aside from offering each other misguided advice about dating and diets, we talked about little other than "the biz." Our friendship was delicately held together, loosely bound by a frayed cord and the chance that one of us would become famous–or die in a fiery crash after midnight on Mulholland.

In truth, if I were in a fiery crash at midnight I wouldn't think of calling Marco. He wouldn't answer the phone if it disrupted his beauty sleep.

When I discovered Debtors Anonymous, it was clear to me that most of my relationships were shallow and anything but stable. I'd become so obsessed with success and winning that my true friends were rare, but mostly because I wasn't willing to be authentic. I wanted to be admired and accepted for my accomplishments. It was all I thought I had to offer people.

I'm not totally over the need to win–some defects die hard–but my friendships today are beautiful and precious to me. They aren't based on the hope that any of us will become rich or famous, or the fear that one of us may die in a fiery crash. They're built on mutual trust and acceptance.

And, while I do my best to schedule my crises during daylight hours these days, I don't have to worry about it, because I can count on the friends I have in recovery to pick up the phone. Even if it is after midnight.

It's Not About The Money:

I love DA because crises rarely happen on schedule.

February 14

VALENTINE'S

Whether or not you're in a relationship, Valentine's Day can be distressing for a debtor.

Some take the easy way out, choosing to ignore the day entirely, or excusing themselves by saying, "I don't do Valentine's Day. It's a sleazy conspiracy created by evil monoliths like Hershey's and Hallmark."

While denial might be perfectly acceptable for some folks, when it comes to debtors, there's almost *always* more to it. Perhaps we refuse to participate because we're cheap, or we're trying to disguise our self-pity with indifference and moral superiority. Or maybe we have such high expectations that we can't bear to be disappointed, so we throw our hands up and say No Way to Valentine's Day.

Instead of ignoring Valentine's Day or defending your cynicism, I'm asking you to consider enjoying it. Like the good ol' days when your homeroom teacher gave out handwritten cards, chocolate kisses, and multicolored hearts that tasted like styrofoam. Except today, your job is to be the homeroom teacher. You get to pass out the love today.

Whether it be a few homemade cards or some chocolate kisses, you get to pick at least three people to honor today. The point is to have fun without getting all neurotic about it. Recovery, like Valentine's Day, depends on our perspective. We can wait for love and cardboard-flavored hearts to show up on our doorstep, or we can hand them out to others. Life is so much sweeter when we pass joy along instead of waiting for it to come our way.

If that fails to tug at your heart strings and doesn't inspire you to participate, then you're being killjoy and you ought to cut it out. Really. Happy Valentine's Day!

It's Not About The Money:

Give some love away already!

February 15

CHECKS

"Son, your ego is writing checks your body can't pay for." – *Stinger, Top Gun*

Like many debtors, I didn't give much thought to how I'd pay my debts back when I was writing checks or signing credit card slips. Debtors understand what I'm talking about. Non-debtors, of course, do not comprehend this, which, incidentally, is why they aren't called "debtors."

When I'd sign one of those pesky long-form loan agreements, borrow money from a friend, or take an advance on my credit card, I didn't have a plan to pay it back. I just figured, *It will work out…someday.* While I wasn't actively trying to rip anyone off, what I was doing was the equivalent of writing a check knowing there weren't funds to cover it. Preplanning, foresight, and organization were my last considerations, as were the consequences of what that debt might have on my future.

I've had to learn the hard way, one day at a time, not to make promises I cannot deliver on. I stay in the here and now and work with what I have today. Owing other people keeps me tethered to the past, and being in debt takes away my serenity.

It keeps me from connecting with God and from being in relationship with others.

It's a big part of my spiritual practice and it's fairly simple. I don't make promises I can't keep and I don't let my "ego write checks my body can't pay for." And while I'm not sure how that quote works in this situation, it puts a nice little bow on this meditation. So I'll just leave it at that.

It's Not About The Money:

Son, daughter, please don't write checks you can't cover.

February 16

ICONS

When I came into DA, I had plenty of emotions about money. All of them were bad.

Now, there are "professional" types who claim there's no such thing as a bad emotion, but the more I thought about money, the worse I felt. When the subject of money came up, there were no joyful emoticons or smiley faces involved. So, one day I created a library of what I like to call "sound icons." Instead of mood icons, I decided to use sounds as a way to articulate my feelings and express my emotions about money.

For example, when I was at a restaurant and the waiter dropped off the check, I would growl. When buying groceries, I would squeal like a baby seal. And when I had to pay the IRS, I yelled every naughty word I can think of.

These "sound icons" really helped me get in touch with my money feelings. And while it made for some uncomfortable moments in public, expressing the way I felt through sounds helped me stay emotionally conscious. It's hard to be vague when you're yodeling or honking like a goose.

Of course, "sound icons" aren't for everyone, but I've found them to be extremely helpful.

Now that I've found my way out of the negative emotions, I've begun to discover some really positive, pleasant "sound icons." I'm currently working on an icon for when I've saved enough to take that Battlestar Gallactica themed Caribbean cruise I've been dreaming about for years.

It's Not About The Money:

Because of DA, I can find ways to express joy when it comes to money.

February 17

TITLES

Look, I know money is an issue for me and the causes run deep and the solution is spiritual, blah, blah, blah, but after some time in reflection, I've decided that this whole "debtor" title doesn't really apply to me. Let's consider the following:

I am generous without being lavish. I know exactly what and whom to spend on. Much more than I used to.

I make good decisions. I mean, I will, once I pay these debts off and start earning more.

Aside from the money stuff, I'm quite wise. Ask my friends. They call me all the time with their relationship problems and the results have been, well, phenomenal.

Unlike most people, I'm not even slightly jealous when my friends succeed. More for us to share!

I'm a creation machine. I can sit for hours coming up with innovative ideas. My productivity will only increase with time and more cash.

Sure, there are those who say recovery is the only way to deal with the underlying issues that cause people to debt, and more money will just exacerbate the situation and hinder long-term spiritual growth. To those people I say, "I can't understand it when you use such big words. Can you just speak English?" Besides, I've found that titles, like labels, can be unhelpful. Unless you're going to using a label maker. I love label makers.

It's Not About The Money:

Is there any part of my recovery where I'm a bit delusional?

February 18

SERVICE

I couldn't afford to pay for a traffic ticket so the judge sentenced me to community service at the local Salvation Army thrift store. I was excited. All those lonely castoffs just waiting to be cared for.

On my first day I organized the women's clothing section by textures and color. Within a week, I had the mannequins in the men's section looking like an Urban Outfitters window display, though most of my time was spent apprehending kids who were hell-bent on destroying pure silk with their filthy hands. It broke my heart to see cashmere treated like roadkill.

"You won't believe how mean people are to mohair!" I cried to my sponsor, a resentment festering. He suggested I become willing to be of service and stop judging the customers. I reluctantly agreed.

Each time I entered the store, I would ask God to show me how to be of service to others. Before my thrift-store sentence was over, customers were approaching me for fashion tips and I was hosting mini-makeovers in the aisles of the Salvation Army.

On my last day, the store supervisor pulled me aside. "We'll miss you," he said. "You're a hard worker and I like how you organized the store by color and textures."

To show his appreciation, he sold me a gorgeous pair of caramel-colored suede boots for a dollar. I cried, because they were marked at $63.00 and I'd never have been able to afford them.

When I show up for service, miracles don't *always* happen, but sometimes they do!

It's Not About The Money:

I'll be of service today, but not just because a miracle might be in store.

February 19

FORMULAS

"Came to believe that a power greater than ourselves could restore us to sanity."
– DA Step #2

Trusting in a power greater than myself when it came to some things seemed reasonable, but when it came to debt, I didn't get it. Was God going to get me a job? Would He clean up my credit score? I needed tangible help, not spirituality. What I really wanted was a friendly, benevolent genie.

Alas, in DA, I learned that Step #2 is simply believing in something bigger and more powerful than myself. That might mean the DA fellowship or the ocean. Anything other than *me*. Just believing in something, no matter how feeble that faith may be, was critical to my recovery.

I had to give up the delusion that I could fix things myself, because I couldn't. I was out of control when it came to debt, underearning and overspending, and I needed something bigger to turn things over to. My solutions didn't work. This was not easy for a control freak like me, who wanted it all now and was always in search of the "formula" for success.

The irony is that those "formulas" for success are rarely that and they seldom work for me. Just ask the friends, family members, and banks that loaned me money before I found my way into DA.

Step #2 is a simple daily choice I make to give up control and allow a Higher Power to work in my life. The best part is, I now have a Higher Power that I trust to do things better than I can. Which is saying a lot, because in all humility, I can do a lot of things pretty well.

It's Not About The Money:

God, I'll let you handle things today, because while I'm good, you're better!

February 20

ACQUIT

For most of my life–say, from the age of six on–I've had difficulty handling criticism.

Like many debtors, I thought I was above criticism. After all, I was a decent person, a pretty good worker, and unless feedback included the words "you're amazing" or "fantastic work," I didn't feel the need to hear it. High praise was all I was interested in.

If I discovered I was replaceable or the work I was doing wasn't considered the best, I assumed the blame belonged on the massively incompetent people around me. No matter what job or position I had, my attitude was essentially "this joint would fall apart without me."

Conversely, I felt so bad about myself that even the slightest criticism made me feel like I was being put on trial. And since my value was solely in accomplishing things, if everything I did wasn't fabulous, I would lose my mind. If I couldn't be perfect, there was no point in being alive.

How can a person have so many diverging opinions of herself? I don't know the answer to that. I'm human, and human beings are complex.

DA has taught me that criticism doesn't have to cut to the bone, nor is it an indication of my value. Criticism can be useful feedback, and if I take time to listen to it without reacting, it can improve the quality of my life. Or I can discard it without turning it into a big deal. Criticism and feedback may be reflections of my behavior, but they do not determine my value.

I don't think I'll ever love hearing criticism, but today I am able to listen to it without falling apart. Unless it's a Monday. I don't "do" criticism on Mondays.

It's Not About The Money:

If the criticism doesn't fit, then I must acquit.

February 21

WITH A SMILE

"Good afternoon," I say, greeting Woman Who Is Ignoring Me at My Massively Underearning Retail Job. *Would it be audacious of me to tell you how it makes me feel when you look away as I greet you? As if I were contagious or something?*

"Just let me know if I can help in any way," I say politely, as I enter the fitting room. *Your refusal to acknowledge me is perplexing.*

"Here, let me pick up those jeans for you." *Yes, those, the ones you've so callously thrown on the floor.*

"Oh, don't worry about the bubble gum your daughter left on the dressing room floor. I'll get it." *My sponsor says I need to be of service.*

"Yes, in fact, I do work here. And yes, I'd be happy to ring those up for you." *Service is my middle name.*

"Well, you're right, I am a bit mature for this job, and you're also right that I don't belong here selling size-minus-zero jeans for three hundred dollars a pair, but it's my job for now." *So let's cut it with the superiority already. I used to be someone. I wasn't always hanging out at the mall with moody teenaged girls and guys who wear silos of hair gel.*

"Yes, your daughter can return this dress." *No doubt after she's worn it to several fraternity parties.*

"Whatever it is, we'll take it back without question, it's our policy. Of course, I'll throw that yogurt cone away for you!" *My sponsor says I need to be of service.*

"Thanks again for coming in today. You have a fantastic day!" *No, I don't mind that you're looking right through me again. It's a good way for me to practice being humble. My sponsor says I need to be of service.*

It's Not About The Money:

If there's no smile, am I still being of service?

February 22

IOUS

I was in the seventh grade and had accidentally left my sack lunch at home. When lunchtime rolled around, I asked my friend Hilda if I could borrow some cash.

"I'll pay you back tomorrow," I promised, albeit begrudgingly, as Hilda handed the money over to me. I wasn't planning on stiffing her but I wasn't all that committed to paying her right away. I'd do it when I got around to it.

Boy, was I shocked when I saw Hilda standing at the bus stop the very next morning, hands on her hips.

"Do you have the money I loaned you yesterday?" she asked as she began taking notes in her Hello Kitty ledger.

"No, I don't!" I said. *What a cheapskate!* I thought as I marched off, swearing to never speak to her again.

I gave Hilda the money the following day but our friendship cooled. *If she's a real friend,* I reasoned, *wouldn't she give me the money without strings or expecting me to pay her back? Don't I mean anything to her? More importantly, who wants a friend who has a financial ledger at age eleven?*

My irresponsibility, combined with my sense of entitlement, had damaged many of my close relationships. By the time I came into DA, I was in massive debt but attributed it to my low self-esteem. The truth is, my esteem was low because I refused to take care of myself. I expected others to do it for me.

Maybe if I hadn't been so arrogant, I would've learned from my friend Hilda, who was a shrewd little businesswoman. Keeping track of her money is what made her the person she is today–a hugely successful money manager who married a prince of a guy. And I mean, a real prince. Her husband is royalty from a small country in Eastern Europe.

It's Not About The Money:

Real friends don't let friends write IOUs.

February 23

PASSIONS

It began innocently after college, starting as a line of credit on my debit card. The bank had advertised it as a thoughtful way to help me out in case of an "accidental overdraft." I remember laughing because I couldn't help but notice how much "accidental overdraft" sounded like "accidental overdose."

At first, I resisted, but ultimately they got to me. Soon enough, I was dipping into that sweet little line of credit, and before I knew it, I was unable to keep up with the payments. Which, of course, led to fees, penalties, and all sorts of financial hemorrhaging.

So, I did what any self-respecting debtor would do. I swore off all credit cards. And for years, I stayed debt-free. Until one day–the exact details are hazy –I got this letter in the mail. No interest and no fees for what seemed like an eternity. I held on to that card for a long time, but it was always there, in my handbag, like a dark-haired, lantern-jawed lover just waiting to be devoured by me.

One day, I simply couldn't hold out any longer. That's when the affair with the new card began. I'd waited what seemed like a lifetime for something that would make me feel important and special. The card was beautiful and uncomplicated, absolutely drama free.

I never saw the end coming. There were no disagreements or shouting matches, no stomping around the house or door slamming. Just a twelve-page letter in very small font, with something about a "final demand." That was it.

I was blindsided. Frightened. Lost. Sometimes it still hurts when I think about it. Did I miss the signs? Was it something I said? Or was it just bad timing? Alas, I will probably never know.

It's Not About The Money:

When details get hazy, I can get crazy.

February 24

BIAS

It's called commitment bias–a phenomenon that involves people justifying a decision they've made based on the amount of time and energy they've put into it, despite evidence that the cost of sticking with that decision outweighs the benefit.

I simply didn't know when to cut my losses and move on, especially if I'd already invested a lot of time in something, whether it be a project, an idea, or a relationship. It affected me most when it came to decisions about money. Diminishing returns never factored into my choices or commitments. Walking away with grace and dignity, and accepting defeat, was never an option for me. Instead, I'd spend all my energy trying to make things work, which made the situation worse.

Not everything is meant to work out, and occasionally they stop working for no particular reason. Situations and opportunities change, and–I have a particular disdain for this one–people change, too. Even if a situation has worked well for months, years, or even decades, it just might stop working one day. I do not say this lightly and I am not pleased with this aspect of life. I want things–when they're good for me, of course–to stay exactly as they are.

This is why I'm glad I have DA and a community of people who remind me it's okay to move on. They often have to give me a swift, gentle shove as they're reminding me, but it's okay. Because if they didn't, I'd be living in a constant state of commitment bias, clinging to situations that don't work, and saying "yes" to useless activities, or what my Irish kinfolk like to call a "whole bunch of malarkey."

It's Not About The Money:

God, show me where my biases might be keeping me stuck.

February 25

R.E.S.P.ONSIBILITY

Recovery is hard work. Going to meetings, putting up with irritating people, apologizing for mistakes I may or may not have made, tracking my daily spending, keeping my commitments, and being of service. It can be downright tiring.

There are times, like yesterday, when I feel like shouting, "Hey, why can't I take it easy for a day and for once in my life, not do the right thing?"

Then there are times when I do scream those words and skip my meetings and stop praying. But eventually I find myself *wanting* recovery again, and missing my DA meetings, and feeling uncomfortable about my financial vagueness.

I liken recovery to being on house arrest, only without the ankle bracelet and the probation officer. Even though I don't have a prison record and I've never been on house arrest, I imagine it would be a bummer to be stuck in one location all day long. If I don't make recovery a priority, and think I no longer need to put God first in my life, I have a tendency to slip back to my old rebellious, noncommittal, and irresponsible ways.

"Recovery is a lot of work," my sponsor tells me. "But what else are you gonna do?"

He's right. Recovery may be hard but nonrecovery is harder. Not keeping my numbers and spending money like crazy, or even hiding under the covers when I'm overwhelmed, may feel good in the moment, but they seldom result in happiness. Ultimately, I'd rather be doing things that lead to a connection with my Higher Power and lasting peace. Things that do not lead to rude calls from creditors or pushy probation officers.

It's Not About The Money:

Recovery rarely leads to rude calls from the IRS or ankle monitors.

February 26

OBSESSIONS

I used to hate having extra money lying around doing nothing at the end of the month, so I was constantly conjuring up ways to spend it all.

Shoes, clothes, a trip, an advanced college degree, a new career, whatever it was, it felt very important to have what I wanted in the moment. It was the "dis-ease" of debting that wanted to convince me *I must* have something. Now.

Ironically, the moment I gave in to it, the wanting changed and became a *need*. Getting what I've obsessed over is never as gratifying as the wanting, and when I give in, it only gets harder to say no the next time.

It can take hours, days, even weeks for the urge to pass because it's an endless vortex of wanting, and resisting it usually requires the support of other people. Recovery begins when I start with prayer, a DA meeting, and plenty of outreach calls. Recovery requires that I take contrary action and find a way to be of service to someone else. It's the only thing that gets me out of obsessing.

Perhaps I'm making this obsession stuff sound like a total bummer, but that's because it can be. It's difficult in the moment, but the more I practice not giving in to my obsessions, the stronger I get. What I *want* is more shiny objects, but what *I need* is spiritual connection, peace, and solvency.

You know what I've discovered? Peace is ultimately much more gratifying than the things I crave, like a new car and a trip around the world, or never having to work again. Okay, I lied, it's much more gratifying than a pair of new shoes.

It's Not About The Money:

When it comes to obsession, there's never enough.

February 27

OUT THERE

There's a sentence that I often hear in DA meetings that begins with, "I'm putting it out into the universe..." I don't know how the rest of the phrase goes because I usually tune out once I hear those first words.

I've never, ever been able to put anything out "into the universe," mainly because unless NASA's involved, things sent into outer space rarely return.

I understand people want to trust that their money problems and debting issues are better off in the hands of something bigger than they are. However, when you throw something willy-nilly out into the massive black vortex of space, it has a tendency to *stay there*.

I'm all for trusting a Higher Power, but it's my opinion that, as debtors, and as a society, we might want to practice caution and show some respect for the cosmos. Nonchalantly tossing any situation into a system that is also responsible for keeping track of a billion stars and the Milky Way is simply unwise. Trusting that space is going to resolve my little problem is assuming a lot. However, believing that there's a loving God who cares about me personally and is going to take care of things is much more comforting.

C'mon, people, the universe may be friendly, but it is not a dumping ground or conflict resolution center.

Anyway, I'm not trying to be preachy, I just thought I'd "put it out there." God can and does answer prayers. I have no clue what the universe does. That's way over my head.

It's Not About The Money:

God, thanks for caring about my little problems.

February 28

PRECIOUS

It was a downtown meeting in the city, filled with hipsters and artsy types, but as people went around the room, one thing was apparent. The entire group was suffering from "terminal preciousness."

"I'm an Abundant Underearner," "I'm a Unique Visionary," "I'm a Time Drunk," "I'm a Powerful Goddess Recovering in the Program," "I'm Powerless over Vagueness."

Excuse me, but where do the regular, garden-variety debtors go? I wanted to ask, but didn't. Something told me this trendy-looking group would have me for lunch if I made waves.

It was an okay meeting, but getting through the introductions was about as uncomfortable as white-knuckling through an unexpected sex scene on TV with your parents.

"I'm a debtor," I said when it came to my turn. "My symptoms include many behaviors but at the end of the day, I'm not that fancy. I debt. I'm powerless and my life is unmanageable. So, if you pretentious types could try using the word d-e-b-t-o-r, I'd much appreciate it and would be a lot less confused."

I didn't really say that, either, but I really wanted to. I can't stand preciousness. I did, however, ask Powerless over Vagueness Guy if he could give me directions to the London Bridge just for kicks.

It's Not About The Money:

We're all unique, but there's nothing about debting that's precious.

March 1

PAST DUE

Before DA, I never paid my bills on time, aside from those I'd set up on auto-pay through my bank. Even when I had money, I'd always pay late.

A few months after I started to earn consistently, I decided to pay my phone bill a few days early. When I called the phone company to see what I owed, I found it was less than what was written on the bill. I was so used to paying late that I'd automatically looked at the late-pay section with all the extra fees tacked on.

"That's not right," I said snottily to the customer service representative. "My bill shows a different amount than what you said. What kind of con game are you people running?"

The rep finally figured out I was looking at the wrong section of the bill. While she didn't exactly say, "You're kind of lame, aren't you?" she made it clear that's what she thought of me.

I think the fact that I wasn't in trouble with the cell phone company I wouldn't be living with the anxiety of picking up the phone to hear, "your service has been temporarily suspended," made me so uncomfortable that I created another reason to be upset and irritated.

It took a while for me to figure out that the phone company–and other sundry companies–weren't personally targeting me. I was addicted to the drama of paying late and living on the edge financially.

"I'm sorry. I guess I'll just pay whatever I owe, then," I said sheepishly. I don't pay late anymore, because the anxiety I feel when I do is too uncomfortable. Besides, I feel good when I pay my bills on time, and my serenity is too important to lose over a past-due notice.

It's Not About The Money:

Today I'll remember: Financial dramas never pay off.

March 2

LIVING MARTYR

I'll admit it. I'm not feeling all that spiritual today, nor am I in the frame of mind to be offering words of encouragement to my fellow debtors.

Without coming off as totally rude and insensitive, why should I bother? I mean, honestly, I sit here, hour after hour, day after day, in solitude, slaving over this laptop. Rarely do I get a "thank you" or even a "good job" for any of my efforts.

Sometimes it feels as if all the stuff I do is all about everyone else and less about me. Things often feel a bit one-sided at times..

I'm not saying people don't appreciate the things I do, but I wonder, *do* people *really* appreciate the things I do?

Nonetheless, I hope you have a fabulous day and I honestly mean that. Just because other people in my life don't show a stitch of gratitude for the hard work I put into everything I do, doesn't mean I'm going to stop doing a fantastic job. No, I won't stop, because *I'm* trying to live a spiritual Program, and being of service is crucial to my spiritual Program.

Even when *other people* don't reciprocate it or appreciate the things I do, I will still continue to do them. That's just the kind of person I am.

It's Not About The Money:

Do something for someone else today without concern for the cost to you.

March 3

BOOKENDS

One of the things we do in the DA Program is "bookending," where we call a buddy in recovery before and after we have to do a task that's difficult or scary. Oftentimes, we just need some support getting started or finishing a chore so we reach out for encouragement.

Prior to DA, I had my own version of bookending. It went as follows: I would call a few of my flaky friends and ask them how I should handle a certain situation. Inevitably, I'd get completely different answers, which did nothing but confuse me more. So, I would go along with the answer that sounded the easiest. And if things didn't work out, I could blame my friend. *Who the hell is she to tell me how to run my life?*

Today, I use the DA version of bookending. It starts with a call to one of my buddies in Program. We usually begin with a prayer for God's guidance. Together we discuss my situation, talk about my options, and weigh the possible outcomes and consequences of each choice available to me. It almost never involves anyone giving me advice about what *I should* do.

Once I've reasoned things out with someone I trust and made my decision, then I take the next indicated action. If need be, I check back in with my buddy but then I move on with the rest of my day.

I let God handle the results.

This new, saner approach to bookending was hard for me to do at first. Mostly because there was no one to blame if things didn't work out the way I'd planned. And that was when I *really* started to miss my old, flaky friends.

It's Not About The Money:
Flaky friends don't make good bookends.

March 4

WILLS

"Made a decision to turn our will and our lives over to the care of God as we understood Him."
– DA Step #3

Turning my will and my life over to God was a major decision, because when I came into recovery, I was plenty pissed off at God. In fact, He and I weren't even on speaking terms. Until I admitted the truth–that I was angry and had no clue about who God was–I could not move forward. And that could only have happened after I'd worked the first Two Steps.

In Step One, I admitted my powerlessness over debt - that it had made my life unmanageable - which was pretty easy to do. I knew I'd screwed things up. In Step Two, I acknowledged there was a Higher Power that could restore me to sanity. While I couldn't define, understand, or even talk to God at that point, I did know something else was in control of the universe, and I needed help.

When I started working on Step Three, my Higher Power was the fellowship of DA, and God stood for "good, orderly direction," meaning I'd take actions based on the principles of the DA Program and let the rest go, believing something "out there" could (and would) work things out. As time went on, I discovered a new relationship with God. I began to have faith that I could put my life into His care and trust that I'd be given what I needed, which was, often just enough money for dinner. As time went on, it became easier to turn my life over to God, because I'd had many experiences where I'd trusted and He came through.

I'm no longer as apprehensive about the future as I was, nor am I as preoccupied with what might happen. I try to live one day at a time. That said, I'm always open to receiving a sign from God with details about what I can expect in the future.

It's Not About The Money:

God, you can send me a sign if you want to. If you don't want to, that's okay, too.

March 5

BORROWED

The first time I read about the signs of compulsive debting–"frequently 'borrowing' items such as books, pens, or small amounts of money from friends and others and failing to return them"–I thought, *Wow, those DA types sure are militaristic!*

Who *doesn't* borrow a pen and fail to return it? And books–aren't they meant to be shared? I loan mine out all the time and *never* expect them back. It's called book swapping.

And whatever happened to *su libro, mi libro*? Or, as I used to say, *su dinero, mi dinero?*

In DA, I began to see how my "borrowing" was debting. I borrowed things I never intended to return, because I was selfish and liked knowing I was getting away with something. And why shouldn't I be able to take what I could get? Life had been hard, really hard. If people knew what I had been through, they'd offer me more than a paltry pen or a damn paperback. Heck, they'd probably throw a house into the deal!

I had a debting problem, and it manifested itself in taking whatever I could from life, without considering what I was giving back. It had cost me relationships and opportunities and I was in bondage. Until I could admit to myself what I was doing and turn it over to God, I knew I would never be free.

As part of my recovery, I rarely borrow pens or books. I never borrow money from friends or family and don't incur unsecured debt for any reason. If I don't have the money to pay for something, I don't buy it. It keeps me honest. Besides, there's nothing–especially not a pen–that's worth my serenity. Unless it's a Visconti pen, which might be tempting. Thank goodness I don't hang out with people who can afford Visconti pens.

It's Not About The Money:

Su dinero no es mi dinero.

March 6

BALANCE

I once heard someone say that you can't be in "save-a-nickel mode" and "make-a-buck mode" at the same time.

Without getting into a detailed explanation, it's simply not scientifically possible for matter to expand and contract at the same time. And since human beings are made of matter, the same must be true of us. Ergo, I can't be growing and expanding if I'm clenching my fists and pinching pennies or worried about losing the things I have. Along those same lines, if I'm withholding generosity or hoarding my time, my heart is not open.

Alternatively, when I become obsessed with making a bunch of money, I start getting weird. I lose perspective about the important things in life, like standing on a dock looking at a lake, gazing up at the night stars, listening to sweet little birds chirping in the morning.

When I get off balance in my relationship with money, I can feel a shift in my body. I stop being emotionally vulnerable and I get stingy with my time and attention. And I shut God out. When I feel that happening, I've learned to go straight to the Tools and the Steps of DA.

Recovery not only keeps me on track with my spending and savings, it helps me remain receptive to spiritual and relational expansion. To use a sports analogy, a basketball team that is only focused on defense, has stopped focusing on scoring. You can't be in two places at the same time. You're either in or out, you're either up or down. I'm either open or I'm closed.

Okay, you get the point. Recovery teaches us to stay balanced and avoid extreme thinking and behavior. This is the way we stay sane. Saner. Sane-ish.

It's Not About The Money:

Today I'll try to remain balanced and sane-ish.

March 7

FAILS

I've heard it said that we grow the most and learn our best lessons after we've failed. To which I say, "No, thank you. I'd rather be dumb, shallow, and happy."

Failure happens. There are hundreds of stories about exceptionally bright people who've had major failures. Dumb people have failed, too, but we don't hear those stories as much. And mediocre people also fail but I digress.

There are no guarantees in life. Plans and dreams fall apart and we don't know why.

Just because something seems like a failure in the moment doesn't mean it'll seem that way in the long term. The same goes for success. What looks like a victory today may not prove to be one in the years to come. I've been in situations that seemed perfect in the beginning, but turned out to be total disasters, and I've experienced things I was certain would destroy me but they gave me knowledge I never would've gained otherwise.

It's impossible for me to be objective when I'm in the middle of a situation I've already labeled a failure. That's why I need help from a Higher Power and people I trust to walk me through the difficult times.

There's no denying it–failure blows. But I must admit some of the biggest failures have brought me the most growth and ended up as huge blessings. Am I still more excited by lessons that are simple and easy than the difficult, soul-crushing situations that turn out to be miracles? Yes. Yes, I am. That's just the truth.

It's Not About The Money:

God, help me stay open to the lessons, even when they look like failures.

March 8

TOWELS

Today is National Throw in the Towel Day, and the purpose is to honor the fact that sometimes life is simply too doggone hard. Some days, it's just not worth *grinding it out* or working harder to improve things.

Perhaps you're worried about your job or paying your rent on time. Or maybe you feel you're lost and too far from home to ever recover (my personal favorite). You might be angry at your boss or your lack of progress. You may be bummed out about how much you're earning. Whatever you're frustrated or upset about, take time to identify it.

Now write those things down, and do absolutely *nothing.*

It's Throw in the Towel Day, which means you have every right to do nothing. Below are a few activities you might consider doing today. Or not. They include:

1. Going back to bed
2. Taking a nap
3. Complaining about every aspect of your life
4. Refusing to have a good day
5. Asking your Higher Power to take over.

It's up to you. You can throw in the towel if you want to. You can also hand the towel and your frustrations over to your Higher Power and see what happens. I'm gonna give number five a try today.

It's Not About The Money:

Today, instead of throwing in the towel, I'll turn it over to God.

March 9

CHASED

When I came into DA, the bank that had "Chased" all my money away was calling me every fifteen minutes. As if they didn't have enough of my money, they were demanding more.

"Give it a break," I'd scream as soon as I picked up the phone. "I'm broke and I don't have your money, so stop calling me, for godssakes!"

But they kept calling, and inevitably I would apologize for screaming and promise to pay the minimum on my credit card, and whatever else they manipulated me into agreeing to.

The light finally came on two years later when I heard a woman in a DA meeting say, "My needs come first. I have to be able to take care of my basic needs and some of my wants, before I can begin a repayment plan."

That's funny, I thought. It sounds like she's putting her needs before her creditors'. Is that ethical? Is it legal?

"It's not only ethical, it's advisable," the people leading my pressure relief group told me. They suggested I hold off on paying my creditors until I was clear about what I was earning and spending. They recommended I send a letter to my creditors and ask them to stop calling me, and tell them I'd pay them back when I had a plan in place.

"Debt repayment happens in God's time, not in the bank's time," they reminded me.

I'll admit I didn't want to do things their way. I was looking forward to the day when I could pick up the phone and say, "Hi, Chasing Away My Money? I've got news. You're not my Higher Power. I'll pay you when I can so, for the love of God, stop being so obnoxious. Have a nice day!"

My friends in Program suggested I not call the bank and yell at them, "Your old, crazy ways of handling things no longer work," they said.

I was with them until they used the word "crazy," because I thought I was being reasonable. After all, I'd planned to wish the teller a nice day before hanging up on her.

It's Not About The Money:

My debt is not my Higher Power.

March 10

SOMEONE

My way of dealing with the hurt I'd experienced in life had been to "be Someone." I was attracted to books, seminars, and anything having to do with success. I read every biography written about successful business leaders and politicians, and if an article contained the "Top 10 Things Successful People Do," I'd do it. In my opinion, the biggest crime I could commit was to be a nobody. I'd lost my mojo and figured DA would help me get it back. I thought if I could get some financial stability, pay off some of my bills, and get a good job, I'd put a game plan together and move on.

When my sponsor stated, point-blank, that a career was just an aspect of life, not the purpose for being or a reflection of my value, I ignored him. When he told me my hardship might serve a bigger purpose, I figured he was cute but highly misguided. When he told me his greatest satisfaction came from the small things, I smiled, but when he suggested I take time to savor good times instead of rushing through them, I almost threw up. "Nothing is more important than the way you treat yourself, the people around you, and your connection to your Higher Power," he said. I wanted to hate him but I couldn't, because he was living the life he described. And he was pretty happy. Happier than I was.

It took a long time for me to see that my purpose in life wasn't to "be Someone." Today, I honestly can say that I find pleasure in the small things: laughing with friends, talking to God, listening to music, being of service to others, building the kind of life that sustains me and makes me happy.

Oddly enough, I kind of feel like Someone now.

It's Not About The Money:

I might not be Someone and that's fine with me.

March 11

YES, MAN!

In the comedy *Yes Man*, Jim Carrey plays a lonely, withdrawn man who says "yes" to every offer that comes his way for an entire year.

The film's based on a British man named Danny Wallace, who vowed to spend six months without saying "no" to anyone, all because some random guy on the bus told him to say "yes" more often.

In the movie, Carrey's character attends a motivational seminar, then afterward he says "yes" to everything: people on the street, credit card offers in his mailbox (not recommended for debtors), and solicitations on the Internet. He furthers his career by saying "yes" in a meeting with an executive who offers him a big promotion. He says "yes" to a spontaneous weekend excursion with a cute girl, which ultimately leads to a collision and stint in the hospital.

In the real-life experiment, because Wallace couldn't say "no" to anything, he ends up in Amsterdam to claim the millions he's supposedly won in the Spanish lottery. (Surprise: There's no money.) Wallace also says "yes" to a woman, and they end up falling in love and get married. I recently decided to say "yes" to all requests for a week. It included an ankle tattoo and an ten-hour car ride with a new friend whom I won't call "nuts," but will say might benefit from medication.

As my cousin said, "You know, you could have started with coffee, instead of going away for the whole weekend." To wit, saying "maybe" works better in certain situations.

For you, my friends, I'd like to present a challenge. Unless it's illegal, immoral, or mean-spirited, or will cause you to debt, try saying "yes" to every request that comes your way, today.* Every request for help. Every opportunity to earn or learn. Just say "yes."

**Email misti@mistibwrites.com if you'd like to share your experiences with me.*

It's Not About The Money:

Today, I will say "yes" as often as I can.

March 12

DEBTING, SCHMEBTING

There are times when I get confused and I'm not sure when I'm debting. Is thinking about debting, debting? Am I debting if I'm late for an appointment? Am I debting if I fantasize about making outrageous amounts of money from my book of haiku poetry or plan a crowdfunding campaign to pay my rent?

"Can't you just give me a list so I'll know when I'm thinking about debting?" I asked my sponsor. "Then I'll just stop thinking about it."

"The definition of debting is up to you and your Higher Power," he said. "God will reveal those things to you when you're ready."

"Well, I think I'm ready, so let's stop with all the vague talk and tell me so I'll know when I'm debting, or at least thinking about debting!" I shrieked. "Just give me a clue!"

"Here's a clue. Stay solvent, work the Steps, and go to meetings. That's all you need to know," he responded with a smile.

I'm still not always sure when I'm debting, but I do know this: When I don't connect with God, and I stop keeping track of my numbers, or I start getting vague about my spending, I'm close to debting. And likely on my way to initiating a crowdfunding campaign for my rent.

I've come to the conclusion that debting is–forgive the analogy–a bit like porn. It' isn't easy to define, but I know it when I see it. Not that I see it a lot or anything. I'm just saying it's one of those things you don't need someone to draw you a picture of to know you're looking at it.

I hope that wasn't too crass for a meditation book, but sometimes it's necessary to be specific. Although I could try drawing a picture.

It's Not About The Money:

I don't need a picture to show me when I'm debting.

March 13

HAPPY DAYS

Several years ago, Harvard did a study that suggested the human brain has no ability to predict its emotional reaction to changes that haven't happened. According to the study, the things we assume will make us happy–wealth, fame, beauty, creative genius, or power–don't bring happiness. While we all want to be magnificent and adored, we've heard about celebrities and artists who self-destruct because they can't handle the transient nature of fame.

As for prosperity, new wealth often attracts new "friends" who seem to pop up from out of nowhere. Consider the story of the lottery winner who was targeted by a hitman–hired by his brother – because he wanted the winner's money. Even beauty is relative. You may be the most gorgeous person in your family, but there's always someone better looking.

The reality is, we spend a lot of time thinking about what will make us happy, but most of us have no idea what we really want.

So what does make people happy? Glad you asked! The study showed that friendship, altruism, and a spiritual or religious practice leads to tangible happiness. I'm living proof of this. The moment I take the focus off myself and what I think will make me feel good, I immediately feel better. I won't lie–it is nice to have my finances in order, to have consistent work and a spending plan, but true happiness is having God in my life, knowing there are people who care about me, and being of service to others.

I don't need a hoity-toity study to tell me that!

It's Not About The Money:

I know what I want: a relationship with my God, peace, and lots of love.

March 14

BLOCKS

I recently received an e-mail from a man named Robert that I'd met at a networking event. In the email, Robert called himself as a "transformation specialist." Since I'd never met such a specialist, I opened the e-mail.

Dear Friend,

Do you wonder how you can clear the blocks that keep you from manifesting what you want? The answer is: when you feel confident that you'll have it! Whether it's money, the right job, a relationship–the key to having it is feeling like you already have it. If you don't know in your heart you'll have it, then it's time to clear those limiting beliefs, emotions, and conflicting desires that are blocking you.

My new "friend" had selected me to receive a special offer. For a mere thousand dollars, he would clear my consciousness. I was tempted, as I often worry I'm not living my best life, or getting the things I want because of my unconscious blocks.

I sat down, got quiet, and said a prayer asking God to show me what I should do. Within an hour, I received a phone call from a friend in DA. I told her about the special offer to clear my blocked consciousness.

"That's a pretty good price, is it not?" I asked her.

When she stopped laughing, she reminded me that debtors are insatiable. And for us, the solution is a connection to a Higher Power, period. She reminded me that when I'm grateful for what I have, those "subconscious blocks" aren't nearly as worrisome to me.

Yes, I have a few obstacles to prosperity and doubts about what I'm doing most of the time. Yes, I might be living less than the Best Life Ever, but how the hell would I even know?

One thing I do know is, the answer doesn't require a transformation specialist to release my "blocks." The solution is simple: more God, less me.

It's Not About The Money:

I'll let God clear the "blocks" when He's ready.

March 15

GO BIG?

Reach for the stars! Dream big! Success requires risk, I used to tell myself, as if I was living in some running-shoe commercial.

Like marathon runners or Olympic athletes, I pursued my dreams in spite of exhaustion. I also incurred a massive amount of debt, which ultimately led to misery and grief.

When I came to DA, I was in total despair and bitter as heck. I thought God had abandoned me, not recognizing that I had abandoned *myself*. My go-big-or-go-home approach to everything in life had led me to take foolish financial, emotional, and physical chances. I believed taking huge risks was the only way to be successful. I didn't do *anything* small.

As I worked the Program and the Twelve Steps of DA, I began to see that most of my dreams were rooted in fear, ego, and self-will. My gigantic plans had to take a backseat to solvency. In time, God began to reveal different things to me. They weren't grand visions, merely dreams about being of service and inspiring others. My Big Plans became secondary to being sane, calm, and kind.

I'll always be a big planner and dreamer, and sometimes I still have to remind myself I'm not living in a running-shoe commercial. When I hear myself saying things like "Go big or go home" or "Reach for the stars," it's a reminder that I might need to slow down and take a deep breath, because there's no race and nothing to chase after.

I already have everything I need.

It's Not About The Money:

There's no race when it comes to recovery. It's all in God's time.

March 16

INCIDENTS

There was a story years ago about the A-list actress who stole a hundred thousand dollars in clothing and jewelry from an exclusive department store. When she was apprehended, she showed absolutely no remorse. Not even a "Gosh, I'm so sorry, I totally forgot to pay for that!" or a "Wow, how did that eight-karat diamond fell into my purse?"

When the story first came out, I was in the prime of my debting, and though I'm not proud to say it, I secretly admired her. There was a romantic quality to the story. I could safely watch from the sidelines as this young woman pulled one over on "the man" (although, technically, she didn't pull it off, she ended up doing some jail-time and community service).

Later, more details of the story came out. Then I wanted to punch that entitled, obnoxious celebrity, with her blatant deception and thievery. How dare she be such a jerk?

In hindsight, it became clear to me that this was not just some woman fighting "the establishment," she had a serious psychological problem.

Now, I'm not a practicing psychiatrist, I'm just a debtor, and my acting out is no better or worse than this celebrity's was. I don't steal jewels–or anything, for that matter–but when I'm not solvent or connected to my Higher Power, I do reckless, risky things. I take more than I deserve, I cut corners, I find ways to get more than I need, and I start to romanticize ways I can pull things over on "the man."

When I leave God out and start to rely on my own devices, I can get, for lack of a better word, "slippery" myself. Like I said, I'm not a practicing psychiatrist, so I'll leave it at that.

It's Not About The Money:

Am I being rigorously honest about my own "incidents?"

March 17

SPECIAL

My resentment over being broke often led me to overspend so that I could make up for what I was lacking. One place where I would blow through a lot of money was in the food category in my spending plan. It made me feel special. For example, I could've gone to a big box store to buy a bucket of pickles for say, ten dollars, but instead, I'd overpay for tiny jars of "artisan" pickles from the hip grocer my friends lovingly referred to as "Whole Paycheck."

Dammit, I thought, *I'm tired of being broke! I'm tired of dollar tacos and I deserve something good.* So, I'd go to the hip grocer and spend ridiculous amounts of money on things like air-popped truffle mushroom fries (twelve dollars a bag), and Ginger-Cured Smoked Salmon for forty dollars a pound. It was my way of treating myself.

Why shouldn't I eat things I like? I have nothing else going on in my rotten life. I reasoned. *Besides, withholding organic super foods today will inevitably lead to a self-loathing, shame spiral tomorrow.*

I grew accustomed to paying more for things due to my "self-love"-fueled immaturity, and when I sat down and looked at the numbers, I discovered I was spending forty percent of my income on groceries.

It was self-sabotage, or as I lovingly refer to it, "a way to really screw myself over." I don't have to sleep on the floor and live out of a Dumpster, but I also don't have to be the kook who pays forty dollars for a jar of cold-processed virgin argan oil. I don't need to buy the cheapest thing on the shelf, but I won't be permanently damaged if I don't buy myself the absolute best.

Wanna know what makes me feel really special these days? Sticking to my spending plan.

It's Not About The Money:

Give yourself a big hug and stick to that spending plan.

March 18

AMISH-ISH

Sometimes I wish I were Amish. Not only are they lovely people, they're gentle and tidy, and I just discovered they have their own brand of romance novels called bonnet rippers.

The thing I love most about the Amish is, they don't worry about keeping up appearances. They aren't stressed out over the make and model of their cars, nor do they appear to be ashamed about the fact they don't have electricity or iPhones.

I, on the other hand, spend way too much time worrying about what other people think. My need to "look good" and "keep up with the Joneses" was the reason for most of my debt.

DA has taught me–although slowly–that I'm not my possessions, nor do the things I posses have *anything* to do with a successful life. Things make my life more comfortable but they don't make me more valuable or lovable. And my Higher Power most certainly doesn't care what I have in my bank account. For that matter, what other people think about me and my possessions is none of my business.

I'm a people pleaser who wants to be liked, but I'm learning to care less about what others think of me, my career, or my possessions, thanks to recovery. Still, there are times when I fantasize that life would be a lot easier if I just gave it all up and became Amish–aside from having to learn the Pennsylvania German dialect.

Perhaps someday I'll embrace the Amish lifestyle and move to a tiny village, give up modern comforts like electricity and running water, and convert to the horse and buggy. Or, I can just pretend to be Amish by being more thoughtful and gentle, and not placing so much emphasis on my possessions.

It's Not About The Money:

Today I'll be thoughtful and gentle, like I'm from an Amish village.

March 19

THE LIFE

The speaker at the DA meeting said, "I don't have the life I wanted, but I want the life I have."

I get it. The life I have today is not what I expected. Granted, when I was young, my idea of success was getting paid obscene amounts of money to be creative and brainstorm all day long, or to eat pepperoni pizza and spend my time window-shopping.

My life is totally different than how I'd imagined it would be, and despite what my feelings tell me at times, my life is the way I want it. I can't imagine what life would be like if I hadn't found the fellowship and help of DA. Actually, I can imagine it, and it involves jumping from a very tall bridge or eating mystery meals and Dumpster diving for my clothes.

Because of DA, I've been able to connect with a kind, loving Higher Power, and I wouldn't want to miss any of the experiences I've had. Aside from the identity-theft part that happened a few years ago. If I had my life to do all over again, I would never want to relive the identity-theftt, because it's a pain in the ass to try to get your life back once your identity has been stolen: contacting creditors, changing all your pin numbers, telling the IRS, the banks, the post office, etc. It's a complete nightmare.

I might not be living the life I thought I wanted, but, alas, the life I have is very good and it's just fine with me. Sans the identity theft part.

It's Not About The Money:
I have the life I want today. Thanks, God.

March 20

FAVORITE THINGS

Last night I watched *The Sound of Music* again, and I began to wonder: could Maria von Trapp have been struggling with debting and/or underearning? Now, I'm the last person in the world to judge, because no one loves Maria as much as I do. In fact, I left my handsome Greek suitor on the shores of Santorini when I was 23 to travel to Austria for *The Sound of Music* tour.

However, now that I'm in DA, I've begun to notice a few things about darling Maria that heretofore, I'd missed:

- "Brown paper packages tied up with strings" are among her favorite things.
- She's "late for everything, except every meal." At least that's what the nuns claimed.
- Her entire wardrobe is made from curtains. By hand.

Oh, Maria, that I could step back in time and explain to you what DA has taught me about debting and self-worth.

If I had my choice, I'd take Maria – who'd undoubtedly still be in that dress made from green and white damask drapes – by the hand and say, "Sweet, angelic-voiced Maria, I want you to want more for yourself. I speak from experience when I say, 'If you're a debtor, get some help.' Don't expect some strapping, rich naval captain to rescue you and assume life will become some romantic Rodgers and Hammerstein musical production. Real life doesn't always end like it does in the movies."

I'd then ask Maria to sing my favorite *Sound of Music* songs, which I'm sure she'd do, because she had a hard time saying "no" to people. But that's a different program and I'd best not take other peoples' inventories.

It's Not About The Money:

I'm so glad I know how to identify my favorite things these days!

March 21

GOD'S NUMBERS

By definition, a spending plan is a "charting of predicted and actual spending, a way to plan monthly expenditures and ensure spending doesn't exceed the total monthly net income."

Yawn.

Imagine my surprise when I learned that spending plans were a core part of recovery in the DA Program.

"Can't we skip over spending plans and just do the spiritual stuff?" I asked my sponsor.

"A spending plan is spiritual," he sang back. "God is in the numbers."

"Yeah? So, God's going to reveal the hidden calculations of the Great Pyramids and the mathematic miracle of Stonehenge?" I snapped back.

My sponsor explained that a spending plan would bring clarity. The more clarity I experienced in my finances, the more empowered I'd feel, and eventually I would enjoy the process of managing my spending plan.

He was half right. I don't exactly get giddy over the thought of keeping and maintaining my spending plan, but it does feel good to know where my money is going.

I decided to do an online search for the term *God is in the numbers,* and I learned that Mozart was rumored to have been a Freemason. I also read about the Fibonacci numbering sequence, which is the basis for perfection in nature. I got a little confused when I started reading about the planetary revolutions and spiral arrangements, so I stopped reading. Then I went back to tracking my spending plan. I felt much better.

While I'll never be giddy about managing my spending plan, I can appreciate that God is in the numbers.

God is all up in the numbers.

March 22

CROWD FUN

I've decided to launch a crowdfunding campaign–funds collected from a large pool of backers on the Internet to pay for a project –to cover the cost of my trip to Paris next summer.

You see, before I came into DA, I promised myself that every few years I would get back to my European roots, and it's been ages since I've even ventured out of my backyard. So, as I was doing my meditation this morning–the term "crowdfunding campaign" kept coming up for me. And it seemed like a brilliant way to pay for my upcoming trip. Paris can be pricey, especially in the summer.

I've not yet spoken with my DA sponsor, or anyone else, about my plan, and I most surely will consider it. Nevertheless, I've done some research and it appears my crowdfunding campaign idea might be allowed under the DA "gifting clause."

Next week I plan to start shooting my first video for the campaign, which is going to be super cool. The video will open with a shot of a couple kissing on the Champs-âlysées. Then there'll be a montage of French people riding bicycles, holding French baguettes and smoking French cigarettes. Of course, there will be plenty of people sitting around in French bistros, eating croissants, and a few people French kissing. And I'll include a few good French songs, if I can get the rights to them.

All in all, I'm super excited about my crowdfunding campaign idea. It'll be amazing to see what I can achieve when I allow other people to contribute to my dreams.

It's Not About The Money:

Am I sharing my "bright ideas" with people I trust?

March 23

SELF TRUST

"I don't think you trust yourself with money," my DA sponsor said to me recently.

"What is that supposed to mean? You make it sound like I'm some kind of lecherous cheat or something, like I can't be left alone with a credit card or I'll use it. It's not like I borrow money from myself and don't pay myself back," I said, laughing.

"That's exactly what I mean. You have done all of those things," he said gently.

"So what is your point?"

"Your relationship with money is like any other relationship," he said in his deep theatrical voice. "When you're trustworthy with money, you don't borrow money from your savings and fail to pay yourself back. You don't hide money from yourself, because you're confident you'll make good decisions. You also don't have a dozen accounts at different banks because you've forgotten about them."

"What is it you're trying to say?"

"I don't think you trust yourself with money–"

"You've already said that!" I snapped. "What do you suggest I do to become more trustworthy?"

"Start paying attention to the ways in which you hide money, or get vague or overwhelmed. Notice your feelings and write about where you are and what you're doing when it happens"

"Okay, I'll give it a shot." I sighed.

Imagine that. Insinuating I don't trust myself, and I have a bad relationship with money. He gets that way sometimes, my sponsor. Esoteric. Theatrical.

It's Not About The Money:

Of course I trust myself with my money!

March 24

EMPLOYED

Even as a child I knew I'd be best suited for "creative" work, the kind where I could show up to work around 10:30 a.m., toss around clever sounding ideas for a few hours, take lavish two hour lunches, and finish the day with a facial. And be highly paid.

I've held those "creative" types of jobs for short periods of time–usually until I was replaced by someone related to the owner of the company. The thing about "creative" jobs is that you work for "creative" people, who tend to be unstable and highly inconsistent.

When I quit my last "creative" job–I was tired of hanging out with artistic jerks that were more self-absorbed than me–I decided to get help from a career coach. After subjecting me to a slew of personality tests, she confirmed I was meant to work in a creative field. The other options included shoe sales or private investigation.

I was distraught, because I'd been forced to face my ultimate fear: that my abilities simply didn't translate into the real world. And I started to worry that, not only was I not destined for greatness, I wasn't destined for anything that might include long-term employment.

I went to a DA meeting and shared my fears about being unemployable. At the end of the meeting, someone shared with a quote from the Big Book, which says: God is my employer. "Being all powerful, he provides what we need if we keep close to Him."

I'm not sure what God has planned for me. It may include selling shoes. Or it might involve me hiding in an unmarked car outside an apartment building, binoculars in hand. I don't know, but I do know that I'm ready to let God be my employer. Which is good because I imagine God is a much better boss than the wackos I'm used to working for.

It's Not About The Money:

God's my employer, which means I should probably start taking shorter breaks.

March 25

HEAD HUNTS

Tell me who your friends are and I'll tell you who you are," said the sumg Headhunter, leaning back in his chair. I wanted to kill myself right there in his smug-looking office.

I was new to DA and I didn't have the energy to take on another high-stress job, but I couldn't admit that I was burned out. I'd been laid-off from another difficult job, the last in a series of Internet companies that were cutting costs due to poor management and an open disdain for Marketing–types like me. If I couldn't achieve Herculean results or turn the company around within a few months time, the mood would turn dark. I'm not necessarily complaining, but the grind of knowing my head was on the chopping block before I'd gotten comfortable in my new parking spot had become too much for a neurotic, people-pleaser like me.

I'd committed the sin of being out of full-time work for too long, and hadn't stayed in touch my old co-workers. The customers I dealt with had left their companies, too. Everyone in my network had disappeared, and I was in the twilight zone of unemployment. I had no past, no future and was certain I'd never be found again.

I looked at the Headhunter and started to sob, which sealed my fate. He ushered me out of his office without even offering me a tissue.

In time, DA taught me that I didn't need to worry about being a better "networker," I just needed to be willing to be of service and trust that it would be enough. As long as I continued to take action, God would bring me the right opportunities. It took a while, but it worked out, and I found something new and very rewarding. Work that no smug Headhunter could ever have found for me. Take that, smug Headhunter!

It's Not About The Money:

My fate is never sealed, as long as I keep taking action.

March 26

FRAUD ALERT

Deep down, on some level, I knew this day would come.

There's no way to explain how I felt when I woke up this morning, other than having an eerie sensation that my biggest fear had finally come to fruition. Today I knew I was going to be outed as the complete fraud that I am.

I have no tangible proof, but I'm fairly sure that when I arrive at work this morning, my boss will make the announcement–over the loudspeaker, of course–that I am unqualified for anything other than shredding envelopes or licking stamps, and that everything I've done up until this point in my life has been a total waste.

At that point I'll be escorted out of the office building as my colleagues stand by. "We've been on to you for years," they'll hiss as they toss staplers and paper clips at my head.

I've considered calling someone in DA to talk about how I'll handle this situation, which I assume won't occur until close to the end of the day–my boss will try to get all the work she can out of me–but I'm sure they're all too busy, living useful, authentic lives to talk to me.

I would call my sponsor, but I won't be able to handle his disappointment when he discovers he's been sponsoring an impostor, a hack, and a sham of a human being.

Nope, I'll go in to work today and face the music, which will, no doubt, be sad. And very, very slow.

It's Not About The Money:

Am I creating music that I'll never have to face?

March 27

DO-OVERS

I used to be a road-rager. Not the get-out-of-your-car and punch someone type of road-rager, but I was definitely passive-aggressive when I drove. You know, you ride too close to my bumper and I tap the brakes? You cut me off, I honk and flash you the middle digit?

I was so proud of myself when I went twenty-two days without flipping another driver off. It was proof that I was finally achieving spiritual maturity. Then I went to work on the twenty-third day and my streak was broken.

The solution to my road-rage problem is similar to my recovery in the DA Program. I take things one day at a time, because success from the day before doesn't carry over. I have to start each new day with the help of God and the Twelve Steps.

To some that may sound depressing, having to start life over every single day. But for me, it's actually kind of fun, because when I've been a jerk on the road–or anywhere, for that matter–it's comforting to know I can get a do-over if need be, which, some days is necessary before I've gotten out of bed.

It's Not About The Money:

I love the fact that life allows me do-overs.

March 28

RAINBOW PEEPS

Sometimes I get so tired of thinking about money that I fantasize about living with the Rainbow People–the wealthy bohemian hedonists who put on Rainbow Gatherings–and camp out in the forest. There, I'd pay for my dinner with pinecones and make tie-dyed scarves in exchange for toilet paper. No money trading hands, no greed, no power mongering, no structure. Most importantly, no "masks."

Just peace, harmony, and free love.

Going off the grid with the Rainbow People seems like so much fun, until I consider the fact that the people I'd be sharing the communal kitchen with folks who don't practice any sort of daily hygiene, nor do they believe in wearing clothes when they cook. The drinking water is filtered from open streams, and sanitation has been known to be a problem.

When addicts want to escape, they take a drink or a hit. I create fantasies in which the things I want magically appear when I need them and I don't have to put effort into anything. I'm very sensitive and creative, and dealing with trivial things like bills and money tends to bum me out.

DA has taught me to deal with the real world in a healthy, mature way, because I live in the real world and not in the forest.

Despite my protestations, I've discovered that the real world is kind of fun at times. For instance, I like paying for my clothes with real money. It's kind of neat to look at my checking account and see all those numbers before the decimal point. And I like knowing that I am capable. Today, I have the support of a Higher Power and a recovery Program that gives me the Tools to manage my money. So, when it comes to shopping for things like dinner and toilet paper, I no longer fantasize about paying with pinecones anymore.

It's Not About The Money:

Thanks to DA, today I use cash instead of fantasy.

March 29

UPSTANDING

Some people don't enjoy planning for taxes. I'm one of them.

So imagine my shock when my sponsor said, "You're going to start having your taxes done two months before they're due."

"In October?" I asked.

"Huh?"

"Well, I always file my extension in mid-April, which pushes things to October. If I'm lucky, I get it all done just before Christmas. So early would be October."

"No more extensions," he said. "The rest of the nation pays its taxes on April fifteenth and so can you. You need to have your taxes filed by early March next year."

My sponsor and I worked on that as a goal for several years. Not we, exactly, I mean *I* worked on that. All my sponsor did was call to remind me of the dates things were due. And when I told him I'd done it, he congratulated me.

This year I paid my taxes on March 12. I'll admit, it felt pretty good, like I was all pulled together. Normal. An upstanding citizen.

It's a sweet feeling, kind of like when you find a canvas bag filled with gold coins in your attic, or a bunch of money in an old IRA account that you'd forgotten about? Okay, it's not that sweet, but it definitely feels good. Like in the way you feel when you go to a really great DA meeting and you feel connected to God, to others, and to life again?

Yeah, kind of like that.

It's Not About The Money:

Thanks, God, for showing me how to be upstanding.

March 30

GREENER PASTURES

If a path is well groomed, lined with primroses and bluebells and daisies, nesting birds and blossoming orchards, it's probably not for me. I prefer paths that are bumpy, broken, and jagged. If a passage looks pristine and easy to travel, chances are zero that I'll follow it.

Is it because I'm uncomfortable when things are peaceful and uncomplicated? Is it because I'm familiar with trails that are jagged and difficult? Is it because those well-groomed routes don't appeal to me? I mean, of course they *appeal* to me, but someone's got to do the planting and pruning. And I'm not really big on pruning.

Or, is it because, well, life is harder for me and people like me have to toil, trudge, and struggle?

Ding! Ding! Ding! That's it. It's only easy for *other people*. Everyone else gets to travel the green paths surrounded by meadows, smothered in flowers. Okay, that's an exaggeration, not *everyone* else. Just *mostly* everyone else. All of *my* friends. They all get *everything* they want.

That's how it looks from the cold, lonely, beaten down, jagged, rocky path I've been forced to traverse. But don't get me wrong, I'm not complaining. That's just how the pastures over there look–easier, lighter. Way greener than they are over here.

It's Not About The Money:

No matter how rocky it is, my path is no less green than anyone else's.

March 31

JOYEUX ANNIVERSAIRE

Today is Celebrate a Debtor Day. Even if it isn't your DA recovery birthday, you're gonna celebrate. And since I can't possibly cover everyone's birthday–although a meditation book with nothing other than a daily birthday message could be fun–I'd like us to celebrate our debtor birthdays together.

Even if you have no idea when your DA birthday is, you're going to celebrate it today. Because let's face it, most of us can't even make it to a dental appointment on time. Remembering our DA birthday is highly unlikely, so why not just choose to celebrate today?!

Unlike some of the other Twelve-Step Programs, I've noticed that DA doesn't make a big deal out of birthdays. Is it because we don't like being the center of attention? Or, is it because we're broke? Too cheap, perhaps? Or is it because we can't keep track of time?

Alas, there could be a host of reasons, so I'll not spend our precious time today dwelling on the why. Instead, I'll say, "Hey, debtor baby, happy birthday! I'm so glad you're here. I'm so happy you didn't give up and let the fear get to you. You are amazing!" And if I could, I would give you a big, bear hug right now, because you matter!

There, do you feel a little better now? I sure hope so. Because you, Mr./Ms. Recovering Debtor, do the hard work. You show up to meetings and you keep track of your numbers. You offer your hand to others and you stay at that job until you find something better. You don't just quit without a plan anymore. You're a champ. And you are the reason I say today is Celebrate a Debtor Day.

Happy birthday, you adorable, amazing debtor!

It's Not About The Money:

Celebrate you and your awesomeness today!

April 1

LIES, LIES, LIES

One of my favorite lines comes from an episode of the show Seinfeld.

Gary:
The truth is, George, I'm living a lie.
George:
Just one? I'm living, like, twenty.

When I came into DA, I was living a lot of lies. Of course, nothing criminal; it isn't like I had severed body parts stuffed under the cushions of my couch. I just wasn't all that transparent about what I did with my money or how I spent it. But I was able to rationalize.

What's the big deal? This world has gone entirely mad! Isn't everyone living a lie or two? Or twenty? I figured doing Step Four–"a searching and fearless moral inventory"–would be a piece of cake. I didn't have that much to hide.

I didn't realize a searching and fearless moral inventory would include the ways in which I was deceiving and *cheating* myself. I was surprised to discover that I lied to myself much more than I did to others. I spent a big chunk of my life denying how I felt about certain situations and relationships. I was terrified of making choices, so I accepted whatever life gave me in those areas of my life and as a result, I became skilled at hiding my true feelings from myself. Ultimately, I learned that those seemingly pint-sized lies were wearing away at my soul, and it was painful. I had to grieve the things I'd missed out on or denied myself because of my debting problems.

Today I aim for rigorous honesty with God and myself above all. And although I'm not perfect at it, I'm doing much better than I used to. It feels so good to not be living, like, twenty lies anymore.

It's Not About The Money:

God help me remember that honesty begins from within.

April 2

PERSPECTIVE

I was working at minimum wage for a high-end retailer. What perturbed me most were women who would leave a dressing room filled with designer clothes all over the floor. Inside out. And expect me to pick them up for them.

The part of me that was dying to follow them out of the store and scream, "Do I look like your mother?!" had to constantly be held in check. Sometimes the dark side of my personality won the fight and I did follow them out of the store, whispering snide comments under my breath. Not surprisingly, I hated going to work.

Slowly by slowly, I began to apply the principles of DA to my work life. I'd get on my knees each day before I went to work and ask God how I might be of service at my job. The prayer started out as, "God, show me how to be of service to these totally inconsiderate, entitled women who think the world is their laundry hamper." I said the prayer every day, even though many days I didn't mean it. But, after a month or two, the prayer became, "God, show me how to be of service to all of my customers, no matter what that means, and help me to really mean it."

One day, I was at work, collecting a pile of designer clothes that had been thrown on the dressing-room floor. I didn't even think about sighing loudly or following the woman who'd left them on the floor–inside out. I simply picked up the clothes and went about my day.

My perspective had changed. I no longer thought of myself as a victim or a flunky for spoiled, entitled customers, but as someone who was of service to God. And I learned that my serenity is more important than trying to teach someone else a lesson about entitlement. And I stopped it with all the sighing and the snide comments. For the most part.

It's Not About The Money:

Slowly by slowly, I will practice being of service.

April 3

CLARITY

I still remember my DA sponsor saying, with complete sincerity, "I love tracking my numbers. Financial clarity is pure joy."

What is this guy smoking? I thought. *The day I'm excited to look at a spreadsheet, my spending plan, or bank statement is, well, let's just say it'll be a cold day in h-e-double toothpicks! What kind of person gets excited about recording and reconciling numbers, aside from rich hedge-funders and their wives?*

It took me three years in DA to calm down enough to consistently keep track of my numbers. It's still not easy, but my sponsor is right–it does feel nice. As nice as, say, taking a trip to Australia or getting a Swedish massage? No. For a debtor like me, there are many, many things that are more enjoyable than looking at my numbers, but it is no longer painful. Or as painful as it used to be.

I do it because it's an essential part of my DA recovery. I feel saner when I know how much money I have and where it's going. No matter how bad the situation seems, when I sit down and do my numbers, I always feel calmer after having done it. Kind of like the way I feel after having gone to the gym.

I doubt I'll ever be as gung-ho as my sponsor about tracking my numbers or anything having to do with financial clarity. It's not even close to being a blast for me but I'm grateful because it could be worse. I haven't, like, died from doing it. Yet.

It's Not About The Money:

Today I'll work on my clarity so I can keep my sanity.

April 4

WALK AROUND THINGS

Today, April 4, is National Walk Around Things Day, the point of which is to avoid problems and risks, which for most debtors isn't a huge stretch. Avoiding problems is second nature to us.

And while this day focuses on the physical aspect of walking around anything that poses danger (ladders, feral cats, exposed wires) it can also be applied figuratively. Which is what I am recommending.

Today, I suggest we utilize those well-developed avoidance skills to stay out of and not initiate conversations about difficult topics or issues, unresolved debts, or anything that might create discomfort or a potential argument. Today is definitely not the day to call the IRS and admit you haven't paid the past five years' taxes or to show up on the doorstep of the cousin you owe a lot of money to. And if the sight of banks cause you stress, avoid them today as well.

If anyone tries to lure you into a discussion about anything difficult, including money, simply say, "I'm honoring Walk Around Things Day. Can we take this subject up tomorrow?" Then offer to buy them a cup of coffee.

If you want to get literal about today, you could find a park or a mall, bust out your new orange Converses, and go for a walk. Or a run. Anything to avoid conflict at all costs today, because this is National Walk Around Things Day, and you have permission to avoid dealing with anything that is risky today!

It's Not About The Money:

Feel free to walk around anything that's particularly stressful.

April 5

HAPPY TALK

It's been proven in numerous scientific experiments by some very smart people that human beings, especially debtors, tend be poor predictors of what will make them happy over the long run.

In fact, people are often more disappointed after having received the very thing they claim to have wanted. Sound familiar, oh friend of mine *who was sure that promotion was all she desired?* Or other friend of mine *who promised to invest that inheritance instead of frittering it away?*

When it comes to wanting, our imaginations can be elusive, and yet we still continue to want. I'm sure there's some very specific evidence about why that is, propagation of the species and that sort of stuff, but really, the takeaway is that old adage: Be careful what you wish for, as you just might get it.

Or, in DA speak: Stop being a self-centered, greedy derelict and thank God for what you have. There are children in Mozambique who would love to have your outdated Adidas running shoes, and people in North Korea who'd give anything to be driving your fifteen-year-old Kia.

Pull yourselves together, people! In this moment, you have absolutely everything you need. So please be grateful, because, if you're anything like me, one thing is certain: Once you get what you want, you'll be grousing about it soon enough.

It's Not About The Money:
God, please help me to want recovery.

April 6

CAVE JOBS

I used to despise people who'd say, "if something isn't serving you, let it go." I've always had a difficult time letting things go, whether it be old ideas, shoes, broken cups, or sunglasses. I also had a hard time walking away from jobs that allowed me to stay small and hide my talents, positions that left me financially and emotionally unhappy.

So what? You may say. *Plenty of people take jobs they hate. What's the big deal?*

It all boils down to *why*. As an underearner, I was addicted to negative thinking and would instinctively take work that didn't serve me. Or, worse, I'd get a fantastic job and sabotage it, only to end up in another job I hated.

The questions for me were: Did I stay in unfulfilling jobs because I was afraid of criticism? Or did I stay in unfulfilling jobs because was I afraid of taking a chance on a bigger life?

The answers were a resounding "yes" and "yes."

In order to overcome my addiction to underearning, I have to get out of the emotional "cave." I can be aware of my negative emotions without getting stuck in them. It requires commitment, consistency, and a connection to a kind and loving Higher Power. Besides, when I'm hiding in a cave, I can't be of service to the world because I'm caught up in my own misery and depression.

I'll probably never like people who say things like, "If it doesn't serve you, let it go," because it sounds so sanctimonious, but I'm working on letting those self-important types–like my underearning–go.

It's Not About The Money:
I'm going to let go of the cave today.

April 7

PASSED

My version of the past is not–and never has been–totally accurate. For example, I have a tendency to romanticize former relationships, places I visited or jobs I've had. I've also been known to lament about how much better things were "back in the day."

It's hard to have a good present when you're living in the past.

The reason the past seems so great in hindsight is because I know how things turned out. And it's easier to look back now, because I know what I'd've done if I had it to do things over. The irony is, I often don't know even what to do when things are happening in real-time.

For me, finding a Higher Power keeps everything in perspective: my past, my present and my future. When I remember that God has a plan, I don't have to make up romantic stories about how great the past was. I can let go of the past, because, in reality, I know that things weren't necessarily any better "back in the day."

Yes, the present can be difficult at times, but because of DA I have Tools for living in the moment, so I don't have to regret the past, nor fear the future.

In fact, I can say with absolute certain that the future holds fantastic things for me. And I believe the future is looking pretty bright for you too, my friends. Especially if you wear sunscreen and avoid chewing tobacco.

It's Not About The Money:

The present is a present. Treat is as such.

April 8

MONEY TALKS

Money Finally Talks Back to the Debtor.

Dear Debtor,

I thought I'd take a moment to share a few of my thoughts with you. I know how often you talk about me, probably not with the respect I deserve, but I'll get to that in a moment.The point here is to offer you some feedback. Instead of the usual talk about how much, as you like to say, you "struggle" with our relationship, might you consider another subject: say, how fun it would be to try CrossFit? Or, about how people who take "knee defenders" onto planes with them are impolite? I'm sure any of those subjects would be substantially better topics of conversation than little ol' me. At the very least, how about you try talking about me with less contempt?

You say you don't like talking badly about me, but you do. A lot. I'm what you talk about when there's nothing else going on. Honestly, you spend so much time talking about how I let you down constantly, but there are many other things going on in the world, maybe you could talk about those things? Like, the bikini-cleanse diet you've just started. Although I hate to tell you, a bikini cleanse is just another diet. It's eating things like raw vegetables and cutting out sugar and meat and drinking a lot of juice. There, I just saved you a lot of money, so perhaps now you will stop talking trash about me.

You say that authenticity is important to you, especially now that you're going to those DA meetings, and while I don't doubt your sincerity, how can you be authentic when you're always worried about me?

How's about we call a truce? You won't talk about me in a negative way, and I won't talk about you. We won't talk about our "relationship" for a while, or try to figure out why you never seem to have enough of me. For the next few hours, you do your thing, and I'll do mine. Capiche?

It's Not About The Money:

Today I'll focus on something that isn't money.

April 9

AVOIDANT

"I think I'm a love avoidant," I told my DA sponsor while having coffee with him and another friend.

"Do say more," he said, smiling.

"Well, some debtors love too much. Others love too little, and others are love avoidant."

"She's right," my friend chimed in. "A lot of debtors have problems with other compulsive behaviors. It's very common. Process-based addictions, they call them."

My sponsor laughed.

"Anyway, there's a seminar for love avoidants," I said. "It's only five thousand dollars. Should I go?"

"How much do you have in your educational reserves?"

"Umm...I have four. Dollars."

"I can loan you fifty," said my adorable friend.

"Is it technically considered debting to borrow money to go to a seminar?" I say to no one in particular. "When it's recovery work? If I'm love avoidant, I should probably take care of that, don't you think?"

"I think some people take their own temperature way too often," my sponsor gently said.

Huh? I've never once taken my own temperature, I thought. *I don't even own a thermometer. What's this guy talking about?*

"I suggest you do some praying and writing about it, then schedule a PRG about how best to spend the four dollars you have in your educational reserves." He paused. "Although I suspect you already know the answer."

As I was driving home, it hit me–what my sponsor was trying to say without saying it. And he was right. *I was* love avoidant and I *did* need to deal with it.

It's Not About The Money:

God, help me pause and listen to what is really being said.

April 10

CONSPIRACIES

Although my "friend" wasn't a conspiracy theorist, recently she'd become convinced the reason she was unable to pay her bills was due to covert manipulations coordinated by some major corporations. It seemed these efforts have spanned decades and multiple continents.

My "friend" began to track the roots of the problem back to her childhood. It began when her father told her she needed to "learn the value of a dollar," which didn't make sense at the time. Until she started to think about similar patterns with people in authority: employers who expected her to show up on time and earn the money they were paying her, corporations trying to manipulate her into paying for things she'd purchased at crazy interest rates. All this, after having offered her free money! Then there were the "friendly" offers to gain her trust and friendship by loan officers who quickly turned on her and began sending rude letters demanding immediate payment.

True friendships are hard to come by these days, my "friend" thought.

The only plausible explanation she could come up with for her situation was "an exceptionally coordinated, high-level effort" to get her to join a game of epically dangerous proportions. She believes the conspiracy to destroy her credit and keep her down involves friends and family members, as well as the upper echelons of American society. How else could she explain why she's now instantly rejected when applying for credit?

On the surface, this theory might make my "friend" seem strange or crazy, or at the very least, irresponsible. Which is, of course, exactly what "they'd" like you to believe about her. My "friend" never used to believe in conspiracy theories. Until now.

It's Not About The Money:

Am I running any conspiracies in my head?

April 11

MISS UNDERSTANDINGS

I was setting up a new business account at my bank and the teller suggested I open a savings along with the checking account so I could earn a few hundred dollars.

I was perturbed when, two months later, I discovered the teller had forgotten to mention that the savings account would cost thirty dollars a month, although I had a daily balance of $10,000. I decided to call the bank.

Normally, my conversation would've started with: "What the hell is wrong with you people? Why are you always trying to rip me off? And why are you charging me when I have so much money in my account? Isn't keeping my money kind of, you know, a bank's job? One of these days, I'm gonna drop you like a hot potato!"

As you might imagine, things would often go downhill from there. But because of my work in recovery, I have learned that things generally go better when I don't start off insulting someone. I've learned to bring God into those conversations–most of the time. I ask for my Higher Power's help so that I approach the other person with kindness, and refrain from acting like a jerk. I say a prayer of blessing for the person on the other end of the line. Because, contrary to what my head tells me, I'm not dealing with some inherently evil person who lives to make my life miserable. I'm dealing with a human being who has feelings and frustrations, too.

Instead, I began the call with, "Hello, there! I was wondering if you could help with what I think is a misunderstanding." I went on to ask the bank to reverse the charges. They agreed, and things worked out nicely. No sighing, no screaming, no drama.

My interactions with the bank don't always go this smoothly, but they go better than they used to. Even though I might not get what I want, when I'm kind to another human being I feel good. The people at the bank aren't personally trying to ruin my life. At least I don't think they are, and for today, I'm going to assume that's true.

It's Not About The Money:

God, help me remember that other people are doing the best they can.

April 12

BIG CAPTAIN

I was so embarrassed. One of the people listed on my bankruptcy report was the woman who led the From Broke to Billionaire course.

Most of the people I'd taken the course with had gone on to success. I, on the other hand, was an unrecovered debtor. I had no clue why I couldn't make it from broke to …not broke. Within a year after I had "graduated" from the course, I was in bankruptcy court.

I couldn't figure out what was wrong. *Why couldn't I just "create wealth" and have a great life?*

I wanted to blame the instructor for my lack of progress, because I'd done everything she'd suggested. Yes, she was a little too cheery, trying to trick us into making cold calls by substituting the word "ship" for phone, using nautical analogies to distract us into marketing ourselves. Yes, I was annoyed by her excitement over making a stupid spending-plan as well, but deep down I knew it wasn't her fault.

I had to lose everything before I finally understood what debting really was. The solution to my problem wasn't cold-calling with a smile, or setting bigger goals, or pretending I was the captain of a large boat and my staff was my crew, and my potential clients were sea mammals. The solution was admitting I have peculiar responses to money, writ large.

Today, I set goals, make the calls and sent out "ships," but I put the results into the hands of the Big Captain in The Sky, trusting that I'll be led in the right direction. It's a daily surrender, the only one that leads to emotional and spiritual freedom.

I admit, sometimes I do still wear my captain's cap when I have a lot of phone calls to make. It's just more fun that way.

It's Not About The Money:

All right, already. Understanding comes from the inside.

April 13

HALF-ARSED

In the Big Book of Alcoholics Anonymous, it talks about "half measures… availing us nothing."

Before I found DA, I was a big believer in half-arsed measures.

It takes a lot of work to make dreams happen, I told myself. It requires focus, weekends working while everyone else is out at parties having fun. Let's face it–it's just not worth it to give myself over to anything a hundred percent. How many people have wasted years of their lives in pursuit of an Oscar or to run for a public office and never achieved their dream?

When you do everything half-arsed, you never have to fear you've wasted your life giving it your all and failed.

Thanks to DA, I don't do life half-arsed anymore. Because of recovery and a renewed connection to my Higher Power, I am able to commit to at least trying my best and to be of service to others. My best at times may just mean smiling at someone, or not leaving work early when I want to and know I can get away with it. Or my best might be just refraining from being snarky to someone else. My best may not be a hundred percent and that's okay. But I can guarantee that I never settle for doing anything half arsed anymore. It's simply not very fulfilling.

It's Not About The Money:

If we're willing to give life our all, we will see changes.

April 14

SELF-GOVERNING

"Each group should be autonomous except in matters affecting other groups or DA as a whole." – *DA Tradition #4*

At first, this Tradition sounded boring, kind of like reading the directions on a TV remote or a prenuptial agreement, or any of the other various contracts I've signed without reading.

When I finally sat down and read the Fourth Tradition, I found out how important it is to the DA fellowship, and even to my own life.

I've heard it called "self-governance with responsibility." While each meeting is independent, it must remain considerate of the whole group. This gives each meeting the freedom to decide the topics and content of the meetings. The group decides when and where the meeting will be held, and if it will be open or closed. The group can change the format and has the authority to spend the money it receives.

Each meeting has its own format while remaining within the overall guidelines of DA, but must be careful not to focus on any particular philosophy, religion, political viewpoint, or hidden agenda. Which is nice, because that means I don't have to worry that the sweet old lady who's giving me her phone number will offer her opinion on fracking or con me into some bogus multilevel marketing scam.

Tradition #4 keeps DA meetings safe and shows us how to govern the groups responsibly. Now, if I could learn to *govern myself* responsibly, that would be something!

It's Not About The Money:

Today I will try to govern myself responsibly.

April 15

TAXING

It's tax day. Since the dawn of time, human beings have done their best to avoid both death and taxes. I understand why. Both are anxiety producing. And if you're like me, doing anything on an "official" timeline just doesn't work.

So, today, instead of caving in to pressure to pay my taxes–on some arbitrary date because the government has designated it so–I've chosen to spend the day honoring the champions who courageously argue against the legality of taxation. Although their success rate has been minimal (unless you include those who got out of paying taxes because they've been incarcerated), I'd like to salute those visionaries and their completely bogus arguments that they earnestly believe will cause the federal government to say, "You know what? You're right, dude. Let's just drop the whole taxation stuff. It's completely illegal!"

Don't get me wrong. I'm not a freeloader who wants to get away with something. I'm not above the rules. It's just that doing things simply because everyone else does it has never been my style. And the fact that I'm an American does not prohibit me from pointing out how easy and stress free tax day is for our Canadian friends. Why shouldn't it be? In Canada, tax day's a celebration, with neighborhood parties and music and dancing. I've heard that egg dishes and Canada Dry are served at tax-day events.

If you happen to be one of those who will be filing your taxes on time today, please know that I'm totally thinking good thoughts for you. I hope this day is as pleasant as it can be, all things considered. People like you make the world a better place to live, and you make me proud to be a debtor. Well, not exactly proud to be a debtor, but honored to live in a country where there are people who gladly pay their taxes on time.

It's Not About The Money:

Do I think I'm above the rules in any area of my life?

April 16

PASSION

Early on in recovery, when I was down and busted out, certain I'd be a big fat zero for the rest of my life, a friend of mine said, "Success is just a matter of doing what you feel passionate about."

"For the love of God, enough with the passion clichés," I screamed at her. "My passions are having fun, sleeping, and eating peanut butter and banana sandwiches. Who's gonna pay me to do that?!"

I know my friend meant well and I probably could have been gentler with her, but sometimes I get tired of the whole be-passionate-and-you're-guaranteed-to-make-a-lot-of-money-and-be-a-huge-success culture we live in. That I live in.

The truth is, we may not make a living from what we're passionate about. No one really knows. Recovery has shown me that passion doesn't equal or guarantee success. Besides, too much passion can make people crazy. I know a few passionate folks who are certifiable.

I was in recovery for a while before I even figured out the things I was really and truly, down-in-my-heart passionate about. It took me time to figure out what I enjoyed, because when I first came into recovery, I was so broke and depressed the only thing I knew to do was to read a book or watch the cars pass by on the street. I lived on a busy street.

If I do what is in front of me, and do it in the most loving way possible, satisfaction will be an outcome, and satisfaction is a pretty cool outcome. I don't always feel passionate but that doesn't mean I'm not successful. In fact, I feel kind of successful today.

How about you? Are you pleasantly satisfied with anything today?

It's Not About The Money:
What can I be pleasantly satisfied with today?

April 17

PLANS

In Debtors Anonymous, we use the term "spending plan" instead of "budget," because "budget" tends to freak us debtorly types out. And no wonder. Budget reeks of discipline and deprivation; it's the dark hallway of finances. It's eating leftovers in the back alley while your friends are inside a cozy French restaurant dining on fine wine and cheese.

"Spending plan" is abundance. It's peacefulness. It's me in the sunlight, lying in the soft, lush grass amidst jewel-colored flowers, hummingbirds hopping about, scattering dewdrops and chirping merrily as they preen their plumage.

Okay, that's an exaggeration, but "spending plan" doesn't make me feel like "budget" does, like I'm being pulled into a powerful undercurrent, being swept down into a vast underwater pocket, leading me to a watery grave where my body will never be found.

A spending plan gives me categories like: entertainment (yay!), personal care, education, and vacations (double yay!), things I denied myself–thinking I was being noble–while under the influence of debting. Today, I take care of my needs first, then pay my creditors. This allows me to have a life.

I suppose, then, that debting is the watery grave, the massive undercurrent of despair that pulls me down. But a spending plan gives me hope and serenity, a connection with my Higher Power. It guides me back to the terra firma, along fertile banks bursting with sweet-smelling thyme.

I'm glad I was able to pull this analogy back because it was getting pretty dark there for a moment. I know, not every meditation can be light and this is an intense subject. But I'd say I got us back on track, wouldn't you agree?

It's Not About The Money:

I'll stick to my spending plan and away from the currents of despair.

April 18

TALE OF TWO DEBTORS

"I know what's needed to get you out of this funk," Marco, my celebrity-stylist friend coos over the phone. "Girl, we is goin' shopping!"

"I can't buy anything, you idiot. I'm broke!" I start to hang up, but he piques my interest with, "Don't worry, we'll go to the outlets. And since we're friends, I won't charge you for my styling advice."

Marco picks me up in his brand new Range Rover. "Why are you wasting your life playing small? Wearing off-the-rack, cotton poly-blends?"

"Because I'm broke, and I came from a screwed-up family that had no taste. For goodness sake, they bought boxed wine for special occasions!" I sniped.

"Nuh-uh. You can't blame your parents forever, nor can you let them define who you are." This, from the man who took me home on Christmas to pose as his girlfriend. When he ran off to grab his Chanel boots to wear on the annual family snow-sledding excursion, his mother winked at me and said, "It's okay, honey. I know. We all know."

"You have got to get over this poverty mentality, and the first step is in opening yourself up to abundance." Marco croons as we traverse every square inch of the mile-long outlet mall.

Since most of our shopping trip is spent discussing Marco's relationship issues, he only charges me for three hours of his time, and gas. Still, I'm out two thousand dollars, since he convinced me a Fendi wallet is key to attracting wealth and vital to opening myself up to abundance.

Yes, I spent every last dime I had that day, but I felt so fortunate to have a friend as wise and generous as Marco.

It's Not About The Money:

Am I sabotaging my efforts to be abundant?

April 19

TRIES

"Would you mind picking up my mail while I'm gone?" my neighbor innocently requested last week.

"Umm, okay, I'll try," I said sheepishly.

"Try?" She laughed. "What's so hard about picking up the mail? The mailbox is a hundred feet from your door."

I wanted to explain that many debtors share an intense fear of opening the mailbox, but I couldn't.

I'm not "arguing for my limitations," as the proverbial "they" say, but being vague is part of what I do. I still work on it in DA, but for someone who used to check the mail once a month and bought a p.o. box so she could avoid checking the mail for three years, the fact that I get to my mailbox once a week now is an utter miracle. Opening bills is scary. I've never once gotten good news from the IRS, a utility company, or a bank via the mail. But I won't give up hope.

In recovery, I've learned to take contrary action, and I have a Higher Power and friends who help me. It's nice to know that my DA pals understand my seemingly bizarre fears, and they're always there to walk me through the hard actions required for growth. I know that if I continue to take action toward solvency one day at a time, I'll have so much peace and recovery that one day I may enjoy going to the mailbox.

"Okay," I said to my neighbor. "I'd be happy to pick up your mail while you're gone." And I meant it. Sort of. I mean, I'll do it. I might not like it, but I'll do it. Contrary action and all that.

It's Not About The Money:

I won't argue for my limitations. I'll just take the action.

April 20

THE GAMBLER

I remember watching Kenny Rogers sing his hit song "The Gambler" on The Muppet Show. There he sat, next to a bunch of craggly faced Muppets on a train, passing around a whiskey bottle and a cigarette. The whole scene filled me with a sense of melancholy.

I knew things were going to end badly for the crusty, beak-nosed Muppet with a gray wig when he looked at the camera and sang:

Every hand's a winner
Every hand's a loser...
The best that you can hope for is to die in your sleep.

When the Muppet snuffed out his cigarette, leaned back, and closed his eyes, I burst into tears. First, because he had the same gray wig as my great uncle Aaron and looked exactly like him, and second, because I'd just witnessed the death of a Muppet on national TV.

I felt so sad as that lonely old Muppet, so thin and broken down, took his last breath, while Kenny Rogers sat there without even reacting!

I was a little confused when the old Muppet ghost jumped up, slapped his gangly legs, and started singing:

You got to know when to hold 'em
Know when to fold 'em
Know when to walk away
And know when to run.

He died broke and yet he was so happy! What were they trying to say? Gambling is fun? Drink and smoke all you want? Or was it, Watch how you spend your money, otherwise you'll end up broke and alone and dead on a train while people just stare at you?

That episode of the Muppets traumatized me for many years, and I'm convinced it played a huge role in my distorted relationship with money. And death. Fortunately for me, I was never big on cigarettes or whiskey.

It's Not About The Money:

Folks, don't gamble. You'll never beat the house.

April 21

FREAK OUT!

Someone in DA once told me that when they were in the throes of fear about money, they would set their alarm and do what they called a Five-Minute Freak-out. They'd spend an entire five minutes kicking, screaming, crying, whatever. But at the end of the five minutes, they'd have to stop freaking out. They wouldn't allow themselves to think about that problem again for the rest of the day.

For the first three months in DA, I had to set my alarm for a Five-Minute Freak-out every single day. The first time I tried it, I imagined various terrifying scenarios, including homelessness, prison, selling the mercury in my teeth for cash, and donating one of my kidneys to the Russian mafia. I cried, screamed, punched my pillows, threw ice cubes at the wall, and worried as much as I could. But once that alarm rang, I had to move on. I couldn't think about that subject again until the next day.

Are you worried or stressed about something? Set your alarm for five minutes and completely obsess about anything related to your debting, spending, underearning, or your future. Imagine every possible horrible scenario that could happen and feel as rotten as you want. Give it every ounce of energy you have and completely freak out.

If you're like me, you'll see how the Five-Minute Freak-out helps release those fears and frees up your energy. More importantly, you'll discover how agonizingly long five minutes can be.

It's Not About The Money:

Five minutes to freak out. Then you get to turn it over to God.

April 22

SANE-ISH

Sanity: soundness, rationality and healthiness of the human mind, as opposed to insanity.

I thought sanity would come when I got more money. I'd be calm, gracious, generous to a fault–someone completely and utterly unlike who I am deep down inside. I didn't quite get that, when it comes to debting and compulsive spending, I do not act sanely.

I could not, nor can I now, modify my spending and underearning behaviors. It's only through attending DA meetings and working the Twelve Steps that I experience the miracle of sanity – not through getting more organized, strategic, or finding a new therapist. I can't do it without a Higher Power, a community of others who are committed to staying solvent, and remaining free from resentments.

It took a lot of work for me to understand what sanity means when it comes to debt. I may not be foaming at the mouth, or even hanging out on a ledge, these days, but my behavior around money can get crazy pretty quickly.

I had to discover the hard way that there is no fail-proof system that leads to sanity in this area of my life. Sanity is a daily reprieve from compulsive spending, underearning, and self-debting. A daily reprieve from resentment, envy, laziness, entitlement, unforgiveness, and selfishness–all things that trigger my debting behaviors.

So, instead of trying to pretend I've got it figured out, I start every day by turning my will over to my Higher Power. Sanity is a daily choice, not a permanent state.

Drats.

It's Not About The Money:

Today, I'm not even going to pretend I'm sane around money and debt.

April 23

INSIDES

"You'll know you've made it when you understand that there's nothing anyone else can give you, no matter how grand or fabulous, that you can't give yourself."

– Anonymous

"What is it I would want me to give myself, if I could?" I asked myself. "Self-esteem? Humility?" I replied.

"Ugh."

"Self-love?"

"Meh, it's overrated. The only thing I really want from myself is a big fat bank account and a lot of jewelry," I said.

"But up until this point, you haven't really been able to give that to yourself, have you?" myself chirped back at me.

"You're right. I've had great jobs and it wasn't enough. So then I went off on my own. And I tried asking for more money, and raising my rates, and that didn't work. I tried convincing myself I deserved more by citing a bunch of dumb affirmations and attending hokey motivational seminars."

"Those didn't really work out so well, did they?" myself whispered back.

"No, so what are you trying to say?" I replied.

"They didn't work because you didn't think you deserved them."

"You could be right," I said to myself.

"Maybe there's something to this whole concept of recovery being an 'inside job.' Maybe I need the help of a Higher Power."

"Okay, what else?" myself asked.

"Maybe there is a God and it's not me. Perhaps I can just take the action and let God handle the results."

"You're pretty smart at times, you know?" I said to myself.

"Yeah, and at times, so are you." I replied.

It's Not About The Money:

It is an inside job, but it's not all up to me.

April 24

HELP

The Program of Debtors Anonymous can get heavy on the tactical and tangible stuff at times, so today I decided to concentrate on the impractical, intangible aspects. No talk of spending plans or numbers, or checking accounts or credit cards. Instead, we'll focus on the softer, more spiritual aspects of kindness.

Sometimes little acts of service–a smile or a compliment, or a call to a friend–are as important to cultivating abundance as keeping the numbers. Being thoughtful, generous, and kind are like little seeds we plant throughout the day, and the result is a fuller life. When we share our joy or show compassion to others, we sow the seeds of intangible prosperity.

Today, focus on how much you can offer others from that intangible realm, and do something nice for someone, whether it's a hug or a phone call or a kind e-mail. The one thing we can control, no matter how bad our financial state, is our attitude.

We might not be able to increase our earnings today, but we can always reach out and be of service to others.

Some of the biggest changes I've experienced in DA occurred as a result of helping others. I can't break it down or explain how it works, but thoughtfulness and a willingness to help someone else always improves the quality of my life.

Please go out and be helpful to someone else today. You can even go wild and start hugging random people you see on the street. Just be helpful. This concludes today's sermon.

It's Not About The Money:
Today, I'm gonna give away some love!

April 25

PROMISES

We will begin to live a prosperous life, unencumbered by fear, worry, resentment or debt. – *DA Promise #4*

When we work the Steps, go to meetings and use the Tools in DA, we're promised we will experience prosperity. I've heard countless stories of people finding fantastic jobs, increasing their wealth, falling in love and, for the first time in their lives, experiencing a feeling of abundance.

Because of recovery, I've redefined "prosperity." Prosperity, for me, isn't about having by a chunk of real estate or a monstrous savings account. It's having an abundant spirit, increased creativity and fulfilling relationships. My definition is different today than it was in the past, when my definition included fame and wealth.

As a result of the work I've done in DA, I'm less encumbered by fear and worry. It doesn't mean I don't worry at times, but I no longer feel like I'm being held hostage by the anxiety I used to feel day in and day out. I still get resentful at times, but I don't let those resentments weigh me down. I'm able to let go of the things I can't control, which is a lot of stuff.

The best part of the freedom I've gotten from Program? I'm no longer encumbered by those resentments, fear and worry. For the most part. On average, I'd say that I'm unencumbered 80% of the time. And 80% is a pretty good average, is it not?

It's Not About The Money:

It feels great when I'm unencumbered.

April 26

PRESENT

Most of us are familiar with the phrase, – *"What happens when you stand with one foot in the past and the other in the present?"* – The answer, of course, is that the present is gonna be plenty messy, if you know what I mean.

So, please remember there is a God, and it is not you. Make a commitment to let God figure everything out on your behalf today.

I know, you've got major problems, serious worries, valid concerns, and pressing issues. You can't just go throwing caution to the wind, hoping everything will pan out.

Well, my sweet little chickens, yes you can.

Just for today, let go of whatever is bothering you, whether it be money, work, relationships, or health problems. For this day only, you're going to act as if whatever's nagging at you has panned out, and your issue(s) has been solved. You can even pretend to be one of those optimistic types who believes that everything is working out for the best and it's going to be fantastic. If that's too much, then just go with the acceptance that yesterday is over, tomorrow is not here, and for today, things are *exactly* as they should be. Because, even if you're not feeling optimistic, that *is* the truth.

It's one foot out of the past and the other foot out of the future, it's keeping both of your tootsies firmly planted in today. There'll be *no messing on the present,* if you know what I mean. And I think you do.

It's Not About The Money:

Things are exactly as they should be today. Even if they aren't pretty.

April 27

DA-WHAT?

Most of the time when I tell people I'm in Debtors Anonymous, they assume I have a problem with gambling.

"Good for you," they say. "So, can you still go to Vegas with us?"

"Sure," I say, and then wait for the relief to turn into confusion. I usually leave it at that, because it's kind of hard to explain DA. Some people ask for clarification, and when they do, it usually goes like this:

"See, I have a strained relationship with money. I don't take care of my money, I quit jobs without having a backup plan, and I avoid making decisions. I'm unclear about my finances and I live on the edge financially..."

Silence as they try to absorb all this. The next comment is usually about how *everyone* is broke and hates their job.

"Yes, I know a lot of people are in debt and hate their jobs, but for a debtor, it's a *thinking problem*. We don't want to be responsible, we don't pay bills on time, and don't manage money well. Some us are afraid to check the mail–"

At that point, they often recommend that I just walk to the mailbox and pick up the mail.

"I know how to check the mail; it's not that simple. You see, I'm often angry at the world, the government, my job, other people. This attitude affects all areas of my life and it causes me to isolate. So I go to Debtors Anonymous meetings."

I inevitably get a question about what happens at a DA meeting.

"Well, we sit in a circle and everyone shares. And when we're done, we hold hands and pray. There's usually a lot of laughter and hugging ."

Then what?

"No, of course we aren't drunk!"

It's Not About The Money:

God understands me, and that's all that matters.

April 28

THANK YOU

My sponsor told me the first thing he does when he wakes in the morning is open his eyes and say, "Thank you."

"Thank you' is a complete prayer," he said.

Then he suggested that I do the same thing throughout the day, no matter how badly I felt. I didn't know whom I was thanking, or what I was saying thanks for. But I was desperate so I agreed to give it a try.

For two years in DA, I said "thank you," every day, over and over, almost all day long. It was the closest thing to a prayer I could manage when I was in the midst of the chaos debting had caused.

"Thank you," I would say to no one in particular. "Thank you for the basics: my fingers, my toes, my bed, my favorite pair of socks." I would like to have said "thanks" for my bicycle, but I couldn't because I'd lost my car and wasn't yet thankful for "being able" to ride my bike to the bus stop.

Eventually, I started looking at my bike with love and honestly meant it when I said "thank you." I began to look at the scowling bus driver with appreciation and was able to thank him and mean it. I don't know how or when, but my "thank yous" eventually became genuine.

"Thank you, God," I'd say, "For nothing and for everything. For the recovery and hope I'm experiencing, and for the spiritual program that has given me back my life."

Now, it's your turn. Try saying "thank you" as many times as you can today. You don't have to understand why, or even mean it–just say it. Your world may not change immediately, but I promise that your cynical little heart will feel a tiny bit better.

You're welcome.

April 29

LOOK BUSY

Debtor 1:

How are you?

Debtor 2:

Super Busy. You?

Debtor 1:

Literally insanely busy!

Everyone is *so* busy these days. It's gotten to the point where it feels like another layer of competition in this overactive, cutthroat world. It's people's way of saying, "I'm a way bigger deal than you are."

Most of us debtors are so consumed with "being busy," we feel guilty when we take some time to ourselves. Recently I took a few days off and noticed something: I'm a lot nicer when I slow down and take time to connect with God before I start the day. When I get up and out of bed and start pushing myself to get more done as fast as I can, I don't feel that great.

Must we buy into the pressure to be busy or more productive all the time? Must we constantly be working toward something, promoting something, or talking about how busy we'll be once we get something going? Must we assume that we can't possibly be valuable unless our calendars are completely booked or we're in demand every hour of the day?

I think not.

Listen to me, please. Insanely or literally insanely busy or not, you are valuable and lovable as you are. Not because of what you do. You're doing enough–at least the last time I checked, you were. Besides, you're *so* much cuter when you relax a bit.

It's Not About The Money:

Stop trying to look busy. You're doing just fine.

April 30

LETTER TO CREDITORS

Just for fun, I thought I'd offer a glimpse of letters I've considered writing to my creditors. This was before I found DA, so it's not advisable nor is this approved by DA, or anyone who has their head on straight.

Dear (insert name of creditor here):

This letter is in reference to my outstanding account. I wasn't able to find my account number, as I'm looking for work and my stuff is in storage. Also, I don't have much time to go looking through my old records. You'll probably do better to just look me up. In reference to my account, please note:

1. *I've already spent the money I owe you, or I may have lost it–I don't remember. But there's not that much I can do about it now, is there? I'd prefer that we stop focusing on the negative, because I've moved on and I sincerely hope you will as well.*
2. *You aren't the only one who's having a difficult time. Things in my world haven't been great lately, either. Maybe you could try walking a mile in my moccasins. Imagine how horrible you would feel if you weren't able to pay me money you owed me.*
3. *If you could, for a moment, get out of the whole "money as currency" aspect of this situation, you might just consider forgiving the debt. And I would consider such an offer. I know you think this money is yours, but honestly, there are things that belong to me that were taken away and I know I will never, ever get them back. I'll let you ponder that for a moment.*

Really, I just wanted to start a "dialogue," as they say. If you're open to letting go of this negativity about who owes what to whom, I'm willing to talk.

Very sincerely,
Me

It's Not About The Money:
Am I really willing to listen?

May 1

DISCOUNTED

It used to be that whenever I bought something on sale, or used a coupon, I felt compelled to enjoy it. After all, it was cheap. The least I could do was be grateful, right?

A McRib sandwich for a dollar? Sure, I'll take that, even though it tastes like mesquite-coated earwax and I'd really rather have a chicken burrito. I mean, it was practically free. These shoes? Yes, they are one size too small but I'll make them fit. They were half off! I know this coffee has been sitting here since last Tuesday and it smells like pipe cleaner, but if I don't drink it, no one else will.

Normal people don't eat McRibs–thank God–just because they're on sale. When people want a chicken burrito, they order a chicken burrito. Normal people also don't squeeze their feet into shoes that are the wrong size because they're half off. When I deny myself the things I want because the things I don't want are cheaper, discounted, or free, I feel less valuable and I'm never satiated. I get snotty and resentful, and I stomp around like the world is trying to take advantage of me. And then, to make up for how badly I'm being treated, I start overspending in other areas.

Part of my recovery has been learning to admit what I desire. There's something healing about giving myself what I want, when I want it. I'm not talking about going hog wild and buying a Rolex or a small island in the South Pacific online, but allowing myself to have things that are important to me.

When I give myself what I want, I'm much less likely to force myself into buying the wrong-size shoes, eating food that's Mc-anything, or drinking coffee that tastes like pipe cleaner.

It's Not About The Money:

You deserve a break today!

May 2

KNOWLEDGE

Yes, sir, I found everything I was looking for, thank you very much. Will I be paying with cash or credit? Um, actually, I was hoping to use the currency of personal understanding I've gained in DA, in exchange for these groceries.

Feel free to ask me anything you want about why people debt. It's complicated, though. What's that? Oh, you require a different form of payment? In that case, how about my understanding of why I debt? Can I pay with that? No?

Well, maybe you don't understand how valuable self-knowledge is. True, it's not cash, but in some places it's like gold. For instance, I can analyze you and tell you why you aren't living up to your potential. Not that what you're doing isn't great, I just mean I can offer advice that could be very helpful to you. If you want to take it, that is.

Oh, so you're saying my knowledge counts for nothing when it comes to buying these groceries? What about my earnestness? Would that be fitting payment for these few items? No? Okay, what about for just this loaf of bread? What if we treated the wisdom I've gained while journaling about my own debting issues as a coupon of sorts?

Hmm, not even for these bag of apples? Yes, I realize there's a line forming, but you people might want to reconsider what you call "appropriate." There's no need to be rude. Of course I'll step aside and let these folks go ahead. You know what? Never mind, I'm taking my business elsewhere. Someplace where they'll appreciate me as a customer. Yes, I'll put the items back, but don't expect me to darken your door again. I know good customer service and, believe me, this is the very opposite of that.

Have a nice day.

It's Not About The Money:

Self-knowledge is good, but I have to get into action.

May 3

PITY

Acceptance and gratitude will replace regret, self-pity, and longing.

– DA Promise #5

I come from a long line of self-pitiers. My relatives made a sport of commemorating heartbreaks. They made an art form of their disadvantages and wore their hurts on their sleeves. Literally. I have an uncle who had the words BORN TO LOSE tattooed on his left bicep.

My family was also first in class when it came to discontent. My grandmother was infamous in the neighborhood for saying things like, "What's the point of it all, really?" and "It never works out for people like us." Okay, infamous might be stretching it, but the point is, I was genetically predisposed to self-pity, longing, and envy.

Amazingly enough, even for a dyed-in-the-wool self-pitier like me, the Program of DA worked. When I started to apply the Twelve Steps and Tools of recovery, I began to see life differently.

Despite my allegiance to being a financial wreck, I began to experience the Promises of DA when I committed to change. I found acceptance and gratitude for the life I had, instead of always wishing I was living someone–anyone–else's life. And, yes, even though my childhood was filled with a lot of depressing messages about money, I love the life I have today.

When I make God and my recovery at the center, I feel genuine appreciation for the life I have. In fact, most days I'm filled with gratitude and an enormous sense of abundance.

Every so often, I catch myself smiling and laughing for no reason at all, even when I'm around my self-pitying family. Which usually generates a red flag for them. "You think things are good now?" they say. "Just you wait!"

It's Not About The Money:

I'm going to say "no" to regret, self-pity and longing today!

May 4

RANTS

"One of the greatest lies perpetuated on mankind is the do-what-you-love-and-the-money-will-follow baloney," I said to my sponsor.

"Uh-huh," he said softly.

"Not everyone should shoot for the stars. It's a tragedy that this whole concept is constantly being shoved down people's throats. Not all of us can be the president of the United States."

"This is true," he said, nodding.

"And, well, a lot of people would love to be president, but only one person will get the job every four years. Why tell a child to dream of something like that? It's cruel. Why must people insist that following their dreams and loving what they do guarantee they will earn a living at it?

"I don't know."

"Some people have to work menial jobs, you know? Not everyone gets the opportunity to, say, make their living as a writer, although I'm sure everyone would love to."

"Not everyone wants to be a writer," he said.

"Well, then, they're bonkers, because what better job could there be than making a living inspiring people with your writing?"

"Maybe you feel that way because you have something to say. Speaking of, have you written today?" he asked.

"No."

"Maybe it's time. You're still working on your book, right?

"I...guess. I don't know. Maybe...I will do that now," I mumbled.

"Good idea," he said.

It's Not About The Money:

Is my ranting distracting me from taking important action?

May 5

GROWED UP

Before I found DA, I was the adult all the kids loved having at their parties because I could relate to them, and I was a lot like them: impulsive, irresponsible, always in the mood to play, and highly predisposed to boredom. I could also down as many–if not more–cupcakes in a single sitting than anyone under the age of ten, which made me somewhat of a local hero.

Then, one day, while watching over one of my friend's children's party, a kid fell and got hurt. And I had the shocking realization that these kids were depending on me because I was the adult. Without knowing it, I was an authority to them, which was weird, because in my head I was still a kid myself. Of course I knew I was an adult, but it's not like any my grown-up friends were looking to me for stability or wisdom.

In DA, I had to look at my selfishness, my irresponsibility, and my unwillingness to play the part of the adult. I had done *everything* to avoid being the grown-up. At six years old being childlike is cute, but not at… well, let's just say, after six years old!

Even though I may drag my feet or stomp around when I have to act mature, it feels good to know I'm an adult who can handle things. I have the amazing support of a community and a Higher Power who leads me in the right direction, when I take the time to listen. There are still times though, when I have no idea what I'm doing, and I make stuff up and hope for the best. At least now, though, I admit when I'm making things up, because for the most part I do know what I'm doing.

And yes, I do still take pride in the fact that I can annihilate my friends' kids when it comes to eating cupcakes. I know, because I did it last week.

It's Not About The Money:

Today I'll practice being a bigger person.

May 6

OVATIONS

I was a bit angry about not getting much praise for working on my debting problems.

When people stop drinking or get clean, they get a pat on the back for putting down the drink or the drugs. No one pats a debtor on the back or gives us a standing ovation when we keep our numbers, pay our bills on time, or stay solvent. In fact, when I tell people I'm in DA, they usually look at me and say something like, "I'm so glad you've stopped shoplifting. Or stealing credit cards. What is it you debtors stop…doing?"

"No one in my life gets what it means to be a debtor," I growled at my sponsor over the phone. "I feel so misunderstood."

"You're right, most people don't understand debting," he replied. "So get over the need to be understood. Understanding comes from inside."

What a self-righteous, superior thing to say, I thought, rolling my eyes internally.

"Stop rolling your eyes," he said. *How could he tell?* "In DA there's no substance to put down, manage, or moderate. What other people think about your recovery from debting is up to them, not us."

Recovery in DA is being solvent, taking consistent contrary action, and watching my attitude, especially when it comes to earning, spending, and giving to others.

Even though I think it's kind of a smug thing to say, I agree with my sponsor, that understanding comes from the inside. But I can guarantee you, if understanding came from the *outside*, I'd be pretty happy, 'cause I live in a city where I can find help for fixing my outsides faster than you can say, "Botox party."

It's Not About The Money:

Alright, already. Understanding comes from the inside!

May 7

SECOND HAND

"I'm glad you're a debtor," my friend said to me as we walked through the doors of our favorite department store.

"What do you mean?" I asked.

"Well, you go to those debtor meetings and you're learning all these great things about money. It's like I'm getting therapy for free, because I learn so much from all the work you do!"

"That's good to know…I guess."

"It's like secondhand smoke, except it doesn't cause cancer. It's more like secondhand learning."

"Yeah, well, maybe you should come to a meeting so you can get the benefits. Besides, recovery doesn't really work secondhand. Each person has to do the work themselves," I said, feeling profound as I scouted the sale rack.

"I would, but I'm not as bad off as you are. I mean, I'm not a real debtor. I didn't lose everything and end up in my car. You poor thing," she said, with a slight tsk-tsk in her voice.

"Thanks, I think," I said.

She slipped on the pair of seven-hundred-dollar boots she'd been ogling. "Are you buying anything?"

"No, I've got to stick to my budget," I said dejectedly.

"See, that's what I mean. I'd go to a meeting with you, but I hate budgets and spending charts."

"Uh-huh." I clenched my teeth and held my tongue.

"I feel so much more hopeful since you've been going to DA meetings." She marched over to the cash register.

"Glad to know I could help," I said as she pulled out her credit card to pay for her new boots.

The truth is, *I was* glad I could help her. I don't know if what I did qualifies as help, but I have hope.

It's Not About The Money:

I don't know who I might be helping or how, so I'll stay hopeful.

May 8

POWER

I'd arrived early for my interview with the political powerhouse. The library was filled with photos of her with presidents and world leaders. She waltzed into the library of her mansion to meet me, in a powder blue Christian Dior suit. She was surprisingly small in stature, but lovely. She shook my hand and looked me over, like a naval sergeant inspecting a cadet.

Should I salute her? Is it appropriate to curtsy? I was so intimidated I could barely speak. She smiled. Perfect teeth, flawless skin.

"Eet's so nice to meet you," she said, in her trademark Mediterranean accent, "Tell me about yourself."

"I was born in a town near Claremont College, which isn't to say I went there, I didn't. I didn't even apply there. That place is impossible to get into–"

"You know, it ees very important that I have someone who understands my policies and has a very good knowledge of politics."

"Right. Absolutely. I've read most of your books. I just can't remember any of them right now."

"Did you watch the video of the speech I gave at Columbia?"

"Yes, ma'am, and I took notes. I was impressed with your views on limiting corporate lobbying. It's about doggone time, I say,"–I pumped my fist in the air–"enough of the corporate greed!" After a lengthy pause, she looked at her watch.

"Meesti, did you read my book?" She was growing impatient.

"Yes, I did. I think. I mean, I know I did. No, I did."

"Just talk to meee about me." Her voice was like velvet. "Vhaat can you tell meee about me?"

I had to think fast. "Your skin, I mean, it's so perfect, I could eat off it."

"Darlink, you don't seem to have a clear point of view or the ability to articulate yourself verrry well. Nor do you have a grasp of who *I am*. I don't think this is going to work out." She flashed that smile and summoned her assistant, who ushered me to the door.

What struck me most about the political powerhouse–aside from her skin–was the fact she wanted to know more about *herself*. I figured t knew *a lot* about herself. Why did she need me to remind her?

It's Not About The Money:

If I'm focused on what you're thinking about me, I'm not focused on you.

May 9

CELEBRATTY

I was meeting at the Four Seasons Hotel with the megastar, trying to convince her to let the nonprofit women's organization I worked for honor her at an awards show.

I was relieved when the meeting was over. Beneath the Miss Cutie Pie exterior was a self-absorbed, miserable woman, and the conversation was uncomfortable, and to my shock, after Miss Cutie Pie agreed to let us honor her, she walked out and left me with the bill, which was a hundred dollars for two lemonades and a tiny plate of cheese.

"What is it with celebrities?" I asked my boss as I turned over my receipts for our meeting. "They get everything they want and expect the rest for free?"

"That's how it goes, kid," said my boss, who could easily be mistaken for Bugsy Siegel in a dimly lit room. "Those who need the least are given the most. Get back to work." How ironic that this boss would later be fired for diverting the organization's funds to cover her clothing account at Neiman Marcus.

Thus, began my resentment toward rich, entitled celebrities, around whom I worked for years. It wasn't until I left that line of work that I was able to see how truly angry I was.

In DA, I had to deal with those resentments, which weren't really about the celebrities but about my own feelings of inferiority. Celebrities were just easy targets.

What other people get or don't get, take or don't take, is none of my business. I have to live a life of integrity and honor myself by being solvent, staying connected to God, and not debting, one day at a time. I'm no more or less than anyone who has money. I have my own path and purpose on this planet. And I can have peace, no matter what's in my bank account. And because I would never assume that someone else should pay for my hundred-dollar lemonade, I don't order things I can't pay for.

It's Not About The Money:

I'm not entitled to be angry at folks I think are entitled.

May 10

SAFE

I had been going to Debtors Anonymous meetings for about three years before I was able to start tackling my debt.

I'd received an unexpected inheritance, and of course, I immediately wanted to pay off all my debts. At once. But my sponsor and friends in DA suggested that instead I take things easy. They recommended I formulate a spending plan, then consistently pay back the money I owed.

Over the course of two years I paid off everyone: old accounts, credit card bills that had gone to collection, doctors, hospitals, etc. I also started my business, formed a DBA, opened a checking account, got a business coach, and created a spending plan. I even opened a "prudent reserve" account dedicated strictly for rainy days and unplanned-for expenses.

Throughout the entire process, I was in turmoil. Part of me was overjoyed to have the weight of debt lifted off my shoulders. Another part of me was still very afraid.

I was free, in some ways, but in other ways, I wasn't.

The day I dropped off that last bill into the mailbox, I started to cry. The tears came slowly at first then harder and more persistently. Standing on the corner as I dropped the envelope into the mail chute, I was laughing hysterically *and* crying. The waves of relief, the sense that everything was going to be okay filled my entire body. I was free of the crushing debt, and I felt safe. For about two whole days.

It has taken time, but I *finally* get that safety has *nothing* to do with the amount of money I have. Safety and security come when I turn my will and my life over to the care of my Higher Power. Yes, it's a bit lofty and spiritual sounding, but it works for me. I think it'll work for you, too. Really, I do.

It's Not About The Money:
I've got mine. I'm safe and secure today.

May 11

SPECIAL

I have a secret to share with you.

I'm special.

Special in that way that rules don't–or shouldn't–apply to me. Stupid rules, I mean, like texting and driving, paying the rent on time, or having to stand in line when I'm running late for an appointment. It's not like I deserve to have everything I want right now, but, well, I should be able to have what I want within a reasonable amount of time.

My other secret is that I believe I'm a total impostor who doesn't deserve anything. I do little more than take up space and waste a lot of plastic bags–or, I did until they banned them in my state–but I still have a tendency to waste paper towels if I can get away with it.

When I disclose my secrets to God and another human being, I get out of isolation. There's something healing about telling a friend or a fellow in Program the truth about how I really feel. When I share my faults and flaws with others, I'm reminded that I'm just another human being on this planet trying to do my best.

I realize I'm not the only one who does thoughtless things to get relief from the pain of life.

Sharing secrets is a little like eating a whole white coconut cake. It feels good and yet, it's kind of bad. But, ultimately, it's way more good than bad.

It's Not About The Money:
Go ahead, admit it. You're special, too.

May 12

ENOUGH, ALREADY

We will realize that we are enough; we will value ourselves and our contributions.
– DA Promise #5

As a friend of mine in Program once said, "Before DA I had three options. To be a Supreme Court Justice, a professor, or an Pulitzer-Prize winner."

Most debtors think we have to be Some Big Deal in order to be valuable. We can't just have a job and be someone's next-door neighbor, or that guy/girl in the cubicle at the office.

God forbid we end up being average.

I used to hate anything that reeked of normalcy–I needed drama, extreme experiences. My ultimate fear was being average. So I created scenarios in my life that contained a lot of drama and pain, especially when it came to money and relationships.

It took a long time for it to sink in that It's okay to be normal, even ordinary. I am enough, even if I never have another fabulous job or do anything special.

All I have to do is be a decent human being and try to love other people. Which, in and of itself, is the single most challenging job I have ever had.

There are a lot of weird people out there.

It's Not About The Money:

It's kind of fun being "normal." Try it today.

May 13

MONEY TALKS

My friend was frustrated with God about her nonexistent love life, so her therapist suggested she begin talking to God as if He were her fiancé. Take Him to premarital counseling, if you will.

It seemed to work well for my friend, and since my relationship with money has been dysfunctional at best, I decided I'd take *money* to counseling, if you will.

I started by talking to my money as if it were my last boyfriend. I began with some of the things that were bothering me, including the lack of support I felt, specifically over the past few years. I said I didn't feel my real needs were being met, and that it had been ages since we'd had a good time together.

I was upset because I was the one who took the initiative in our relationship. I got no response.

I said I didn't think my feelings were being honored. I got nothing. Silence.

Then I told my money I had kind of lost the passion. Silence.

I wanted to know what the future held for us. Nada.

Wow, this really is just like my last relationship.

"That's it!" I screamed. "If you aren't going to be there for me when I need you, it's over!" I didn't really know what that meant. It was new to me, the whole therapeutic approach to money.

The next day I received a check in the mail from an old client for a service I'd never bothered collecting on. I still haven't cashed the check because I'm sure it'll bounce. I do have another "session" scheduled with my money this week, but I'm still hurt, and I can't seem to shake the fact that if I wasn't the initiator of things, our relationship would *never* improve.

It's Not About The Money:

If I want things to change, I have to make the effort.

May 14

CONSCIENCE

I was on vacation in Austin. While out on a long run, I discovered a coffee shop that looked exactly like a tree house, set atop a hill, right by a gorgeous lake.

Next to the register in the coffee shop was a stack of books for loan. I immediately found a book I liked and settled in with my cup of coffee. When I emerged from the tree house several hours later, I was in a bit of a crisis. Should I take the book with me, or return in to the books-for-loan pile?

I really could've used the book for work, but the cover price was twenty-seven dollars! I agonized for ten minutes. *Take the book, don't take the book. That's stealing. But it's not like there's a line forming to read it! Besides, you're in a tree house and the guy at the next table just lit up a joint. Who's gonna turn you in?*

I didn't take the book, not because I'm morally superior, but because I didn't want to run five more miles with a book in my hand. And I wouldn't have enjoyed it if I'd taken it ... karma and all that.

My recovery from debting says I don't *borrow* things that don't belong to me, unless I ask for them. I no longer take things that aren't mine, in any area of my life, which started me thinking about that crime TV series I'd been downloading for free. Then I reminded myself that I have a tendency to think too much and started back up on my run.

It's Not About The Money:
Is that my conscience that's whispering to me?

May 15

IMPRESSIONS

I decided to go back to school later in life. I figured it would be fairly easy, what with all my knowledge and maturity.

The first day, old insecurities began popping up. *What if the other people in the class hate me, or my hair, or think I'm dumb? What if I have no one to eat lunch with? What if I fail all the tests? What if I've just wasted all this money on a new career and I still end up broke, alone, and on the streets?*

The amazing thing is, even though I have some recovery, when I start feeling insecure, I get a little…intense, and when I get that intense, I repel people. It's palpable. I can feel them easing away from me.

But once I make the decision to bypass the noise in my head, things change. A slight shift in my perspective, like thinking about how we're all alike instead of focusing on how different I am, lightens things up.

When I remind myself that everyone else, like me, is a little kooky, insecure, and frequently wrong, I stop worrying so much. When I'm "others-centered" instead of "self-centered," I can feel people moving towards me. I am an attraction to others.

I don't have to be the prettiest, smartest, the best, or the brightest, or the most well liked to feel good about myself. And while the voices may continue to whisper in my ear, I can choose not to listen to them. I can even whisper back something like, *Hey, insecurity, I'm doing just fine. So you can just pipe down.*

It's Not About The Money:

Hey, insecurity, take a hike! I'm not in the mood today.

May 16

TALENTS

If you're experiencing any degree of self-pity about your financial situation, today's meditation was written especially for you. Today you are going to start out by thinking of one talent you possess, and it cannot include sleeping, or crying, or watching TV.

Today we're going to practice getting out of self-pity. This will not be easy to do, because self-pity starts with the word "self." And when you're in it, you don't want to get out of it.

To do so, your only priority is to use your talents to improve the life of *someone else*. Let's say you're a cook. Today you get to make dinner for someone else. If you're a gardener, put together a small bouquet of flowers for a friend. And if you're a poet, your job today is to refrain from writing poetry. Just kidding. You can write, but it can't be depressing. On second thought, if you're a poet, find something else to do today.

The point is to reach out, nurture an existing relationship, and use your unique talent to serve *someone else*.

I know, you have every right to feel sorry for yourself. Life is hard and you're struggling. You're thinking, *"How the heck is doing something for someone else going to pay my gas bill?"* Guess what? The only way to get out of misery and despair is to try something different.

Start now. Do one kind thing for someone else. It can be baking cookies for your coworkers or helping the little kid down the street fix her wagon. It shouldn't cost you anything, but I promise, if you do it, you will feel better. And if you do it and you don't feel better, you can be mad at me. But I have a feeling you're going to want to thank me tomorrow. It's all right. I'll wait.

It's Not About The Money:
One small step for you, one giant step for your recovery.

May 17

PATIENCE

Even as a child, I was notoriously impatient. Rarely a day went by when I wasn't told, "Stop being so darned impatient, child!" or "Take it easy. Don't you know impatient kids score lower on their SATs?"

That didn't deter me. So, when I grew up, discovered DA, and saved some money, what did I want to do with it? Pay off all my debts at once, of course! I thought I wanted to do it because I had become a righteous, noble person. Who could blame me for wanting to get rid of my debts? Then I discovered that the desire to pay everything off right away was *more* compulsive debting!

"What? How can wanting to pay off my debts be a bad thing?" I asked my sponsor.

"Because it's compulsive behavior," he explained. "It's classic debtor behavior–impatient, impulsive, and extreme."

"Oh, I see," I said, but I didn't.

"You're the hare, not the tortoise. You don't want to warm up and run around the track every day. You want to sprint across the finish line in a grand gesture."

That, I understood.

In recovery, I'm actually beginning to enjoy doing the more boring things I need to do to be financially healthy, like keeping track of my numbers, not debting one day at a time, going to meetings, and being of service to others.

Delayed gratification is a drag sometimes and paying debts off slowly isn't exciting. It's quieter and calmer than I'm used to being. It's not filled with scary sound effects or mean people calling me at all hours of the night. It's not dramatic. But I'm sort of starting to enjoy it.

It's Not About The Money:

Not everything has to be done right at this moment.

May 18

EASY MONEY

The Quickest, Easiest Money You'll Ever Make!

This not a joke or an exaggeration. You will be paid real money to sit on your bum and do stuff for us. No hooks, no catches.

And here's the best part, folks: You don't need one minute's worth of experience! We'll take absolutely everyone who clicks this link and follows the instructions. The only way it could be easier is if we sent our personal jet to your house and clicked on this link for you.!

Here is a testimonial from someone who clicked this link:

Before I started this job, I was borrowing money, living in my car, and trying to stretch twenty dollars into a week's worth of groceries. Before I even realized what was going on, I was bringing in more money than I could count!

-M.C.

Wait, it gets better!

Two years after clicking the link, I've made more money than I ever have at any time in my life. Clicking the link changed my life!

- P.J.

There is literally no downside, folks. Even if you have no idea what you're doing, you can still do this! All you have to do is stop stalling and *click this darn button*. Soon, you too, will be telling your own story about getting rich!

It begins with one step. Click now!

It's Not About The Money:

Where in my life am I looking for the quick and easy?

May 19

POSS OBS

I recently heard the term "possession obsession" in a DA meeting and decided to research it online.

The first thing that came up was a music video for a song called "Possession Obsession" by Hall and Oates. It's set during the '80s Wall Street greed-is-good era, and features John Oates as a taxi driver who is forced to usher around every rich jerk in New York City. The most hilarious part of the video is that not one rich person is even close to normal. They're all portrayed as obnoxious, indulgent, and abusive. In fact, a group of the rich jerks go so far as to punch Oates's taxicab (pretty bright, no?) after they stumble into the streets, drunk, in front of his cab.

Meanwhile, at an unknown nightclub nearby, Daryl Hall, in a shimmery green suit and a killer pompadour, sings, "Gimme, gimme, gimme," as a torrent of white steam unfurls around him.

I think the video is trying to teach us how to say "no" to the desire for more money, or things, or, as Hall and Oates would say, "The more you take, the less you get back." Or give back. I couldn't read Oates' lips.

I didn't do anymore research on "possession obsession" because when you strike gold with this kind of video, you don't need to dig deeper.

So here, my friends, is your anti-debting meditation for the day: "Possession obsession" is not good. It will ruin your life and mess up all your relationships. You'll end up sucker-punching taxicabs in the middle of New York City at night, or on some reality show that mocks you, only you won't even get it. And people like Hall and Oates will *not* like you.

It's Not About The Money:

God, help me remember my possessions are not worthy of obsession.

May 20

ADMIT IT

"Admitted to God, to ourselves, and to another human being the exact nature of our wrongs." – *DA Step #5*

Step #5 in DA allows us to tell the truth about ourselves when it comes to debting. We examine our distorted beliefs, broken promises, grudges, and long-held resentments. We also take responsibility for the ways we have harmed others and ourselves.

We may have screwed up seven ways 'til Sunday when it comes to money and debting. We may have lost our jobs and homes or ruined our relationships. We may have gotten into legal trouble. Whatever we've done, when we're totally honest and admit our wrongs to another debtor, the burden is lifted. The acceptance and love we get when we're honest allows us the chance to let go of the shame and receive the grace of a Higher Power. It's the beginning of true liberation from debt.

No matter what you've done or avoided doing, you will feel better by sharing it with another debtor. Maybe you cheated on your taxes (done that) or written bad checks (done that, too). Perhaps you were involved in a crime ring that sold stolen laundry detergent on the black market (never done that but I would've been tempted if the opportunity had presented itself). There's always someone who can relate to you, and somebody somewhere who has done it, too. Except for the story about the guy who confessed to removing gold teeth from cadavers and selling them to pawn shops. No one else has ever been able to say they did *that*.

But seriously, I've never heard of anyone who didn't feel a deep freedom after completing the Fifth Step in Debtors Anonymous.

It's Not About The Money:
Go on, admit what you've done. It's okay.

May 21

LOTTERY HAIKU

Haiku, developed by Japanese poets, are short poems that use sensory language to capture a feeling or image. They were often inspired by nature or a poignant experience. A haiku has only three lines, with the first line having five syllables, the second having seven, and the last having five. When a haiku is good, it's really good. But when it's bad, it's even better! Consider this one:

God's my employer
But he won't lend me money
He knows me too well.

Or, this one:

Does money change things?
I will let you know after
I'm back from Vegas.

When you're in debt, there's simply no better (or cheaper) way to have fun than writing some bad money haiku. It can be funny, angry, silly, inspiring–whatever you want it to be. Take a moment to honor the bad poet inside of you!

It's Not About The Money:
Don't give me that face. Give it a try!

May 22

BAD LIFE

I had been talking nonstop about how bad my life was. Problems galore, money was tight, work was hideous, money was tight, my life was pointless, etc.

My sponsor finally broke in and said, "Just because you're having a bad day doesn't mean you're having a bad life."

"But what if I have a really long string of bad days in a row over a long period of time and it adds up to a bad life?" I figured that would shut him up or at least garner me some sympathy.

"Okay, what I'd like you to do is keep track of how many really bad days you have in a row. At the end of your life, I'll read it and let you know if you've had a bad life." Surprisingly, I didn't have a retort, so I agreed to keep track of my bad days and to give it to him so he could do an analysis.

Unfortunately, there have been a few really fantastic days in the midst of my otherwise depressing life since I started keeping track so I can't confirm I'm having a bad life. Yet.

At least, not as of today. But there's always tomorrow. *I am* keeping track.

It's Not About The Money:
A bad day doesn't equal a bad life.

May 23

SLOGANS OR TATS?

DA Slogans or hapless lower-back tattoos? You choose.

1. Get rich or die trying
2. Be kind to yourself
3. To get something you've never had, you have to do something you've never done
4. It works if you work it
5. Start today
6. Time is money
7. I am not my debt
8. Money don't sleep, neither do I
9. Easy does it
10. Cash only

Answer Key:

Debtors Anonymous slogans: 4, 7
Regrettable lower-back tattoos: 1, 8, 10
Both: 2, 3, 5, 9

It's Not About The Money:

God's Got My Back is my permanent tattoo.

May 24

STUFF HAPPENS

One of the things I used to obsess about before I got into recovery–who am I kidding, I still do–was the inevitable "next disaster looming around the corner."

The anxiety began with the simple thought, "I could get caught up if all this bad stuff would just stop happening to me!" Then it hit me: bad things happen. And it wasn't just because God was out to get me and ruin my life, it was because I jerry-rigged things in order to save money. I'd buy cheap stuff that would break because I didn't think I was worthy of anything more.

Plumbing problems? Why waste money on hiring a plumber? I've got some hair clips and teriyaki turkey jerky. That should fix her right up. The check-engine light is flashing in my car? I'll just cover it up with a Hello Kitty sticker. The brakes squeaking a bit? Why waste money on it now? I'll see how long I can ride them before they go out.

DA has taught me how to plan ahead and keep a prudent reserve available, because when I don't handle problems right away, they snowball. Part of my recovery is having an emergency savings account.

I call it my Unplanned Disaster Looming Around the Corner Account so that when "stuff" happens, which it invariably will, I'll be ready and won't take it personally.

There's no disaster that can claim my serenity. Most of the time.

It's Not About The Money:

There is no impending disaster that's worth my serenity.

May 25

PERPLEXED

I'd signed up for a sixteen-week course to increase my income and become more prosperous. Most of the people in the group had experienced very tangible results. I, on the other hand, found myself deeper in debt and growing more fearful and frustrated.

"Why isn't this working for me?" I asked the instructor as the course was winding down. "I do the affirmations, including standing naked in front of my mirror and saying 'I love you,' but nothing has changed. I'm still broke and on the verge of bankruptcy!"

The instructor seemed perplexed. It was obvious he had no idea what to say to me. So, he did what anyone in her position would do. "I'm offering an advanced course for hard-core cases starting next month. You'd be perfect for that!"

I didn't sign up. And things didn't get better. I declared bankruptcy two years later. I didn't realize then that I was a debtor and my solution wouldn't come from affirmations or another prosperity course. There was no class on "wealth building" that would solve my core problem.

I needed a spiritual solution.

When I finally found DA, I was so relieved. While I still couldn't pay my bills for the first year, I began to see that the solution was not in working harder.

In fact, it was the opposite. As I met regularly with other debtors who understood and cared for me, I stopped worrying about the money and focused on my spiritual development. Eventually the money started to come. I still don't get it; I just know it works. And I'm darn glad I no longer have to stand naked staring at myself in a mirror, because that just leads to a whole 'nother kind of craziness.

It's Not About The Money:

I've said it before and I'll say it again: Prosperity is an inside job.

May 26

REASONS

A recent study suggests the reason people love reading articles with lists is because our brains love order. We need to know that information can be contained and organized by subject and classification. We also want to know there will be an end to said information at some point.

In light of those facts, I decided to list Top Five Reasons Why People Debt:

1. They don't earn enough
2. They spend more than they make
3. They earn less than they spend
4. Their mother
5. Their father

I hope you feel better now, knowing that other people are to blame for your financial problems. Unless you aren't earning enough or are spending more than you earn. But I highly doubt that fits your situation. It's more than likely your family's fault.

It's Not About The Money:

I may have to throw out my list of "reasons" for debting.

May 27

MEAN IT

The Big Book of AA talks about the Resentment Prayer, which suggests that if we want to be free of a resentment, we should ask God for the willingness to pray for the person we resent for fourteen days.

The prayer tells us to ask our Higher Power to give the person we resent everything we want for ourselves: health, prosperity, joy, etc., and it promises us we will be free of the resentment.

Part of the reason this prayer works is willingness. With most of my resentments, I had to start with: "Even though I don't mean this at all, I am willing to mean it. I wish for this jerk all the joy, happiness, prosperity, and health I want for myself."

I did this because I was told it worked. I tried the prayer with everything I resented–family members, friends, employers, insitutions, etc.. Sometimes it took more than fourteen days, but ultimately, the resentment was removed. There was inevitably a moment in those fourteen days when the prayer became: "God, I earnestly wish for this person all the wonderful things I desire for myself," and I meant it. I could feel the resentment dissolving.

I've discovered that after a while, where I'd once felt bitterness and hatred, I felt...peace. I don't necessarily become best friends with the person I've been praying for, or resenting; sometimes that just isn't possible, but I always end up with more compassion and an acceptance of the situation.

Some of the bigger resentments took longer, but the resentment prayer eventually works. I know because I've been praying for the IRS since January.

It's Not About The Money:

At least for today, I'll mean it when I pray it.

May 28

LAUGH OUT LOUD!

I was perusing the appendixes of one of my meditation books and noticed something. None of them had entries under the heading "fun." One had an entry for humor but I could barely get through the meditation because it was so boring. It talked about "nourishing gaiety" and "sparking things with a dash of rosy pink." Whatever that means.

While humor can't be analyzed, it can be cultivated. It's about a change in perspective and it starts with our attitude. If you're a debtor who has a tendency to accentuate the negative, even you can learn to lighten up!

Start by paying attention to other people. Be curious and ask questions. Set a goal of seeing more humor in life, because the more you look for it, the more you'll find it.

Try looking at your problems with a new perspective and relate things that don't ordinarily go together. Look at life from the viewpoint of, say, your dog or your goldfish. Find one element of your situation that could be considered humorous and share it with others.

Life is absurd at times, and a slight twist in your viewpoint can turn a tragedy into comedy.

Okay, so humor isn't easy to explain. And as I've just proven, it's impossible to do it in a funny way. But I'm sure of one thing: Humor never includes "gaiety" or "dashes of rosy." And for a debtor, it never, ever includes the letters I, R or S.

It's Not About The Money:

Humor. You'll know it when you feel it.

May 29

PEANUTS

"That's the secret to life. Replace one worry with another." – Charlie Brown

Debtors are sort of like the Peanuts cast of the recovery world. One thing both have in spades is the pervasive sense of separation.

Like woeful, adorable little Charlie Brown, we tend to be anxious and insecure, we're afraid, and we spend a lot of time hiding. Instead of going to a meeting or reaching out when we need help, we stay at home and sulk, or lurk around the DA phone meetings without saying a word.

Some of us debtors are mopey and melodramatic, and with a bit of the grumpy, demanding characteristics of Lucy, who barks and snaps at people, although she'd be happier if she'd shut up and let things go. Some of us relate to dreadfully dressed, academically challenged Peppermint Patty; or the overwhelmed, schizoidal Linus; or the artistic, pretentious Schroeder. In debtors, there's even a version of Snoopy–the idealistic loner who lives in a world of fantasy.

While there are plenty of people who find the Peanuts gang quite endearing and funny, I've always thought them to be depressing and not comical, which is probably one of the reasons I haven't been able to sit through *Why, Charlie Brown, Why?*, or *What Have We Learned, Charlie Brown?*, and even the beloved *A Charlie Brown Christmas*–I have a hard time relating to characters whose expressions of glee, frustration or smugness are made with a dot and a parenthesis.

So, then, I suppose the Peanuts analogy might not be the most appropriate or interesting one possible. I apologize. Carry on.

It's Not About The Money:

No melodrama, no isolation, no worries today. Be happy.

May 30

CARRYOVERS

The idea of a daily spiritual practice didn't appeal to me when I came into DA. I had been a decent person, I'd never killed, stolen–nothing big, anyway–or harmed anyone on purpose. That is, unless they'd talked trash about me or ignored my phone calls, then all bets were off. I was nice enough. I figured that over time I had accrued a decent reserve of karmic credit that I could draw upon to get me through recovery. I probably had a few spiritual "carryovers" coming my way.

I was wrong. Recovery is not for every other day, or one week at a time. It's a daily, conscious choice to stay in contact with God, to stay solvent, to let resentments go, and to not incur debt. When it comes to debting, the only way my obsessive-compulsive mind can do things is one day at a time.

It's called a daily practice, me thinks, because there are no "carryovers" when it comes to recovery. I can't draw from the tank that was full yesterday. I have to begin again anew each day.

It's not easy to do, this spiritual stuff. It's also not easy to live in debt or be a compulsive spender or an underearner. But it is *much* easier and more rewarding to do the daily spiritual stuff than the debting stuff. So I'll stick with the spiritual practice. I'm a debtor and, frankly, I'll always take the easier way out.

It's Not About The Money:

There are no carryovers in recovery. It's a daily practice.

May 31

HANDLERS

Apparently the human brain loves money so much, just touching it can reduce physical pain.

In an international study, two groups of people were told to hold either a stack of money or a stack of blank paper before putting their hands in hot water for a short time. The participants who had touched a stack of bills before reaching into the hot water had a much higher pain threshold than those who handled the blank paper.

The participants who held money found the water to be more bearable than those who held the blank paper. Ironically, the people who handled the cash weren't even offered money as compensation. They just felt better for having held it!

Based on this study, researchers have concluded that touching money can help lessen emotional pain. And I believe them. You know why? Because I just took some money out of my wallet and held it, and boy, do I feel amazing. Although I must say, nothing is quite as soothing as cuddling up with a good book and my Harry Potter in Graceland snow globe.

There is absolutely *nothing* wrong with enjoying and respecting your money. In fact, it's important that we enjoy the financial blessings we've been given. It feels good to be abundant!

Right now, take out whatever cash you've got in your wallet, even if it's just a few bucks, and spend a few moments appreciating it. Touch it, hold it, pet it, sing to it. Get comfortable being around it. But please don't put that money in your mouth. You never know where it's been and who else has touched it.

It's Not About The Money:

Reach out and touch the money. Just don't put it in your mouth.

June 1

NUMBERS?

"God is in the numbers." – DA slogan

"God isn't in my numbers!" I burst into tears when I first heard that slogan. "If he were in my numbers, wouldn't my rent be paid? If He's in the numbers, why doesn't He add a few zeros at the end to the totals in my checking account?"

The idea that God is in the numbers was just plain cracked. How would I ever get to the point where looking at my accounts would bring me peace or serenity? How would I ever get closer to my Higher Power, when people kept saying absurd things like that?

Looking at my financial accounts made me anxious and angry; it definitely did not make me feel close to God. With the help of others and the Program of DA, I began to calm down enough to look at my accounts without panicking. After a while–a long while–it got to the point where doing my numbers and reconciling my accounts felt good.

I'm still not completely sure what "God is in the numbers" means, because it sounds an awful lot like "The devil is in the details," which is what I used to believe. But I do know that I feel more serene when I keep track of my numbers and what I spend.

So, in that way, I guess God *is* in the numbers. Maybe someday I'll move God over into the details. Or not. Maybe I shouldn't read so much into these sayings.

It's Not About The Money:

God is in the numbers, if I allow Him to be.

June 2

RELIANCE

"When a job still looked like a mere means of getting money rather than an opportunity for service, when the acquisition of money for financial independence looked more important than a right dependence upon God, we were still the victims of unreasonable fear." – *DA Twelve Steps & Twelve Traditions*

So, let me get this straight. I take a job to be of service? As in, "Hello, ma'am, would you like some curly fries with that burger?"

A job is not about telling people how they should run their company? I don't take a job so I can act smart and boss everyone else around? It's not so I can get paid a lot of money to not do very much?

You're telling me that acquiring more money and status isn't the means to my independence? That this whole journey is about a reliance on God?

Whoa, whoa, whoa, let's slow it down here. I'm all for lending a hand here and there and checking in with God when I need help, but this is a bit extreme. At least, it seems that way to me.

This whole DA Program is starting to sound, well, extreme, if you want to know the truth.

I was with you until that whole "God dependence" part. Then you sort of lost me. I might need a little more time to think about this.

It's Not About The Money:

The mind of a debtor is a terrible thing to waste.

June 3

GO FOR BROKE

Today is National Go for Broke Day. While it's for you to decide if you're a debtor, if you are, it's not recommended that you celebrate this holiday in the literal sense. You might be better off honoring the day figuratively. While those without a debting problem would consider today the perfect day to take a big risk, if you're a debtor, Go for Broke Day might be your opportunity to take absolutely no risks at all.

Please remember that Go for Broke Day doesn't have to be about money. Who says going for broke has to involve buying, selling, or negotiating anything? It might mean trying something new, like taking a class. Maybe you have a particular project on your mind. Make the decision to go for it.

Perhaps your challenge is with a relationship. Is it time to move on? Or, maybe you're ready to take a step into a deeper commitment. Today might be the day to do it! Go for Broke Day might be the time to think about traveling to a foreign country, or somewhere you've never been before. If you're feeling it's time to find a new job, you might explore new career ideas. But please, think it over carefully and decide if the risk is worth it. You don't want to do something that you'll regret, especially if you don't have a backup plan. Of course, it's entirely up to you how to celebrate today.

If all this talk about "going for it" is too much, feel free to make it Don't Go for Broke Day. Celebrate the day however you want to, even if it means staying home, doing nothing and eating pop tarts. Which, in that case, would make this If It Ain't Broke, Don't Fix It Day.

It's Not About The Money:
It might, or might not be, Go for Broke Day.

June 4

HUNTING

Recovery from debting is a bit like job hunting. It often requires the same steps: plenty of hard work, a ton of tiring research, and a lot of waiting around for something to happen. Without any pay.

In recovery, as in a job search, the harder you grasp at results, the farther they seem. And when you finally give up trying, you get multiple offers.

In DA, we discover that the answers don't come by grinding it out. Recovery comes when we acknowledge and accept our powerlessness. It's also known as surrender. We allow God to guide us, we stop trying to control the outcomes, and we accept life on life's terms.

The thing is, when you're on a job interview, you can't exactly say to the hiring manager, "I don't need to get into details about why I'm unemployed or try to convince you how great an employee I'll be, do I? Because I'll let you in on a little secret. You're not the one who'll be deciding if I'll get this position. That's God's job." And you can't just show up on your first day of work and say to your new boss, "You may not know it but you're not really in charge here. God is my employer."

No, you wouldn't do either of those things, because while they may be true, there are some things we keep to ourselves in recovery. So, in that sense, recovery and job hunting are wholly and utterly unrelated and have absolutely nothing in common. But, on the other hand, in recovery you never have to grasp for results because God is in charge. Also, you never have to spend *any* time with a human resources person. That is, unless you want to. But, why would you?

It's Not About The Money:

No grasping for results today. I'll let God handle things.

June 5

HACKS

I used to work in advertising, and I was often surprised by how shallow and self-aggrandizing my colleagues were.

Rarely a day went by that I wasn't forced to sit through a meeting where I'd look around and think, *We're responsible for shaping the marketing messages for the world's biggest brands, yet we're the most confused, insecure people I know. What a bunch of "hacks" we are!*

I was in constant conflict. Why were we lucky enough to get free lattes and expensive lunches while other people had to work in factories? I'd ponder this as my creative colleagues would throw out things like, "We'll start with a closeup on the cleavage of a twenty-year-old model, and then a voice-over in a British accent will talk about the new model, the engine size, how fast the car is, as we pan over the model's body..."

"Love it!" someone would exclaim. "Just make sure it doesn't sound too scientific." It's not as if we didn't work hard; we worked twelve-hour days upon days and months on *things that meant nothing*. Or so I thought.

The truth is, when I was debting, I was never satisfied. I couldn't simply have a job; it had to have some virtuous significance or it was pointless. The funny thing is, when I finally got a job doing something "virtuous" or, at least, not as cheesy as trying to drum up excitement for flavored yogurt, I missed my old job! I even missed that fortysomething creative director who would show up at creative pitches with a skateboard in hand.

My perspective about work that is "necessary" or "noble" was not reliable because I was never satisfied, and the fact that a company would hire me confirmed its stupidity. At least, that's how it used to be. Now, when I get a new project, I think, "Well, they hired me so they must have their act together. I'm going to do a quality job." I show up, do my best and stay grateful, and I never have to worry about being a "hack" anymore.

It's Not About The Money:

When I'm doing my best, I don't have to worry about what I am or I'm not.

June 6

SACRED

Recovering from debt is agonizing at times, and it isn't unlike recovering from a physical ailment. Yet the suffering we experience when we're healing can have a sacred element to it.

In recovery we not only change, we are restored.

When I do what is required of me in DA–work the Steps and Tools; keep my numbers; stay out of debt; try, above all else, to be rigorously honest and spend time with others who are struggling–my pain begins to take on a deeper meaning. I can't determine how the grief, loss, and hurt I have experienced will help others. And when I become willing to share my story with others, I am healing.

The more recovery I achieve, the more I feel responsible to react well to the challenges I face. The right response becomes more automatic the more I focus on serenity, and my suffering can have an element of sacredness to it.

Even when I'm feeling tranquil and serene, though, I'm still aware that everything, even my recovery, is beyond my control. I can't determine the course of my recovery, my problems, or what is going to come my way, but I can choose my responses. That is something that can't be quantified.

Do I always feel grateful for the healing? That's a resounding "no." As I've stated before, I'd prefer the easy, breezy way. But when I consider that my pain might be a gift to someone else, it definitely lessens the burden, and reminds me that my experiences *can* be a gift to others.

It's Not About The Money:
My losses can be a gift to others.

June 7

CHICKENS

Harland Sanders held many jobs, from motel operator to an army mule tender. He aspired to practice law but failed, and his political career went nowhere due to the fact that he dropped out of school in the sixth grade in order to care for his brothers.

By most peoples' standards, he was not a success. At age forty, Sanders was operating a rundown gas station and decided to make extra money by serving meals to busy people. He called it Sunday Dinner, Seven Days a Week. The place was so small that people practically ate in his bedroom. But they always came back because he made great chicken.

It got to the point where Sanders (named a Kentucky colonel in 1935 for his fine cooking) could no longer cram people inside his house, so he moved to a bigger place across the street. His restaurant was a hit and everything was going well, until a new highway was built and directed traffic miles away from his restaurant. He went bankrupt at the age of sixty-five.

The colonel cashed his first Social Security check and used it to open a franchise. And then another, and another. Sanders was so confident in his ability to fry chicken that he used his final check and invested it in his restaurant. Within ten years, Sanders had six hundred Kentucky Fried Chicken franchises. In 1964, he sold his interest in the company for two million dollars to a group of investors. He was in his mid-seventies.

Today, the colonel's face adorns buckets of arguably the best extra crispy chicken you can get for a few bucks The moral of the colonel's story should be obvious, but in case it isn't, I'll clarify. No matter *how* old you are, no matter *where* you've been, or *how far down* you may be today, never, ever give up, my little chickens. Your Higher Power has a plan. Just keep showing up, and the plan will become clear in time.

It's Not About The Money:
Don't give up. You're just getting started!

June 8

SERIOUSLY?!

I was reading an article about Debtors Anonymous's message being diluted because there were so many different viewpoints about what debting was.

The article suggested people were clinging to their "symptoms": time-debting, cluttering, or underspending. The writer made a few pithy comments, then closed by saying, "But enough humor. Recovery is serious business."

I wanted to say, "No, there's really not enough humor. We debtors need more!" Yes, recovery is serious, but as I've heard it said, "The only difference between tragedy and comedy is time." Or timing. I don't remember now.

I say, "We debtors need more fun! More laughter!" And while it's not easy to laugh when the guy from the power company is standing at the gas meter, hovering over the cutoff switch, there *are* things to smile about and ways to have some fun (hint: it doesn't include shopping), even when things aren't good.

Today, try to find something that will make you smile, if not laugh. Maybe it's watching funny YouTube videos or renting *Blazing Saddles*. It might be listening to your favorite song and dancing around your kitchen. It doesn't matter what "it" is. Just laugh for five full minutes today. Five minutes. On purpose. Then you can go back to worrying about the power bill, the rent, or what the future may hold for you. But I'll you bet you won't.

It's Not About The Money:

God, help me remember it's okay to laugh, even if it doesn't seem like it.

June 9

DREAMIN'

A few years ago, one of my screenplays was optioned by a hotshot production company that had just won an Oscar. After many rewrites, we were ready for casting. We had lunches at swanky hotels, threw around A-list names as leads. I was feeling pretty cool.

Suddenly, my calls stopped being returned. After a year of this, I finally figured it out. They weren't going to make the movie. Two years later, the company went out of business.

Around that same time, another screenplay of mine was in preproduction, and the lead actress–a huge star–bailed out and declared bankruptcy. The following year, the executive producer who was financing my third script died unexpectedly. I was so disheartened I vowed to stop dreaming–note the victimization and self-obsession–about making it as a writer.

After a lot of work in DA, I've come to realize that, while life has not turned out the way I want it to, God has a plan for me. Believe me, this is a hard-won lesson, but "making it" might not mean writing another film. It might mean just being a decent, honest, kind person.

I don't know what my Higher Power has in store for me. I just keep showing up and try to keep my feet planted on the ground. Which isn't always easy when you're prone to fantasizing and avoidance. But I've had some coffee today and I'm feeling pretty grounded. I hope you are, too. If you aren't, it only takes a few moments, and it starts with a prayer. Go ahead, I'll wait.

It's Not About The Money:

God, help me stay firmly planted in this moment.

June 10

IMPERFECT

"We were ready to have God remove all these defects of character."

– DA Step #6

When I first came into recovery, I couldn't handle the fact I was imperfect. I mean, I knew I wasn't *perfect,* but I definitely wanted to fix a few aspects of my personality and get better at things I was horrible at. I thought I would use the Tools of DA's Program to get a handle on these defects of character.

The thing I didn't get was the fact that I wasn't in charge of removing my own defects. It wasn't about me doing the "right" things. I had to trust that God would remove my defects when He was ready and the time was right.

Did I want to have the defect of envy? No. Of entitlement? No. Selfishness? Nope. Irresponsibility. Nah. I'd preferred to have the defect of, say, being too thin or too rich–not really defects but that's the way I thought when I came into DA.

When I finally began to see that the operative word in Step #6 was *God,* I had to surrender. My defects may serve a purpose, or even exist to help someone else–which was a tough one for me to understand–but I have no clue what God will use. I didn't get to choose my defects, and I don't get to take them away.

God will remove my defects when the time is right. I can act better but my defects won't be removed by my own actions, willpower, or striving. Strangely enough, the more I try to "fix" my defects, the worse I feel. And, the less I try to "fix" them, the better I feel. I can't give this too much thought, if you get my drift. Change comes when it comes.

It's Not About The Money:

Who's in charge of fixing your defects? That's right, God is!

June 11

QUITTERS

"You don't get to quit because things didn't turn out the way you wanted," my new life coach told me over the phone. I would've hung up on her but I would have lost my $150. I'd remember that next time I hired an online coach.

"What do you think about what I said?" She was very pushy for a woman I'd never even seen.

"Guess I'd better get a job," I snapped. I hated her already.

"This isn't about a job. It's about your art."

"Writing isn't an art. It's just what I do. I need to make money!" I could hear my whiny voice slip out.

The picture on her website was no doubt fake. In it, she and her husband were standing outside a gorgeous brownstone in New York City. They're perfect. They're rich and happy. Easy to tell me not to quit when she was earning millions from the Internet off of losers like me.

I pretended to drop the call and hang up. I was gravely disappointed in myself because I didn't consider myself a hang-up type of person.

Pride and envy were hugely affecting my ability to earn when I came into DA. By doing the Steps I was forced to uncover parts of myself that were not pretty, mostly the fact that I hated anyone who was doing really well. I wanted to be thrilled for other people's success, but I wasn't. Envy was part of what kept me stuck.

The thing is, withholding kindness because someone else has it better does nothing but hurt me.

Don't worry, I'm not going to pull out the old there's-enough-for-all-of-us cliché, but I will say this: It's none of my business what someone else has or doesn't have. It doesn't matter where other people live, how much they earn, or what they're doing. Or, even if they're charging way too much for their coaching services. I'm on the road to recovery and I'm going to using my experiences to become better, not bitter.

And I am not quitting. So there.

It's Not About The Money:

Thanks, God, for helping me out when I want to quit.

June 12

POSITIONING

If there's one thing that reveals a person's true nature, it's when they are put in charge of other people. There's no better way to learn about yourself than by seeing what you do when you have some power.

I've held some powerful positions in my career. And while I would never have admitted it at the time, in hindsight I see I didn't handle it very well. I was kind of like Napoleon, if he were female, tall, and blonde. Yes, I was a big control freak when I was put in charge of a lot of people. I was power hungry, insecure, and a pain in the ass at times.

The truth is, before I got into DA, I wasn't a good leader. I didn't let people do their jobs; I was a micromanager. I was pretty sure I could do a better job than they did. If possible, I would've replaced everyone with more of me because I was that damn good!

In DA, I was able to see how those actions cost me relationships, and, as a result, opportunities. Man, that stung!

In time, I was able forgive myself and make amends to the people I had harmed. Until I learned how to be a worker among workers, I would never be a good leader. I'm not perfect by any stretch, but at least now I can recognize when I'm getting off track, and when I am, I reach out and get support from someone in Program. I get on my knees and ask God to help me remember that my purpose is to be of love and service to others.

My purpose is not to be the boss of everyone. Although these days, *I am* a pretty good boss. As far as bosses go. I mean, I've had some bad bosses and I am nowhere near that bad. Not anymore, that is.

It's Not About The Money:

I don't need to be the boss, I need to be of service.

June 13

BRIDGES

I've burned quite a few bridges during my time on this planet. Not that I'm counting but, if pressed, I'd estimate the number to be 12,408. Give or take a few. There have been times when I've taken the match to those bridges gleefully and stood by watching them all go up in flames. And there have been times when I've burned the bridges out of ignorance, unable to stop myself. I've made major decisions knowing full well I was destroying the only remaining route home and blowing any chance for a future.

I simply didn't know better than to douse everything I loved in kerosene and ignite it. DA shows me how to do things differently.

Today, I avoid creating disasters or crisis in my life and in the lives of others, by walking away from situations with as much dignity and grace as possible.

Most of the time.

There are times when the temptation to pull out the gas can from the back of my trunk is strong. That's when I ask for God's help and I take contrary action, by picking up the phone and calling someone who'll understand. Someone who will talk me out of the urge to start burning things, because they've been there and they know it's hard to go home when you burned all the bridges behind you.

These days, when I see a bridge, I hardly ever feel the urge to set it on fire.

It's Not About The Money:

I won't even think about burning that bridge when I come to it.

June 14

STUPID ACTIONS

My first year in Debtors Anonymous went like this: I'd wake up in a panic, worried about not having enough money to pay my bills. Then I'd spend the rest of the day writing about how excruciating it was to be an underearner and a debtor.

After I did my writing for the day, I'd spend hours online researching unemployment and homeless rates across the nation, or searching terms like, *What if I never get another job again?* or *Am I employable?*

Clarity did not come from Google. It came by praying for guidance from my Higher Power, and putting myself out there, even if my intuition was off and I did stupid things. In order to change my life, I had to take action. Even if it was stupid action.

Taking stupid action rattled my inner drill sergeant, because I wanted a linear, direct answer to my efforts and it never happened that way. I had to keep going when nothing made sense. The results usually came as an indirect action not always related to the action I had taken.

Even today, I can't always draw a line from actions to results. I just keep taking actions and they often add up to something.

It's Not About The Money:

Just take the action, already.

June 15

IDLE

Most of us debtor-ish types are busy. Insanely busy. Doin' the deal, making things happen. Because, don't you know, busyness is a sign of productivity!

Being idle, especially to a debtor, feels like, well, death.

But studies have shown that idleness is as indispensable to the human brain as vitamin C is to the body, and if we don't take a break every so often, we may suffer from mental afflictions.

When we're idle, we create the space and quiet that's necessary for making unexpected connections. We see life more objectively, which is necessary to making changes.

Idleness is also a way to create. History is full of stories of inspiration that came from idle moments and dreams. Kind of makes you wonder why the slackers aren't responsible for more of the world's great ideas and masterpieces, no?

So, why not put it in idle and give it a rest today? Relax. Chill out. You might get more accomplished. Then again, you might waste the whole day, get absolutely nothing done, and turn into a complete loser. While I'm too busy to spend a whole lot of time on this subject, I have a feeling that won't happen if you just take it easy for the next twenty-four hours.

Go on, take it easy today. It'll be okay.

It's Not About The Money:

Sit still for a while, why don'tcha?

June 16

SEXY MONEY

When I first admitted to being an underearner, I was kind of embarrassed. It was so…unexciting, melancholy, sad. "Underearner" just didn't have the je ne sais quoi of, say, "compulsive shopper" or "overspender" or even "gambler."

The underearner was like the crazy old aunt of the debting world, the one with the creaky arms and hairy moles on her cheek, who covers all her furniture in plastic. The compulsive shopper, on the other hand, was the sexy, tanned, wavy-haired high roller, and the overspender was the tall, handsome hedge-funder who's extravagant, glamorous, and hangs out with rock stars and supermodels.

The truth is, no matter where someone falls on the debting scale, a debtor's life is unmanageable. We all suffer from isolation, impatience, fear, and emptiness, and the only way we get relief is from a Higher Power. The pain, as well as the solution, is similar for all of us.

Sure, I would've much preferred to arrive on the doorsteps of DA in a racy new Jaguar with a booty of treasures, as opposed to than a twenty- year-old pickup truck with containing all of my worldly goods on my back, but that wasn't the way things went down.

Yes, there are times when I envy the freewheeling, big-time spender who drops the equivalent of a month of my salary on dinner, because it's tempting to believe that person's lifestyle is more glamorous than mine. But when it comes to debt, there's no such thing as "exciting" or "sexy." Unless you're the amazing-looking man who sits in the front row at my Monday night DA meetings. But that's another story.

It's Not About The Money:

When it comes to debt, there's no such thing as "sexy."

June 17

NOTE TO SELF

I put a yellow Post-it note on the dashboard of my car this morning. It read, Do I WANT TO LEARN TO PLAY AN INSTRUMENT?

It was a reminder to do something constructive with my life, because I'm the type of person who needs to be reminded to do constructive things. I also need to remind myself to have fun.

There are those folks, who, given all the time in the world, would watch TV in their pajamas and eat potato chips all day long. These people would sit instead of stand, and walk instead of run. I'm not one of those people. I must be doing something profound every single hour of the day. Yes, this need to be productive is tiring at times. I often exhaust myself and, no doubt, the people I love. And the people who can't stand me? I exhaust them, too. I know, because they've told me.

Sometimes I wonder, *Am I compensating for some inherent laziness, or am I really just a super productive perfectionist personality?* I do not know the answer, but in DA I've come to see that my value is not connected to being more productive or successful. My "doing" does not make me more lovable.

While I'll never be a couch potato, I've learned to slow down and enjoy more things than I used to, which means taking time to play. I can do things because *I want* to, not only to improve myself or to feel I'm being constructive and therefore more valuable.

Today, I can honestly answer a note that says Do I WANT TO LEARN TO PLAY AN INSTRUMENT? with a "maybe." I might want to take a painting class instead. I suppose, then, the real question is: Do I want to enjoy life and take the time to discover what brings me joy, no matter how weird it might seem? The answer is yes, yes, yes.

It's Not About The Money:

What do you want to do today for fun? No pressure, just asking.

June 18

MONOPOLIZE

Every since I was a kid, I've had a love/hate relationship with Monopoly. While I loved the game, I hated going to jail, and I never understood how it was possible to be thrown into jail when I'd done nothing wrong except roll a pair of rigged dice.

It didn't seem fair. There I was, having a great time with friends, drinking all the sodas and eating all the Pop Rocks a body could digest, when all of a sudden BAM! My little wheelbarrow was locked up and thrown into the "joint."

I'd sit there fuming while everyone else was laughing and buying up all the good properties like Park Place and Boardwalk. It was either rot away in the slammer or cough up fifty bucks to get out. How's that for paying your debt to society? When I was finally released from the "joint," I'd come out bitter and way more determined to succeed. I wasn't just playing a game anymore; I was compelled to crush the competition. My goal was total destruction.

After I'd stockpiled entire blocks of land, I'd get really bossy and snotty. I was obsessed with keeping all the money, the properties, the sodas, and the Pop Rocks to myself. I'd go from a happy-go-lucky kid to an evil, money-grubbing little slumlord, howling with laughter as my friends were carted off to jail for landing on my properties.

Then, as if the hand of God was at work, after I'd bought everything I wanted, I'd roll the dice and end up back in jail. I wanted so badly to be a millionaire magnate but could never maintain it. I had no idea how to handle the money or the power, and I'd always end up broke. Or in jail.

It's probably best that I rarely won at Monopoly because I had plans, you see, and those plans did not include sharing my pad on Park Place or filling my friends' wheelbarrows with cash or soda, never mind Pop Rocks.

It's Not About The Money:

It's always better when I include God in my plans.

June 19

LATTE FACTORS

Much has been written about the "latte factor"–you know, the warning financial advisers give about how your four-dollars-a-day latte habit will rob your grandchildren of their future?

Before DA, I was like, "Look, I know the money I'm spending on this latte could go be going into a retirement account, but I'd rather have the latte now than four bucks when I'm old and too tired to enjoy it."

Recently, I decided to do the math on this whole latte-factor business.

It turns out that if a guy spends four dollars on a latte on his twenty-fifth birthday, that money is gone forever. If, however, he puts it in an investment that earns five percent over forty years, he'd have $28.16.

If the guy bought one four-dollar latte per week from age 25 to 65, that would be 2,080 lattes, or $8,320 (assuming no price increase) a year. If he invested that $8,320, he'd have $26,590.67 by age 65. If he bought three lattes a week (6,240 in total), it would cost $24,960. If he invested that at five percent, he'd have $79,772.01 upon retirement. Instead of earning five percent, if he put that money in an index fund, which has earned twelve percent annually since 1976, he'd retire with $558,690.42.

A latte a day is a $931,150.69 loss when he retires. Two lattes a day–$1,862,301.38, in future dollars with four-percent inflation. Basically, he'd spend $387,897 on two lattes per day. It's not the latte that's so pricey. It's the regular purchase of the latte combined with compounded interest that's scary.

Overwhelmed yet? Me, too.

So let me break it down. One day at a time, we make a choice to live within our means and consider the future costs of our spending. Lattes go bad, but good habits don't. It's okay to have the latte, just don't do it every day. At the risk of sounding like one of those superior financial-ish types, make time for the treats, but keep them in check.

It's Not About The Money:

God, help me stay balanced with my lattes and my numbers.

June 20

FORGET IT

I often forget I have friends. It always happens on a Sunday, which is the hardest day of the week for me. I'm convinced the rest of the world is having brunch at some hip new restaurant, looking like models in *Vanity Fair* magazine, and I'm at home, alone, eating stale sunflower seeds and tropical flavored Otter-Pops.

That's when I start to spin out. *Oh my God, I'm such a loser. No one cares and I'll be alone forever. Broke and alone. Forever.*

No matter how many meetings I go to, there are things I still struggle with and this is one of them. *Everyone else is having a fantastic life,* I think, *except me. I should have stayed in touch with the bitchy girls from my sorority.* I know for sure a lot of them live in homes that belong on the cover of *Architectural Digest.*

It's a bit dramatic and slightly immature. Although I don't want to sound pathetic, I kind of am, and the result of this thinking causes me to hide or isolate, or to go out and spend a whole lot of money. Anything to try to fill the void.

Which is why I love DA. Because it reminds me I have a spiritual program and a lot to offer. And even though I don't have a home and friends that look like they belong on the cover of magazines, I have people who love and care about me and they're precious to me.

Deep down inside, I know that even if I were at one of my old sorority sisters' *Architectural Digest*-y parties on a Sunday afternoon, I probably wouldn't be having fun. Because I didn't really like many of them, and I can never forget that the president of my sorority – the one who made the pledges walk around campus with eggs in our bras – became a hedge-fund manager.

It's Not About The Money:

Today, I'll remember that I don't always see things as they *really* are.

June 21

BABY STEPS

I totally related to the mental patient named Bob in the movie *What About Bob?* when he'd say things like "baby steppin' to the bus" or "baby steps into the elevator."

When I first came to DA, I had to take things very slowly and constantly remember not to get ahead of myself.

DA showed me the best way to accomplish a goal was by taking small steps. When I had to do something like apply for a job, speak to a creditor, or call a bank, I would meet with my friends in DA. Together we would break the process down into small, manageable pieces.

I've begun to take this approach to everything in my life, and by golly, it works! It's not necessary to take bold or dramatic steps. I can take things in little chunks, or like Bob, I can baby step so I don't get overwhelmed. Besides, when I take on pint-sized tasks and complete them, I feel good.

For instance, when it came to writing this book, I thought I couldn't possibly write the entire thing. When I had a PRG about it, my DA buddies advised me not to worry about writing a whole book. They told me to write fifteen minutes every day and that's exactly what I did. One day, I realized I had completed a whole book. More or less. It'll never be as good as I want it to be, but for all intents and purposes, this book is done, because I baby-stepped it into being.

I just kept on baby steppin'.

Before I came into DA, my first question used to be: What's my next gigantic leap? Today it is: What's my next baby step?

It's Not About The Money:

Baby stepping is nothing to be ashamed of.

June 22

HOT WAX

I was new to DA, and working for a day spa for minimum wage. The salon was owned by a woman who employed two teenage interns–except they didn't get school credit, money, or supervision. The place was a petri dish for human bacteria. It was hard for me not to giggle when the owner, who came in twice a week, told me I wasn't allowed to leave the premises for lunch, lest there be some sort of hot wax emergency.

I couldn't help but wonder whether my boss's hysteria about missing a chance to do a bikini wax was an attempt to cover up the fact that our services didn't really matter in the grand scheme of life.

Then one day, it occurred to me that my boss was a lot like me. She was always afraid she wouldn't make enough money, ergo she used cheap wax, bought low-thread-count towels, and ran the place like a sweatshop. I began to see many similarities between this woman and the way I behaved before recovery.

My sponsor told me it didn't matter whether my boss had money issues; my job was to show up and be of service. I didn't have to tolerate abuse or bad treatment, and I didn't get to be resentful or a bad employee.

Whenever I started to feel resentful toward her, I'd remind myself of the times I'd let fear cause me to offer less than my best to others.

DA teaches me to stay "right-sized" and reminds me I don't get to analyze someone else or tell them when they're failing or falling short. Even if my boss was being cheap or acting strange about money, it wasn't my business. And nothing was an emergency. Unless they *really needed a hot wax.*

It's Not About The Money:

My only job today is to stay right-sized.

June 23

GENEROUS

I used to enjoy giving–as long as it didn't make me uncomfortable or put me out. And I'd expect some credit for what I'd done, usually in the form of applause. A lifetime of deference and loyalty was acceptable as well.

I *meant* to be generous. I *intended* to be the person who did things without expecting anything in return. I *wanted* to be the one who loved others unconditionally. I just found so few people worthy of it. And, you know, things happened. People would irritate me or let me down, and I'd have to focus on other important things like making more money or refurnishing my office or updating my wardrobe.

By the time I came to DA, I had given up on "brotherly love." But the kindhearted folks I met in recovery showed me what it meant to be generous. They gave me rides to meetings when I needed them, they took time to help me create a spending plan, and they answered my phone calls when I was hurting so much I didn't think I could face another day.

The people in DA restored my faith in humanity. And because they helped me without expecting anything in return, it made me want to do the same for others. I'm convinced now that my joy increases and I grow exponentially when I give without expectations. When I give to you, I reap the rewards. When I help you, I help myself.

So, come on, put your hand in my hand and let me help you out. I mean it, and I don't expect anything from you. Not one thing.

It's Not About The Money:
The reward for giving is giving.

June 24

STUCK

"When you get stuck, lower your standards." – William Stafford

I remember at one point in my life when I had a great job, a wonderful man, and lots of friends, I looked around my gorgeous condo and thought, What if things aren't as good as they could be? *What if there's more to life and I'm not experiencing it?*

I didn't know I was a debtor. I just knew my expectations could never be met. My standards (read: perfectionism) kept me in a perpetual state of discontent. I was stuck with a lot of unfulfilled wishes and I was very resentful.

Before I found recovery, I was constantly reassessing my situation, in fear I might have settled for less. My lofty expectations were out of control. My insatiability contributed to my debting behaviors, because for most of my life I was driven by the pursuit of something more. I'm sure I wasn't a lot of fun to be around. It's hard for people to be their best when they feel they are being judged and failing to meet the mark.

I'm learning to accept life on life's terms now instead of constantly reassessing how it should be, which is much healthier, especially because I think people with lower standards generally have better lives. I mean, how can you be disappointed when you aren't expecting the moon and the stars?

Thank God for DA, because I'm enjoying life a whole lot more since I actively decided to lower my standards.

In fact, I'm having a delightful time writing today's meditation, because I'm in total acceptance that it might not meet *anyone's* standards. That kind of feels good!

It's Not About The Money:

Let's try lowering them standards today.

June 25

VAGUENESS

"What happens in vagueness, stays in vagueness." – Anonymous

Financial vagueness really is a lot like Vegas. When I'm in vagueness, I can leave behind my daily life. I have an unlimited budget, I can stay up 'til five a.m., eating fried foods, drinking all the soda I can, shopping up a storm, and in general, indulge myself in whatever I want without fear of repercussions!

Vagueness is shiny and exciting. When I'm there, I'm confident, focused, sexy, and charming. I can (fill in the blank) and I don't have to (fill in the blank). In vagueness, I am invincible.

When I'm on one of my vagueness trips, I have no responsibilities. I'm free to act out without worrying what my neighbors or friends will think. No one cares what I'm doing when I'm in vagueness. There are no consequences. In fact, just fantasizing about vagueness makes the bad aspects of my life seem to fade away.

I used to spend a lot of time in vagueness, the only problem was coming back from those trips. While it's true that what happens in vagueness, stays in vagueness, the credit card bills always came back with me.

It's Not About The Money:
Don't spend your life in vagueness.

June 26

DEA OR DA?

Six months into a project I had secured venture capital funding for, I learned that one of my investors was being indicted for securities fraud. He'd been accused of masterminding a massive scam and had stolen hundreds of millions of dollars from investors.

It's a long story, meant for more than a daily meditation book, but suffice it to say, I have a history of falling into business dealings with people whom other folks might see as being surrounded by *red flags*.

DA has taught me to be more selective about the people I do business with. I take my time before getting involved and I don't accept everyone at face value. It's not like I *always* run credit checks on acquaintances–that is, not all the time–but I'm definitely more discerning than I used to be.

When I consider a new financial arrangement, especially when I start to question something, I make sure I get support from a trusted friend in DA before moving forward. Because of the work I have done in recovery and the wisdom I have gained, I take a lot of time to get to know people before jumping into business with them.

Now that I have some time in recovery, I never partner with people I have questions about, no matter how persuasive they are. For example, the next time I'm considering working on a project with someone and officers from the DEA stop by to investigate my future partner while we're meeting, I will give our proposed arrangement some thought. A lot more thought.

It's Not About The Money:

When red flags are waving, stop, or at least slow down.

June 27

SHUT UP

"Keep your mouth shut, especially when you know you're right about something."
– Anonymous

I heard this quote recently at a DA meeting and wrote it down immediately. I'm right a great deal of the time, but I still think this quote will come in handy.

It isn't always easy for an exceptionally reasonable, wise person like me to stay silent when the folks I love are obviously screwing things up–debting and compulsive spending, staying in dead-end jobs, and using too many credit cards. It's especially hard when I can see it and know they could use the help of DA. After all, it worked for me and I was a hopeless mess when it came to money.

But I'm committed to keeping my mouth shut. At least for the next twenty-four hours. I will say nothing when the people I love do things like hide or lie about their money, or overspend. Even better, I'll keep quiet when these very people make the kind of mistakes I know are going to ruin their lives over time. I'll be silent, even when I know I'm right, because most people don't want to be told they're wrong, and believe you me, I know that one firsthand.

I've asked my Higher Power for the courage to carry this out, because I am exposed to so many people on a daily basis who need my help. Most people have no clue about their spending or debting problems. I can count on one hand the people I know who have a good relationship with money.

Yes, I have a lot to say, but I've learned to keep my mouth shut, even when I'm right.

Today's going to be a great day. More than likely a very quiet day, but a fantastic day, nonetheless.

It's Not About The Money:

It's okay to say nothing, even when I'm right.

June 28

NO CYNICISM

Today is No Cynicism Day!

It has been decreed throughout the land that today we shall all curb our cynicism. Enough already with the been-there, done-that attitude. Instead, feel free to let your hope flag fly high, your anticipation shine bright, and refuse to see the possible negative consequences!

Say, for example, you're walking down the street today and there's a man raising an axe and it looks like he's going to lower the boom on the next person he sees. Most folks would run to the other side of the street or call the police. Others might take a picture on their cell phone. Jerks.

The less cynical type would continue down the street and ignore the man with the axe, assuming he would never hurt them. They might even strike up a conversation and convince the man to put the axe down.

Have these people lost their grip on reality? I think not. I think they're simply saying "no!" to cynicism.

While I doubt you'll run across a man with an axe today, and I'm not encouraging you to stop and chat with him if you do, I am saying he could merely be having a bad day so let's try to stay positive. Because it is, after all, No Cynicism Day!

It's Not About The Money:

No matter what's in my bank account, I'" let my hope flag fly high today!

June 29

BANK SCRIPT

In an effort to ensure smoother and more enjoyable phone conversations with creditors, I created a script for the next time my bank "reaches out" to me.

"Hello, Stagecoach Bank!

I'm so glad you took time out of your busy day to call me. Before we get started, I want to let you know I've prepared a few talking points so I don't get off track. Is that okay with you?

(Don't wait for reply.)

Great! What I've done is create a breakdown as to how my income is distributed. Yes, it's a pie chart and I know how dry those things can be, so I won't go into details now. I'll e-mail it to you later.

I've also created a really colorful infographic that charts the course of events leading up to my financial demise, complete with a description of how I found Debtors Anonymous, which, by the way, I would highly recommend to your other customers–only if they need it, of course.

In my presentation you'll also find a timeline that includes my various employers and subsequent job searches over the past three years.

(Brief pause.) *As you'll see, the presentation concludes with slides of things I find super calming, like my dog Sam, the ocean, and the mountains. Who doesn't love mountains?*

Wow, time has flown. I've gotta run. (Smile.) *I'll just need your e-mail address so I can get this document to you after we're done here.*

Thanks again for the call. I've really enjoyed our chat. Toodles!"

It's Not About The Money:

Don't be scared. Be prepared.

June 30

STABLE

I told my sponsor the reason I wanted a lot of money was because I thought it would make me feel safer.

"I never had stability as a kid and some old part of my brain thinks that if I make enough money now, I'll be safe."

"I understand, but there's no amount of money that will make you feel safe," he replied.

"Well, how's about I make a bunch of money and let you know how I feel?" I said, sarcastically.

"The only way to feel safe is to model it for others."

"Huh? My life is a mess. I can't be stable for myself, much less someone else!"

"When I started sponsoring and helping others, I started feeling the very things I thought I was missing. Safety, security and love."

My sponsor tends to be lofty, so I wanted to dismiss what he was saying. Ironically, I found out he was right. Honoring my commitments and being of service to others gives me the feeling of stability and safety I crave. Things I once sought through money and achievement.

The notion of getting a huge stash of cash still tempts me at times, but not nearly as often as it used to. I guess that's why they say, "keep coming back."

It's Not About The Money:

I can create the good I want to experience today.

July 1

FLAWLESS

Many of us debtors buy into the concept of what I like to call the fatal flaw. You know, the flaw that, once discovered, will repel anyone who gets to know the real you? Whether it be a bankruptcy, massive credit card debt, depression, our less-than-perfect home, a bad job history, or long-term unemployment, we believe we are undeserving.

Hear me, my sweet little chickens–there is no such thing as a fatal flaw. You are not defective or undeserving. You are exactly who God created you to be.

Sure, we all have a reflection process we go through and we have to challenge ourselves to change. It's natural to want to improve, but we debtors can get a little crazy with the navel gazing. When all the analysis leads to a need for constant improvement, we stop enjoying life.

For the next twenty-four hours, your job is to not think about or focus on anything you think is lacking or wrong with you. You can't spend one minute trying to fix anything about yourself. Not a thing.

Instead, you're going to imagine that you are perfect right now. You're in the midst of growth, and you have a Higher Power that is leading you to exactly where you need to be. Your pace is as it should be. Acknowledge your efforts, accept the fact that you can't go faster, and give yourself a pat on the back. While you're in this state, look around and see if you can do something nice for yourself. This doesn't have to mean spending the last fifty bucks in your bank account. You can do something small for yourself. Afterwards, you might find that your judgments about how flawed you are will fade away.

So, go out and make it a great day. Because you can and you're perfect as you are. At least God thinks you are.

It's Not About The Money:
Nothing's fatal, nothing's flawed.

July 2

REMOVALS

"Humbly asked God to remove our shortcomings." – *DA Step #7*

When I came into DA, I wanted to get down to business and clear up my shortcomings, because I knew they were interfering with my ability to have a bigger life. I didn't want to waste a bunch of time doing the first Six Steps, so I just moved directly to working Step Seven on my own.

"I've been praying for God to remove my shortcomings. It's been three months and they're still there," I whined to my sponsor. "Why the heck's it taking so long?!"

"Aren't you on Step One?" my sponsor asked.

"Yes, but I'd like to skip through the other stuff and get to work on my defects. I need to start making money again."

"One Step at a time, my friend."

"But I could die before all these defects are removed!"

"You could," he said, chuckling, "but you're not in charge of removing your own defects and you can't rush your recovery. Let's just do this in order. Start with Step One. You're powerless over debting," he said.

Duh, even I know that, I thought. But when I'm back on my feet, I'll be done with this whole powerlessness baloney. I want to be self-sufficient again.

As if he'd read my thoughts, my sponsor announced, "Self-sufficiency isn't the point of recovery."

"Remind me, then, what is the point again?"

"God-sufficiency, connection. Solvency and serenity."

I seriously wonder if he can read my mind at times, so I said a silent prayer: *"God, these shortcomings are really throwing me off. I know I'm not in charge of my recovery, but just so you know, you can remove my shortcomings whenever you want to."*

"You're right. You're not in charge of your recovery," my sponsor said. I'm keeping an eye on him.

It's Not About The Money:

God sufficiency, not self-sufficiency.

July 3

RESOURCES

"We will recognize that there is enough; our resources will be generous and we will share them with others." – *DA Promise #7*

When I first heard that promise in a DA meeting, I thought, *I don't have any resources, so I guess I don't have to worry about being generous yet!* Then I looked around the room and thought, *I certainly wouldn't want to share resources with* these *people. They're weird!*

Truth be told, I didn't want to share my resources with *anyone*. It was my turn, and I wanted my share. If, at some point on my meteoric rise to the top, I had a little extra to help someone else out, I'd consider it. Maybe.

I was in DA to make up for lost time.

One day my sponsor suggested I stop focusing on earning a bunch of money and try to be a kinder, more thoughtful human being. As if I wasn't already thoughtful enough!

"What does being kind have to do with getting my life back together and cleaning up my credit score?" I asked him.

"Nothing. At least not right now. Just give it some consideration," he said.

As I worked the Steps and Tools, I began to see how integral relating to and caring for others was to my recovery. Some of my happiest times have been when I'm helping out a friend or taking an outreach call. I've learned to share the resources of my heart, and despite my insatiable desire for more money, I've come to realize that my internal resources are way cooler than a fistful of hundred-dollar bills.

My life experience is a resource, and it is valuable. Even though I'm still not rolling in the financial resources, I'm definitely one of the richest human beings I know. Seriously.

It's Not About The Money:

God, show me where to put my resources today.

July 4

HAPPY, HAPPY!

Happy birthday, America! It's your birthday! Are you excited?

On this day in 1776, after years of bitter fighting, which had been triggered when a group of colonists fed up with paying taxes–sound familiar?–sent a message to England and threw tons of perfectly good tea in the Boston Harbor, America declared its independence from the British.

And while it might be in order to note that the colonists and succeeding generations exhibited behaviors (impulsivity, entitlement, anger at authority) that might justify membership in a debting program, I'll refrain today from my usual preachy references about recovery.

Because it is 'Merica's birthday!

Instead of dwelling on the fact that My Country 'Tis of Thee has a major debting problem of its own, I'll take my recovery hat off to offer a figurative kiss to the Land that I Love!

America, no matter how obvious it is–to me,–that you need to deal with your debt and should consider a meeting, today you deserve a party with stars and stripes, hot dogs, hamburgers, ice cream, and blue-frosted cupcakes. And fireworks!

You want to know what I love most about you? You never, ever get mad at me for not buying you a card on your birthday. But then again, you never buy me one, either. You're broke.

I still love you, though.

It's Not About The Money:

Happy birthday, America!

July 5

DISCIPLINE

I used to think my debting problem had to do with a lack of discipline. If I could get some order in my life and pay the bills on time–at least before they were two months late–catch up on my late taxes, stop borrowing money, and stick with a spending plan, I could lick the whole debting thing.

It's not like it was rocket science; there was no algebra or statistics involved. I just needed some good ol'-fashioned self-control and discipline.

Day after day I would start out clutching my little pad of paper and pen, intending to note every cent I earned and spent, only to give up before I had my breakfast.

"To hell with this recording stuff," I'd say, and go on a spending bender. I'd buy candles, coffee, toilet paper, trail mix, whatever I could get my hands on.

I refused to be shackled by a ridiculous spending plan.

It took me two years in DA to figure out this wasn't just a lack of discipline or self-control. I had a spiritual problem that manifested in the form of a whacked-out relationship with money, and behavior that included impulsivity, selfishness, and vagueness. I finally realized I couldn't fix myself with discipline. I had to surrender to a Higher Power and work a program of recovery, which included tracking my numbers as best I could. I didn't and still don't do it perfectly, but I keep trying.

Today, I have peace around my finances. The best part is, I don't have to worry about being more self-controlled or disciplined. I just work the plan of recovery one day at a time.

It's Not About The Money:

I may not be as disciplined as I'd like to be, but I'm better than I used to be!

July 6

'PPRECIATION

Why is it that everything that's valuable these days involves a secret? There's the "secret to building wealth," the "secret to investing," the "secret to happiness," the "secret to the universe."

What is it with all the secrets?! Isn't life complicated enough?

If I had something as amazing as the secret to the universe, or the secret to getting rich, I wouldn't charge you $99.95 for it. I'd share it with you, because I would want you to be happy. I wouldn't necessarily give it to you for free, but I'd definitely give it to you for a discount. At least I would want to give it to you for a discount.

I do have a secret to share. And since you've purchased this book, I'm going to share it with you right now for absolutely no extra charge. It's the secret to a happy life.

Here it is: Appreciate what you already have.

I know, it's not sexy, but it's true. It won't make you thinner or smarter or richer, but it will make your life better. And don't we all want to feel better?

At the risk of sounding like one of those "secret" swindlers, I'd like to suggest that right now, you look up to the sky and say, "Thank you, God, for everything. For all that I have been given, for all that has been taken away, and for all that remains."

You won't mean it. Yet. But try saying it for the next fourteen days, in the morning and before bed. I promise you, your life will improve. If not, I will give you all of your money back.*

*Contact me at misti@mistibwrites to share your stories with me.

It's Not About The Money:

The secret might not be easy, but it is simple.

July 7

FILING

I was making such an effort to work my DA Program, I decided to get my tax information together so I could file them on time. It was December and I had filed another extension. But I was committed to getting it done before the next April filing rolled around.

Imagine my surprise when my accountant totaled up my earnings for that year and realized I'd made more money than I had made in the past three years. I even had a refund coming! I looked over the forms again. Everything looked good; I think he'd added things up correctly. So why was I so stressed? Why had I spent most of the year worried I'd never work again? Why had I let my fear keep me from filing my taxes?

I started crying, because I hadn't had much fun that year. I hadn't taken a trip, bought myself any new clothes, or even replaced my broken hair dryer.

"Why? Why? Why do I do these things?" I cried out to no one.

"Because you're a self-debtor and you live in vagueness," I told myself, but it didn't make me feel much better.

So I went to a DA meeting and shared what had happened. About how much fun I'd missed out on because I was so worried about the taxes I hadn't filed. At the end of the meeting, several people came up to me and shared that they'd done similar things. Even though I was sad, it felt good to be understood and accepted for the oddball I was.

Whenever I operate in fear and try to do life alone, when I refuse to look at the numbers or the facts of a situation, or get help from God and people I trust, things don't go well.

The thing is, situations are never as bad as I imagine they're going to be. Well, almost never. Taxes are the one exception, but as I saw this year, even that can turn out okay.

It's Not About The Money:

I can deal, and things aren't as bad as I imagine they'll be.

July 8

THOSE PEOPLE

Most people see a beautiful home and say, "Someday, that will be my home." Before DA, I'd see the same home and say, "I wonder who that dirty rotten slime bag screwed over to get that house!"

I have a warped viewpoint about money, even when I'm the one who owns the beautiful things. Even if I end up owning that gorgeous house on the hill that I long for, there'll be this voice inside my head that reminds me, – *"You're different from those other people with money."* –

In the past, when I had a lot of money, I thought I was smarter, more hardworking than those people who didn't, and when I didn't have money, I thought I was less than other people. Additionally, there were times when I didn't have money and thought I was better than others, and times when I had money and felt I was useless.

I struggled with balance.

Like many debtors, I was either living large or barely getting by. When it came to prosperity, money, and abundance, I'd get very uncomfortable.

The good news is, DA has shown me how to be content with what I have, no matter how much or how little that is. Also, I've learned not to judge "those people" who have more than me. I don't know how hard they work or what they've done to achieve the things they have, and it's none of my business.

Today, when I drive by a beautiful home, I think,–*"What a lovely home. I hope the person who owns it feels blessed. God willing, I'll have a lovely home again one day,"*–or something to that effect. I don't spend a lot of time thinking about it, because more than likely I'd be stopping traffic and someone would honk at me and then I'd think, *I wonder why that jerk behind me can't relax while I'm trying to be spiritual!*

It's Not About The Money:

God loves "those people" just as much as He loves me.

July 9

PRAYS

Growing up, I'd heard a lot of things about how to pray, including "You can't have any attachment to the outcome when you pray," and "You can't pray and be worried at the same time." Then there's the one that threw me off for the first thirty years of my life: "If you don't have faith when you pray, God won't answer your prayers."

As if God was keeping track of the quality of my prayers or the amount of faith I had in order to determine which ones He would answer. As if God was waiting to punish me for wanting something too much. Or withholding things because I didn't know how to believe. As if there was some formula for faith.

When I came into recovery, I had no idea how to pray anymore.

People gently explained to me that it didn't matter what my prayers sounded like or how much faith I had. Simply making the effort was enough. In the early days of my recovery from debting, my prayers went something like this:

Hey, God, it's me. I just wanted to say thank you for my fingers and toes. Thank you for the fact I still have all my hair and a decent pair of tennis shoes. If you could help out my friend that's having knee surgery and maybe show me what to do today, I'd sure appreciate it. Amen.

When I became more comfortable talking to God, I started memorizing new prayers that I heard in meetings. And I read other, more specific prayers and tried them. I've recently started reading the St. Francis of Assisi prayer but that one's a pretty tall order.

I don't know if God cares what words I use, or how I pray, or where I'm standing when I do it. I also don't think He has a measuring stick or a minimum faith quotient before He'll listen to me. I'd like to think God just wants to hear from me. And you, too, of course.

It's Not About The Money:

Prayer–it's all good.

July 10

OLD LIFE

"I want my old life back" was how I would start every time I shared at a DA meeting. "My old life was amazing. I made great money, I had a sweet condo, and a full life. I was somebody!" I'd say, before bursting into tears.

I did have a great life before it all came crashing down. I lived in denial and vagueness about money. I went through seasons of overspending then long periods of underearning. And then it stopped working and I was sentenced to DA. No, I wasn't really sentenced to DA by a judge–that's not possible–but I had tried everything else and I had nowhere else to go. The only people who could understand my relationship with money were the people in the Program of DA.

Once I paid off my debts and re-booted my floundering career, I'd get my old life back. Only this time I'd be smarter and a better saver. I'd make wiser invest choices. I didn't yet recognize that debting, for some of us, is a spiritual "dis-ease" that manifests itself in chaos around money. And it gets worse with time.

My old life looked good before I landed in DA, but in reality, I felt insecure and unsafe and there were times when I thought the only solution was to end it all.

Today, my life's based on a relationship with a loving God, and the Tools and Twelve Steps of DA. I no longer want my old life back. Except when I have to wait at home for a service representative from the utility company to come install something, and the "appointment" is between 8 a.m. and 6 p.m. With my old life, I had no problem wasting a whole day waiting around for a technician. Then I kind of start missing my old life. But only a little bit.

It's Not About The Money:
I want the life that I have today.

July 11

HALLUCINATIONS

"A vision without solvency is a hallucination." – *Anonymous*

My entire life was one giant hallucination. A hallucination based on the idea I could do everything without God's or anyone else's help. I operated on "self-will" for most of my life.

I would set goals with insane deadlines, refusing to get feedback about how reasonable–or not–they were. I'd push other people to meet my ludicrous deadlines, without respect for the fact they might have time frames of their own, because I had to succeed!

I'd sacrifice anything to pursue my dreams and goals, even if it meant draining my savings, my retirement accounts, or potentially screwing up my credit. Sometimes I pursued a dream for so long, I didn't know I didn't want it anymore.

The hardest part of recovery was pulling the curtain on my hallucinations.

Now, when I think I might be close to hallucinating, I check it out with fellows in DA and trusted friends. It's important to have visions, but if they aren't done with the goal of solvency, they can easily turn into hallucinations.

If you can relate to this way of thinking, it could be a sign you're hallucinating. And not the good kind of hallucination, you know, with rainbow-colored reindeers that fly through the air, leaving streams of starlight behind them? Of course, I know nothing about those kind of hallucinations.

It's Not About The Money:

A vision is a gift I receive, not a demand I make.

July 12

CODES

The Voynich manuscript is an illustrated, handwritten code in an unknown language from the 1400s that no one's ever been able to decipher.

It's not like a group of cavemen threw some symbols on a scroll and dropped it off in the Mesopotamian desert. It's a real language, just one that's never been seen before, or since. Military code breakers, smarty-pants professor types, even mathematicians have tried to interpret the Voynich manuscript but they haven't been able to because it's so intricate and unique.

This is exactly what my brain experiences when it sees numbers on a spreadsheet. It's like an unknown code, a foreign language, except it's worse than the Voynich because other people understand it. I'm not stupid, but I don't understand how some people love numbers and enjoy looking at them.

I don't and I can't.

Numbers make me nervous. I don't want to track them or review them. Ever. They make me want to pull out a magnifying glass, or cry, or die from a million paper cuts.

Sometimes when I get scared because I have to go over a spreadsheet, I call a friend in DA. We might just talk, and at other times we'll pray together. They always remind me that numbers can't hurt me. If I breathe deeply and take the next step, the numbers usually make sense. Sometimes it takes a few phone calls before I can complete my task. But I keep trying because it's the way to recovery, at least for me.

Sometimes I say a prayer and ask for "glossolalia," which is the art of speaking, writing, or interpreting languages that have been channeled by God. I hope this meditation was helpful. I worry it didn't make sense. If not, please try reading it again until it does.

It's Not About The Money:

I may never love numbers but I can always reach out and ask for help.

July 13

OVER

"If I had my life to live over, I'd try to make more mistakes next time. I would relax. I would limber up. I would be sillier than I have been this trip. I know of very few things that I would take seriously. I would play hooky more, I would ride on more merry-go-rounds. I'd pick more daisies." – *Anonymous*

Being in debt can make us debtors overly serious. It also can cause us to write staggeringly corny prose.

Whether you're in debt, overspending, underearning, or not, don't allow it to steal your sense of humor. And please don't use it as an excuse to write hackneyed lines about how you're going to feel on your deathbed.

Let's have some fun today, my little chickens. Spend three minutes doing something that will make you laugh or smile. This meditation doesn't count. You must get up, move around, and *do* something.

As far as I know, we're not getting another shot at this life, so let's try to enjoy the day. Take a walk, run barefoot, pick some daisies ride a merry-go-round. Make some mistakes today, for goodness sakes! Laugh until you cry, or cry until you laugh–it will happen if you cry long enough-trust me, I've done it. Just no thoughts, poetry or discussions about what you're going to say on your deathbed.

It's Not About The Money:

Three consecutive minutes of smiling. No eye rolling.

July 14

BUDDY BREAKS

I've worked on and off with an "action buddy" in DA, as a way to set goals and keep myself accountable.

Things always start out well. My buddy and I schedule daily calls and trot out our to-do lists: be more content with our lives, earn more (of course–we're debtors!), be more spiritual, rid ourselves of negative talk, push through emotional obstacles, etc.

Then it inevitably happens. One of us tires out on the exhausting quest to "git 'er done."

The daily calls taper off and one of us asks for a break. Or the excitement wanes when one of us finds a new job, a relationship, or has to finish a work project.

The first few times this happened, I was quite upset and blamed my action buddy. What a flake! Didn't he/she understand the value of making a commitment?

When I initiated the breakup, I blamed myself. I'd failed my buddy.

After several action buddy breakups, I came to realize that each partnership served a special purpose in my life.

Sometimes our buddies stay in our lives for a long time; sometimes they don't. I don't have to blame myself for anyone else when our time to support each other is over. It doesn't mean we don't continue to support each other; it's just the flow of life.

Or, as Sting might say, I have to "set them free," which is a good reminder for me. I've never been able to let go of things I love or even, simply like. I'll probably never be great at it and that's okay. We control freaks are just as lovable as those love-'em-and-let-them-go types.

It's Not About The Money:

I don't have to hold on to everything, or everyone, forever.

July 15

RESENTMENTS

Sometimes I get bitter about my situation. I watch the people and institutions I dislike from afar, as I sit in the damp shadows of fear, nurturing my resentments like Gollum, or one of those slimy creatures from The Lord of the Rings.

Before I know it, I start building resentments, and usually sooner rather than later, those resentments start to leak out and they affect everyone I encounter. They also activate my character defects, and I get cranky and angry, because – *don't you know I'm a good person just trying to make it in the world, a squirrel trying to get a nut who keeps getting beat down?*– Or, on the other side of the coin, I think, *I'm so filled with talent and potential, and my dreams are so grandiose, I can't possibly accomplish them with all these 'normal' people in my way.*

Resentments trigger negative thoughts, which, if left unchecked, lead me to debting. For instance, when I'm jealous and envious of others and feeling I'm lacking, I'm in danger of compulsive spending. When I'm angry at the establishment, it's usually because I'm feeling out of control or overwhelmed and acting out is almost inevitable. When I'm mad at myself, it's often because I'm doing work I don't enjoy, or I'm not taking care of myself. More than likely, I'm underearning or self-debting.

No matter what the symptoms are, unresolved resentments affect my relationship with God and others, and lead me to dark places. I start resembling tiny creatures that hang out in the mountains, and I alternate between being a hostile jerk to being a simple-minded idiot who's easily confused.

It's Not About The Money:

Resentments motivate me, and not in a good way.

July 16

MANGO TANGO

They called him "The Wolf" of Wall Street. He was a day trader who sold stocks in worthless companies and swindled hundreds of millions of dollars from his victims. He had yachts, private planes, and mansions around the world. And he blew it all on drugs, alcohol, and prostitutes.

What a creep, I thought. *If I had that kind of money, I wouldn't waste it. I'd be generous, I'd save entire countries from poverty and disease, I'd travel overseas where major disasters had occurred and valiantly offer my time and knowledge, building houses, carrying water across depleted villages. I'd be the one person who wouldn't be tempted by too much money or power. I would stand for good and not give in to greed or power mongering. I'd be incorruptible.*

Who am I kidding? I'm preoccupied with money and I don't even have very much! I don't know how to handle a little, much less the crazy kind of money that dubious stockbroker had. And while there are many things this guy did that I'd never do–primarily the drugs, the prostitutes, but mostly, the Mango Tango tan–I have a tendency to think I could handle money better than anyone else I know.

When I start believing money will make me happy and whole, I'm headed for big trouble. Money, power, possessions, and financial security will never fill the void that a relationship with a Higher Power can.

In truth, money has never been my problem, nor will it *ever* be my solution. I have a problem with perception. A Mango Tango tan, though? Not something I have a problem with.

It's Not About The Money:

God, help me remember my biggest problem is perception.

July 17

RECYCLED

Back in the day, before it was considered cool, I was a recycler. I recycled plastic bottles and cans, reused my coffee filters when possible, waited until my clothes wore out before I'd buy new ones. While my things were clean and tidy, I'd keep them until they were unusable.

The only way I'd buy something new was if it was on sale or I found it at a secondhand store. When I'd take that rare trip to the mall, I'd pass by store after store and agonize. If I found something I wanted, I'd say to myself, *You already have a few pairs of pants. Besides, the landfill doesn't need more denim. It's your job to stop the waste.*

It occurred to me while doing some work in DA that I wasn't recycling because I cared about the environment, it was because I didn't feel I deserved new things. I didn't believe I was worthy of walking into a nice big department store and buying myself a beautiful new dress simply because I liked the way it looked. I'd allow myself to have something if it had been handed down or, as they say in the thrift stores, "gently used." I was hiding my self-hatred under the phony cloak of environmentalism, which, probably doesn't exist, and if one existed, I'm sure it'd be made from recycled socks.

Now that I'm kind of over the whole self-deprivation thing, I don't feel one bit of guilt about owning more than five pairs of shoes or buying a hair dryer before the old one shorts out and electrocutes me. It's not like I'm getting 24-karat-gold facials, but I'm no longer ashamed to provide myself with quality things.

And while I still feel a pang of guilt at times for buying things I need, it doesn't happen nearly as often as it used to.

In fact, sometimes when I'm feeling frisky, I'll buy in bulk, simply because I can. For that, I can thank the program of DA.

It's Not About The Money:

I deserve good things!

July 18

REBELS

Although I've never been to jail or had more than a traffic ticket, I'm a rebel at heart. I wanna do what I wanna do, when I wanna do it. I want it easy, and I want it quick.

Damn the torpedoes, screw the consequences, I'm the definition of a rebel without a cause. Entitled, smug, and arrogant, I love to criticize The Man, who's keeping me down.

In truth, my rebellion has nothing to do with a bigger or higher calling to help the downtrodden or make the world a better place. And I rarely think about how I can save the planet by using ethanol fuel. It's because deep down I don't like business. I'm afraid I can't do it, so I rail against convention and refuse to take the small steps over time that lead people to success.

Showing up for my own life, going to meetings, and tracking my numbers aren't easy for me. But without the help of a Higher Power and the Tools of a recovery program, I lack the willingness to go the distance in any area of my life.

The interesting thing is, because of DA I now find comfort in things that used to be a drag, like knowing what I have in all my accounts, paying rent without using a credit card, and making major purchases with cash.

I still wanna do what I wanna do when I wanna do it, but consistency and serenity are much cooler than being a rebel and fighting against The Man. One, because I've never been able to find The Man I'm so mad at, and two, I'm way too selfish to be a rebel with a cause. And finally, I have no clue about the difference between ethanol and biodiesel fuels.

It's Not About The Money:
I don't need no stinkin' cause to rebel.

July 19

VIBES

"You're vibrating at a very low frequency," my friend said, throwing her palms up. "I'd hate to see the negative things being sucked into your universe right now."

She shook her head, as if my vibrations were going to taint her. I loved my friend, but she could be a bit of an airhead and over the top with the New Age lingo.

"My life's out of control and this has nothing to do with my damn vibrations," I snapped. "I'm in a financial crisis, and as far as I'm concerned, it's perfectly acceptable to blame my parents for my mess of a life. If they'd loved me more or showed me love by leaving me a huge inheritance, I might consider forgiving them."

"Honey, you can't blame your parents for your money problems anymore," she said. "You need Debtors Anonymous."

"What? I don't have issues with money!" I whimpered.

"Let me know when you're ready and I'll take you to a meeting. And stop it with all the sad faces. It ages you." She grabbed her Louis Vuitton bag and scampered off.

I decided to give what she said serious consideration. Maybe DA could teach me how to earn more. Or perhaps I could get tips on how to save. Who knew? At the very least, I could probably find someone who'd float me a loan for a couple of grand.

For an airhead, my friend was borderline profound.

It's Not About The Money:
All right, I'll admit it, I do have issues with money.

July 20

EXCELLENT!

I used to aspire to excellence because I didn't want to be mediocre. Mediocrity was average and average was like death.

Excellence for a debtor like me is an endless, fruitless, exhausting pursuit that leaves me hungrier, bottomless, and lonely. There's just never enough excellence on the planet for people like me. Good can always be better. Best is always recommended.

DA didn't take away my desire for great things. I'm still competitive and want the best, but excellence to the exclusion of all else doesn't work in my recovery.

Belief in myself is good, vision and goals are important, but when it gets too close to grandiosity and self-reliance instead of God-reliance, I start to get a little scary.

Living an excellent life isn't always having, doing, and being the best. It might just be doing the most normal, ordinary next thing in front of me.

No balloons, no clowns (thank God), and no striving for the best. That might be the most excellent choice I make today.

It's Not About The Money:

I don't always have to strive for excellence.

July 21

OVER IT

I don't want to meditate today. If my recovery was based on a scale of one to ten, today would have been a minus twenty-five. I was seriously miffed at God. So I called my sponsor and he suggested I start the day over and ask for willingness to just do what was in front of me. I did.

I began the day again. At 5:00 p.m.

Recovery doesn't mean there won't be days when I'm unhappy about some of the situations I'm facing. When I wake feeling out of sorts, the best thing I can do is accept that not every day will be a ten out of ten. In fact, those days are rare, even in recovery. Most days I aim for a solid seven, and if I get to a six, I'm thrilled.

So, what to do when I wake up feeling a minus twenty-five? I do the only thing I know: ask for the willingness to trust I will receive whatever I need from the Higher Power I'm miffed at, even if it isn't what I want. Then I go on with my day and try to be of service to someone else. The feelings still come and go, but inevitably when I turn my will over to God and accept what is, I go from a minus twenty-five to at least a three on the recovery scale.

While I'm no math wizard, being on the positive side of an equation is always better than being on the negative side.

It's Not About The Money:

I may have to start the day over. S'alright.

July 22

PREMONITION

After a great deal of meditation and prayer, I've come away with what I like to call a premonition. In fact, I felt so sure that today's entry is inspired, I'm committing it to print.

Instead of our regular daily meditation, I am offering what I believe is the ultimate answer to every debtor's prayer. The winning numbers to this week's Powerball lottery.

They are as follows:

39, 8, 38, 7, and 87.

I also feel very good about:

1, 2, 23, 5, 90, and 7
(in no particular order or combination)

If you're looking for something that's a surer bet than that, then I suggest you gettest thouest to a Debtors Anonymous meeting immediately.

It's Not About The Money:

Lasting recovery rarely involves winning Powerball numbers.

July 23

COMPARE 'N' DESPAIR

"I've said it before and I'll say it again," my grandma Belle said, taking a pinch of Skoal and placing it between her lip and bottom teeth. "Nobody knows nothin'."

She was a tough old bird who drank whiskey and slept with a shotgun next to her bed. I never understood why she was so negative but it's not like I could argue with her, because I was only six and I was scared of guns. And chewing tobacco.

I think Grandma Belle meant, *We're all making it up,* which is good to know because I often compare myself to others, wondering why I don't have a nicer car, a bigger home, or a better spouse, and it always leads to despair.

The truth is, most people I know don't know what they're doing. Their decisions and opinions are only a soupy medley of other people's regurgitated ideas. Many peoples' best is just copying or reacting to what their parents did. Or following their friends' suggestions.

Most of us do the same thing everyone else does because we don't know any better. Someone recommends we buy certain stocks, so we do. Other people max out their credit cards to take a fancy vacation, so their friends follow suit.

Working the program of DA has given me the courage to make decisions that are good for me, regardless of what other people oing. Nobody else has the answers for me, and no one else is doing it "better" or "right." It gives me comfort to know I'm doing the best I can at any given moment. At least, until I start thinking, *If everyone's making it up, why haven't I made up something better, like the huge house, the nicer car, and the better spouse?* And that's when I know it's time to meditate, read some DA literature, and get myself to a meeting.

Grandma Belle was right–nobody knows nothin', which makes me feel pretty darn good, especially when I encounter someone who thinks they know what *I* should be doing.

It's Not About The Money:

Who does know the answers? My Higher Power.

July 24

DEBTOR OLYMPICS–OPENING CEREMONIES

Although not generally known, debtors around the globe have been gathering once every four years at the Debtor Olympics to celebrate the achievements of the world's finest in Debtors Anonymous.

Since debtors aren't big on documenting things, I couldn't find the official dates for the first Debtor Olympics, nor are there records of participants and winners. So, for simplicity's sake, let's call this one the VXII Debtor Olympiad.

Over the next few days we will pay homage to the crafty, quick-thinking behaviors that make debtors who they are. The lovable debtors who can always be counted on to say, without a hint of irony, "Go the extra mile? Who, me?" or "Look, I may not have lifted a finger but where the heck is my gold medal?"

Whether they're preparing for the intense 200-meter short cut, the debtor pentathlon, or the arduous long distance relay, debtors who compete at the Olympic level don't just push through adversity. They don't push through adversity *at all*. Nope. They simply give up and walk away.

So strike up the debtor band (here's hoping they show) and let's honor the twisted thinking and distorted behaviors that make debtors beloved by credit card companies and banks around the world. Because no matter who wins the gold or the silver, we'll celebrate together–on someone else's dime, of course. Let the VXII Debtor Olympics begin!

It's Not About The Money:

Let's celebrate the gold. Hopefully it'll earn interest!

July 25

DEBTOR OLYMPICS–LONG DISTANCE DEBTOR

The life of long distance debtors is difficult and the training torturous. They wake before the dawn to take calls from creditors, long before the rest of the world rises. On the opposite end of the spectrum, they may sleep in until noon in order to completely avoid the calls. Either way, they're always late for work.

Few are as dedicated as long distance debtors. In fact, they will move thousands of miles without a plan in an effort to avoid paying off loans or returning money to the friends they owe. These amazingly single-minded people spend years avoiding the IRS, fantasizing about that glorious day when they'll win the lottery–the one they don't play–or dreaming of the moment they receive that inheritance from the great uncle they've never laid eyes on.

While most mere mortals view the long distance debtor as a free soul with perpetual wanderlust, one who exists to travel the world, there are those of us who know better: the long distance debtor is extremely skilled at ignoring the wiser inner self, the one that whispers, "Stay put, pay your bills, don't be a cad."

Today, we honor the long distance debtors for their commitment to not committing. To anything. Because these debtors, skilled at slacking, or as they like to call it, being "creative," can get away with pretty much anything when they set their minds to it.

And that, my friend, takes a great deal of talent and skill. Put your hands together for the long distance debtor!

It's Not About The Money:

Lift a glass to the long distance debtor, especially if you aren't one anymore!

July 26

DEBTOR OLYMPICS–"UN"BALANCED BEAM

To be present when a nimble debtor dominates the competition on the "un"balanced beam at the Debtor Olympics is one of the most natural highs imaginable!

This debtor is an artist and a strategist in the purest sense of the word, calm and composed throughout impeccably timed manipulations, er, routines. These debtors approach their targets with utmost precision; they are masters of the verbal twist, the emotional turn, and the subtle walkover. They should be, they've had years of training and practice, dealing with all those banks, creditors, family, and previous employers. The mixture of dexterity and speed that enables these debtors to make massive leaps of logic in midair while maintaining control and garnering sympathy is almost supernatural. They never cease to amaze the crowd with their proficiency, moving on and off the beam with grace and aplomb.

Their determination is often accompanied by a smile and an intense stare. "I will get my way," their eyes seem to say. Even after they've taken home the prize, they still seem to want more.

The beauty of the unbalanced beam event is that although the debtor may have fallen off the beam due to their own mistakes, they're able to make it appear to have been someone else's fault. There's nothing like an unbalanced debtor to remind us that no matter how spiritually centered and honest we strive to be, those who master the unbalanced beam will always be able to pull one over on us.

It's Not About The Money:

I'll try to stay on the balanced beam today.

July 27

DEBTOR OLYMPICS–200-METER SHORT CUT

To place in the top third of the 200-meter short cut, a debtor must utilize a combination of techniques specific to the most agile debtors in order to find the shortest route to the finish line. Only the savviest and shrewdest debtor will take a medal home.

Participants in this event must have successfully competed in other Olympic events, like long distance debting or the unbalanced beam. This is only for the most dedicated competitors wanting to claim several titles.

Rumor has it that the gold in the 200-meter short cut has been taken by an American male eight times and an American female at least three times between 1980 and 2013. Again, this is all unsubstantiated, as no official Debtor Olympics records exist.

As with the other Olympic Games, the short cut is not without its share of controversy. In 2004, the bronze winner was disqualified and stripped of her medal after admitting to using a false identity. While the judges praised her for an ingenious attempt at short-cutting, it was determined to be against the rules. At least, they thought it was. No one was able to find the charter.

Trying to determine what would be considered inappropriate for the Debtor Games proved to be too tedious for the judges, who simply stated, "We're not statisticians or black belts here. Many of us aren't even employed and we don't trust things like data or scores. We just know what works and what doesn't."

Let's hear it for the short cutters!

It's Not About The Money:

Short-cutters tend to make things look so easy.

July 28

DEBTOR OLYMPICS–DEBTOR PENTATHALON

The crowning jewel of the Debtor Olympics, the pentathlon is amongst the most beloved in the history of the Games. The five-event competition combines the skills that make debtors so, well, debtorly: borrowing, stealing, chronic lateness, deception, and manipulation. Talents that the world's most prolific debtors have spent years honing.

As impressive as it is to compete in other Debtor Games, the versatility needed to compete at this level is what makes the Olympic debtor pentathlete the greatest and most admired the world over. In order to participate, competitors must be able to pursue debting, spending, and all the related compulsive behaviors with a mixture of speed, accuracy, and dexterity.

The debtor pentathlon brings together the most compelling display of irresponsibility, complete and total vagueness, while maintaining a masterful level of grandiosity. Only debtors with the belief that they are simultaneously the greatest and the worst at the same time would dare challenge themselves at this level.

While few have ever been able to understand the debtor pentathlon scoring system or the how the winners are selected, we are confident that someone will win. And if we can't figure out who the winner is, we'll make something up. We're debtors!

Traditionally, the title of World's Greatest Debtor has been given to the person who wins the pentathlon at the Debtor Olympics. Mainly because they're the only participants who show up on time and don't leave early.

It's Not About The Money:

Today, I'll honor my inner athlete by showing up on time.

July 29

DEBTOR OLYMPICS–CLOSING CEREMONIES

As the VXII Debtor Olympiad comes to a conclusion, some information about the closing ceremonies has begun to emerge.

While details are limited to the public until the actual event, sources say that the choreographed show performed by fellows in the DA community will be entitled, "A Symphony of Vagueness and a Celebration of Creativity."

The closing ceremony's artistic director is quoted as saying the show "could start around seven. Or eight. It all depends. Most of the band will likely call in sick, so we'll probably run an hour or two later than planned," but he has promised that the show will be a "spectacle, as always."

When pressed for more information about the contents of the show and who'd be performing what, he screamed, "Look, I don't know why you people are harassing me. I'm doing the best I can. I don't have to give you details. I'm the artistic director, for God's sakes!" before storming off.

Sources have suggested the evening's ceremonies will begin with a Cirque de Soleil-inspired piece featuring local street urchins, followed by an orchestral performance from the local symphony.

When we attempted to speak with one of the performers, he merely said, "Those Olympic Committee people better not try to stiff me again." The violinist, who claims to have played at the VXI Debtor Games, stated, "I played the whole show, and when I asked for my money, they told me the check was in the mail but I never got it. All I can say is, they better pay me this time or things are gonna get dramatic, all right!"

The street urchins had no comment.

It's Not About The Money:

Late and dramatic. What else is there for a debtor?

July 30

CUP O' MISERY

There's a song by The Smiths entitled "Heaven Knows I'm Miserable Now." I'd quote the lyrics because they are so fantastic, but I can't unless I want to get written permission from Morrissey and his cowriter, Johnny Marr, and if you know anything about Morrissey, you'd know the chances of me getting clearance are slim to none.

Basically, the song is about a guy who's looking for a job, but once he finds it, he's miserable. Then the guy wants to find love and gets it and he's miserable. He wonders why he has wasted his time on people he'd rather kick in the eye. In essence, once he gets what he wants, he's miserable.

That song was my anthem for most of my adult life. I was constantly looking for something but once I got it, I was miserable. People bothered me. I didn't want them to want things from me. I wanted to be left alone to do what I wanted.

Unlike Morrissey, the quintessential purveyor of woe and misery, I came off as agreeable, but the minute I was asked to do something I didn't want to, I'd dig in my heels and pull some passive-aggressive move.

It took working the Twelve Steps in DA for me to see how I reveled in a misery of my own making.

I still enjoy a cup of misery at times, but with help from my Higher Power I can stop myself before I drink too much. Because when I do, it's not long before I want to kick people in the eye.

It's Not About The Money:

God, help me not pick up the cup of misery today.

July 31

SURRENDER

There have been times when, overwhelmed by the weight of my debts, I have screamed, "I give up! I'm done thinking positively and I don't care about recovery. I just want some damn relief."

I did not think of this as surrender; I thought of it as resignation. Real surrender did not include yelling at other people or my Higher Power, nor did it involve broken dishes or bone fractures. I thought of surrender as a supreme calm that came after hours of quiet solitude and spiritual acquiescence.

Today, I see surrender differently. While I do experience those rare times when my surrender is a sweet, gentle experience, surrender usually comes after I've spent hours, days, even months pounding my head against a wall out of frustration. For me, surrender happens once I've worn myself out with worry, or I find something else to obsess about–something shiny and expensive. Or very good-looking and taller than me. Sometimes surrender occurs because I'm exhausted.

I'm not perfect. That's why I'm glad I have a recovery program that leads me to surrender, although I'll admit that even though I can want it and talk about it until I'm blue in the face, I can't identify it until after I've already done it. I will, however, say it's been quite a long time since my surrender included screaming or bloodletting of any kind. At least a few weeks.

It's Not About The Money:

I won't think about surrender today. I'll just do it.

August 1

WHY?

"Knowing why has never helped me." – Anonymous

I always had to know why, even as a kid. Why was ice slippery? Why couldn't I have M&Ms for dinner? Why did I have to take naps? Why, why, why?

As an adult, I spent an inordinate amount of time asking myself why. Why would I choose to be broke? Why would I choose to self-sabotage? Why would I not want to be rich and successful?

One of the first DA meetings I attended, I heard someone say, "Knowing why has never helped me." I wish I could remember who said it because I'd like to give them credit, but I was new to recovery and not emotionally present.

Now that I've done a lot of Step work and reflecting, I have a deeper understanding of what that person meant: Understanding why I do what I do does not change me. Writing down the reasons why I'm worthy just doesn't cut it for me. Knowing more about me, or why I don't feel like I'm enough, or reading articles from the Nation Association for Self-Esteem has done nothing to increase my earnings.

Understanding why I do what I do *may* feel like I'm doing something, but I'm not. What works? Contrary action. Helping others, keeping commitments, and doing admirable things. Having integrity and being kind to others. Asking God for guidance and going to meetings.

Now, maybe it's because I already know a lot, but knowing more of the why hasn't helped so much.

It's Not About The Money:

There may be a –"y"– but there's no –"why" – in recovery.

August 2

ARE I?

In Step Nine in DA, we make amends for the harms we caused while debting. Not all of these harms are obvious, nor are they always malicious or felonious.

Most of my amends had to do with my bad attitude and judgments, my arrogance, my entitlement, and especially my anger. I'd had expectations about how life, jobs, bosses, colleagues, family, and friends were supposed to treat me, and most of them had missed the mark. I was constantly disappointed and I let people know it whenever I had the chance.

Dissatisfaction was my stock-in-trade and as a result, I wasn't a whole lot of fun to be around. When I made my amends, no one said, "Really? You think you needed some help? You have an attitude problem? You're kidding!"

Most of the people I made amends to responded with, "Thank God you got help. You were a mess," or "It's about time, lady!"

Amends aren't easy to make and I still struggle with making them. Things don't always go smoothly and sometimes I get rejected, but I keep making them, because it keeps me solvent. When I ask myself "Are I or aren't I responsible for this situation?' and there's even the tiniest bit of a "yes" then I make amends. True, my grammar in this instance is sorely, but it helps me to constantly ask myself "Are I, or aren't I?," and it keeps me honest.

How about you?

It's Not About The Money:

Are I or aren't I? The answer is probably yes.

August 3

RISKY

I was a risk-taker, a thrill-seeker. I loved getting close to the edge. I'd take sorry over safe, any day of the week.

Other people saw my risk-taking as funny–of course, they weren't the ones risking it all–and I got a lot of ego strokes for my behavior. My drug was adrenaline. Unless I was risking something, life was dull, too bland, boring. What was the point of living if there was no big challenge?

Traveling to foreign countries alone with no plan or understanding of the local language? Check. Pushing myself to physical exhaustion to stay in shape? Check. Skydiving, bungee jumping? Check. Investing all my money based on a tip from a friend? Check.

But those risks were specific and more or less physical. The one thing I rarely dared to risk? Sharing my feelings and fears. Being vulnerable. So, imagine my surprise when I learned that the turmoil I created was my attempt to avoid deep feelings of abandonment, loss, and grief. The key to my recovery would require emotional authenticity and raw vulnerability.

Ugh.

When I finally accepted that I was powerless over my behavior, I started to see how my "risk-taking" was a way to stay safe. I had to trust that God would show me how to take emotional risks. As I began to heal, I found I no longer needed the adrenaline fix to repress the emotional pain. I began to develop a marvelous power that I'd previously been faking. The power to be emotionally honest.

Who would've guessed that recovery from my risky behaviors would have anything to do with being vulnerable? Or being open and willing to trust a Higher Power? Not me. But it's part of the deal, and it's been well worth the risk.

It's Not About The Money:

Today I'll will risk my heart in a way that matters.

August 4

WOLVES

Without going into too many details, when I was a small child, my family abandoned me in the mountains late one night.

When the sun arose the next morning, I wandered into the mountains, crawled into a cave, and started playing with the wolf cubs there. When the mama wolf returned to the cave later that day, she took me in and raised me as one of her own. For six years, I lived happily with the wolves, until I was discovered by a team of rangers and returned to society.

Okay, things didn't happen that way. I wasn't left in the mountains and I didn't live in a cave with wolves, but it kind of felt like it during my childhood. Resources in my home were slim and, aside from the basics, like food water and shelter, I had to fight to get what I wanted. There was never much so my response was to not need much. And if you'd asked me what I wanted, I'd've thought you were nuts.

The problem is, I *did* want things. I was like a ravenous wolf. And as I got older, I was convinced I'd be happy if I could just make up for the things I didn't have as a kid. My solution to most of my problems was things and more things.

There was never enough to fill that void.

I thought God and life owed me something. It took a while to work through the feelings, but in time, I learned to let go of the past and recognize I wasn't owed anything. As an adult, it's my job to take care of myself.

Today I trust God as my guide and partner. I get to experiment and discover what I need and want, and find ways to provide that for myself. The weird thing is, there still times when all I want is to do is escape to the mountains and explore caves.

It's Not About The Money:

"Hungry Like the Wolf" is a catchy Duran Duran song, not the best life motto.

August 5

IDEAL

Since I'm currently trying to build what I loosely refer to as a "healthy relationship" with money, I decided to make a checklist of the things I'd like to have from my money. I felt odd about doing it at first because it seemed contrived and demanding. But according to the dating book, in order to have the relationship I want, it's important that I write down my desires, so I went ahead.

My list included: trust, mutual respect, shared values. I also wanted total authenticity, no game playing or lying. Chemistry was important. There should be at least some passion.

Did you hear that, money?

I've also started to work on the list of deal breakers in my relationship with money. I won't go into details now because I want to keep today's meditation positive, but I will say the deal-breaker list includes: being unavailable when I'm in need, public humiliation due to comments that include the words "your card was declined," or any situation in which I am forced to dine and dash. I'll leave it at that, because I've heard having too many deal breakers can repel the very relationship I'm seeking.

Yes, there are times when I want to throw in the towel and say, "It's too late for me," or "I'll never have the relationship I want," but instead I stop myself and go on a nice, long walk or have a cup of tea. Green, of course.

I know my relationship with money won't be perfect and will require hard work, but I won't give up hope. I believe that a fantastic, soulful relationship with money is on its way to me right now. *You may say I'm a dreamer, but I'm not the only one. I hope someday you'll join us, and the world will be as one.*

It's Not About The Money:

It's never too late to have a better relationship with money, honey.

August 6

CHALLENGED

There are times when I think, *Debtor is such a harsh word. It's so dark and depressing and so…permanent.*

I prefer to think of myself as someone who is "currency challenged." It's nothing to be ashamed of, and it's not something every other human being on the planet isn't experiencing–except maybe the fear of the future, the vagueness around money, and the obsession about and general discomfort pertaining to financial discussions.

Aside from those few things, I'd guess I'm pretty normal when it comes to money. I'm not terribly different than most people I know. And sometimes I think, Why do I have to go to DA meetings or deal with my money issues? I know plenty of people who are worse with money than I am!

That's when I ask myself: Is debting a problem for me? (It is.) Are my relationships are affected by my anxiety around money? (They are.) Is my life unmanageable as a result? (Check that, too). If so, then I still need the help from the Program and Tools of DA.

Other people may find healing from financial fear and debt in other ways. But DA gives me the hope and strength to improve the quality of my life. More importantly, it's a spiritual program that always leads me back to a relationship with God.

Whenever I find myself spending time comparing my money problems to my friends' money problems, I know I am more than currency challenged; I am spiritual challenged. And that's when it's time to pick up the phone or get myself to a meeting.

It's Not About The Money:

Yes, I'm challenged, but thank God my condition isn't permanent.

August 7

CORRUPTION

I recently did an Internet search of the term "politician arrested for corruption" and found 151,458,000 articles.

It got me thinking: Is it the *money* that corrupts politicians, or is it because they place too much *value* on it? I spent a long time pondering this and came up with: *Money* doesn't corrupt. People corrupt. Money is simply the object of our corrupt desires, whether we're politicians or civilians.

Many people, especially debtors, fear that even the desire for wealth is bad. We've seen the greedy rich person cliché for so long, we've come to believe wealth is a destructive goal and making too much money is bad.

DA helps me keep it in perspective. I don't worship money, but I'm learning not to be afraid of wealth and success, either. I'm not more spiritual if I earn a lot, nor am I less spiritual if I'm broke. It's an inside job, and whatever's happening to me financially has no bearing on my spirituality.

If I seek my purpose and value through what I do or what I earn, I will always be vulnerable to the "quick fix" and lured into questionable situations. If I seek to live honorably, be of service, connect to God, and not debt one day at a time, it'll be easier to walk away from shady propositions.

Recovery has taught me I can pursue success and be prosperous without turning into a bad person. I don't need to fear that money will turn me into a jerk. As long as I put the spiritual stuff first.

Besides, I've met just as many poor jerks as rich jerks.

I haven't, however, met a lot of politicians who aren't jerks. Just kidding. Only 49% of the politicians I've met are jerks. The rest I can't speak for, and making a guess about it would not be working my spiritual program.

It's Not About The Money:

God, help me keep money in perspective today.

August 8

COW TALES

I was at a meeting and a guy was describing the difference between debting and underearning. "The debtor takes the cow but never pays for it. The underearner buys the cow, doesn't feed it, and when the cow drops dead, he blames the cow."

I didn't quite get it. Did the debtor just walk off the farm with a cow or did he put down a deposit? Did the underearner buy or borrow the cow? And why didn't he feed it? Was he broke or just dense?

Although I never completely understood the analogy, it did give me a glimpse into the mindset of a debtor and an underearner, both of which I happen to be. I suppose, then, one might say it gave me a glimpse into my own mindset.

When I'm debting, I'm like the rebellious teen who's angry and feels entitled. I dodge my bills or pay them late, and I take things knowing I'm not going to return them. When I expect someone, *anyone* else to take care of me, I'm debting. When I'm underearning, I'm the self-pitying, resentful child who's shut down and disengaged from life. I don't ask for what I need or want, because I don't *know* what that is. When I devalue myself, my time, or my things, I'm underearning.

Both behaviors are about refusing to be an adult, playing small, and not trusting I'm safe in the world. The antidote is prayer, the Twelve Steps and Tools of DA, taking contrary action, and being of service to others. Even though I can't always distinguish in the moment whether I'm debting or underearning, I can trust that God is the solution. Which is good, because I still don't get the debtor/underearner cow metaphor. I just know that I don't steal or borrow cows, and I never, *ever* expect to get any milk for free.

It's Not About The Money:

If I get the cow, I'm gonna pay for it and feed it.

August 9

PRESIDENTIAL

Many of my job problems had to do with my obsession with becoming president. No matter where I was working, no matter the job, before I'd even finished the first day at work, I'd have my sights set on the president's office.

It never occurred to me that the main thing standing between the presidency and me was the fact *I didn't know what I was doing*. In my opinion, being presidential was more of a mindset than an actual job description, and I was darn good at acting like the boss. Or, so I thought.

The results of living life this way were, as you may have guessed, not stellar. It led to plenty of strained relationships, uncomfortable work environments, and disappointment galore.

DA has taught me what it means to be a "worker among workers," not seeking to be a star, nor hiding out in plain sight, but one amongst many. I learned to appreciate going home at the end of the day and feeling good about having done a fine job. And, while playing the part of the president might seem glamorous and fun, because you get to say things like, "Do what I say because I'm the boss and I know what's best, you nincompoop!," it really isn't. And if you're president, you shouldn't be talking to people like that.

I'm much happier these days because my value no longer comes from my title, or what I do, or what I accomplish. I don't need to be in charge, I can be there to support someone else and their dreams, for the sake of the company.

Also, I've heard what some assistants and one intern, in particular did to get into the president's office. I'm not so sure I'm up for that.

It's Not About The Money:

Will I take orders from the boss? You betcha!

August 10

LIKE THAT

"I love my home. It's so warm and cozy, and it has an awesome view," said the trendy woman at the DA meeting. She looked like she'd just stepped out of a Dolce & Gabbana ad.

She's annoying, I thought, snidely.

"In fact, I love my home so much, I never want to leave it!" she said.

There was something off about her but I couldn't put my finger on it. Then she said those magical words, "I don't want to leave my apartment because I can't stand people!"

"Attagirl!" I wanted to jump up and shout, "I can't stand other people, either!" but I didn't, because that would've been considered crosstalk.

"It's not that I don't love 'other people'," she continued, using air quotes. "I just don't like other people anymore. They're so rude!"

I've got to talk to her after the meeting. She really gets it! Then she did an about-face.

"But I started thinking, I could be someone else's 'other people.' When I'm being thoughtless or short with people, it's rarely intentional. It's usually 'cause I'm trying to get somewhere and I'm running late, or I'm just in my own head and not paying attention. I have to imagine that's what other people are doing when they're being rude."

Guess I had her wrong.

"I have to forgive others, so that I can forgive myself, because when I'm having an 'off' day and being short with people, I might be seen as other people's 'other people'," she said, finishing her share.

Although I didn't want to admit it, I had it in for a few "other people" that day, and I decided to let them off the hook, after hearing her comments. For some reason, I wanted to be more forgiving, because, well, it's the right thing to do, and because she made it seem attractive – in the way that people who wear their boyfriend's oversized Armani silk shirts with skinny jeans make everything seem adorable? - Yeah, like that.

It's Not About The Money:

I'll do my best to be "like that" today.

August 11

WHIP-CRACKING

I have a longtime friend from Germany who loves to chide me. "You arhhhh sooo American, vith zis relentless self-help and zis cracking of ze whip," he often says.

When I told this friend I was going to Debtors Anonymous, he giggled. "Ov course you arhhhh!" (I know, it seems as if he talks like the Count from *Sesame Street*, but he doesn't. I'm just bad at writing a German accent.)

I was always big on setting goals. Starting in the first grade, I would wrap up each school year by reviewing my life and making resolutions for the next year. I was constantly comparing and contrasting how well I was doing with my ideal self.

By the time I'd reached adulthood, every week was a bit like New Year's Eve for me–you know, life reviews, to-do lists, and resolutions? While I achieved many of the goals I set, it was mainly because of my ego and self-will. Things worked fairly well for me until they didn't anymore. Suddenly one day, my will stopped working. I was dead broke, without any goals or hope. I couldn't "will" myself back to the top; I needed the help of DA and a Higher Power.

Recovery required me to examine the relentless striving and my addiction to accomplishment. I discovered some of my motivation was to avoid intimacy. When I began working the Twelve Steps, I was forced to look at–and subsequently heal–those feelings of loneliness, grief, loss and pain I'd been avoiding for years.

I still set goals but I no longer do it in the manic, fear-filled way I used to. No more charts or PowerPoint presentations. Instead, I decide what I'd like to complete, get support in the form of a pressure relief group with fellows in DA, and take the next action. And leave the results to God.

It feels good to be able to turn things over and not constantly be charting my progress, because if there's one thing I know, it's that when a German is telling me I need to ease up, I might want to listen. *Jawohl.*

It's Not About The Money:

No whip-cracking needed today. God has it covered.

August 12

APPROVALS

I used to feel uncomfortable in my own skin. In order to make up for my feelings of lack, I sought the approval of others by having what I thought were the right "enhancements."

I used various things–clothes, friends, cars, jobs, power, and statues–to make me feel better. I thought if I could gain the approval of other people – and by that I mean my family, who paid absolutely no attention to my endeavors – I'd be content.

The more I had, the worse I felt. In truth, I needed to accept myself with or without all the "things," or the praise of people who simply couldn't give it to me.

Recovery in DA taught me I don't have to do or have great things to be worthy. Yes, I want people to love me, but it won't come as a result of the things I own, or what I achieve. And doing things to gain other peoples' approval has rarely brought me peace. It's never caused me to wake up in the morning saying, "Yay, life!" or increased my capacity for joy.

For today, I say, let's stop it with the all the enhancements and remember that we do not require the approval of anyone else besides God and ourselves. We're on a spiritual path, not a self-improvement path.

I have an idea. Why don't we read this aloud together?

Hello, Self. I just want to remind you that you're on a spiritual, not a self-improvement path. You don't have to impress anyone else, because you're rather cool exactly as you are. At least God thinks so. And so do I!

It's Not About The Money:
We're not on a path to approval.

August 13

LITTLE

I used to take great pride in my ability to live on a shoestring and make do with very little. I told myself I didn't want to waste my energy pursuing the "almighty dollar." The irony is, I can't think of *anyone* who spent more time worrying about money than me. When a friend would travel somewhere or buy something, my first thought was, *I wonder how much it cost?* If it wasn't the first question I asked, it was the second.

I was obsessed with money.

Like the drunk consumed with the next drink, from the moment I woke up until the time my head hit the pillow, my days were consumed with money: thinking about it, dreaming about getting more of it, worrying I wouldn't have enough of it. My reasoning was if I could get enough of it, I'd be able to stop thinking about it so much. Alternatively, I didn't want to earn too much money, for fear I'd become a jerk who was all tied up in the numbers. In reality, my entire life was tied up in money.

When I started to work the twelve steps and Tools of DA, I saw how profoundly debting had affected my life and became aware that this was a serious, potentially life-threatening problem.

I had no choice but to turn my life and will over to God and trust that as long as I continued to put the spiritual stuff first, I'd be okay. It took a long time to get out of debt and to see how I had created the problems I had.

Today, it feels good to know that, while I may still have an obsession with money, I get to choose how much power I give it. More importantly, I can choose to be in obsession or spend my time in gratitude for the miracles and gifts I've been given.

I may have a little, I may have a lot, but today, I have recovery and that's enough.

It's Not About The Money:

A little or a lot, I'm glad recovery is what I've got.

August 14

MEANS

"We will live within our means, yet our means will not define us."

– *DA Promise #3*

I read an article written in 2009 about how hard it was to get by on $500,000 in New York.

A local who was interviewed for the story was lamenting how much life had changed for the bourgeoisie. According to her, people living on the Upper East Side were just like the rest of us, and that by the end of the year most of them were zeroed out, too!

The article talked about how many east siders felt they were judged by a certain "way of living," and their identities were entwined with how much they earned. They broke down the bare minimum costs of living in the Big Apple: mortgages, nannies, housecleaners, private schools, summer houses, charity galas that only a seven-figure income would stretch to cover. Between taxes, vacations, cars and drivers, personal trainers, groceries, eating out, and dry cleaning, life was pretty expensive.

Another person interviewed for the story noted that people "at a certain level" understood that if they wanted to get ahead in whatever culture they were in, they'd have to take on the trappings of that culture. The consensus was spending tons of money was an indicator of success, and it was what had to be done. The important thing was to "fit in."

I'll never be accused of being the sharpest one in the Nesmuk knife set, but, even I know better than *that*. In my opinion the live-within-your-means solution seems simple: move, put your prized offspring in public schools, ride the darn subway, and stop using that black AmEx credit cards because "things" shouldn't define us, or determine our value.

But then again, I tend to be a bit judgy at times.

It's Not About The Money:

Where am I living beyond my means?

August 15

FUTURA BOLD

Way before I'd hit bottom, I was excited about my future. But after two years of unemployment, I lost interest in what the future had in store for me. If my life had been a font, it would have been Futura Unbold.

"The last time I was truly excited about life, I was in the sixth grade," I whined to my sponsor. "Other than that, it's been nothing but fear and loathing."

"Hmm. So, when you made a movie you weren't excited?"

"Totally."

"When you had several of your stage plays produced, you weren't excited?" He queried.

"Yes, of course I was."

"Your whole life has not been fear and loathing, then, has it?"

"No, just the last few years when I was forced to sleep on peoples' couches and sell window installations door to door."

"You sold window installations door to door?" He laughed.

"No, but I would have if they'd hired me. I didn't even get a second interview!"

"I recommend a DA meeting immediately. You need more God today."

The people I meet in DA remind me how to live for today and turn tomorrow over to God. Because of recovery, I can wake up in the morning and know my needs will be met. I say "can" because it's a choice I have to make every day.

After the meeting, I found some gratitude for what I had and was even excited about what the future held. I've even started calling my life Futura Bold.

It's Not About The Money:

With my Higher Power's help, the future's looking bold.

August 16

BEHIND

There are times when it feels like I'm making no progress, like I'm so far behind in life that I'll never catch up. This is when I have to remind myself I'm not behind. I'm not at the beginning, I'm not at the end–at least I hope I'm not–I'm just…in the middle.

When I start feeling behind, it's usually because I'm trying something different and comparing myself to others, which I'm apt to do. It's not easy for me to try new sport or activities without assessing my skill level within the first say, five minutes of trying said new sport or activity. I get competitive, judgmental, and hypercritical of myself. Sounds like fun, no?

I liken it to running the Boston Marathon. If I stand at the starting line and look far off into the distance, by all accounts, I'm behind. But once I start running, the finish line gets closer and I start catching up. If I stay focused on what's in front of me and ignore how the runners around me are doing, I feel anticipation and excitement, not dread. When I'm running a marathon, I'm not thinking about what area I haven't covered; I'm focused on where I'm going. I don't feel behind; I'm just doing *my thing*.

I suppose it *could* look like I'm falling behind because there are people ahead of me. I *could* be mad at myself for not being as fast as they are, but I'd lose my concentration and probably trip and fall, or give up.

That's how it works for me. I can't be worried about what other people are doing or where I stand–or, in this case, run–in comparison to them but the wisest thing to do is to put my head down and keep running.

Friends, let this be a reminder: You are not at the end, you're not too late and you're not behind. You and me, we are right on time.

It's Not About The Money:

You are not behind. You're right on time!

August 17

NO RISK

According to my calculations, the latex glove company I invested my life savings in six months ago should be worth somewhere near half a million dollars by now. I'm super excited about that! I mean, where else can you earn twenty-percent interest on an investment? The only glitch is my money's been moved to Belize for safety–that and something about the company being under investigation by the SEC. When I go to the investor's website, this is the message I see:

Greeting to Yous:

While Citadel have still office in China where gloves shall be manufacture, investor funds to be on-held until further notices. We have with certainty that company and individuals are to be absolved, Shortly of any wrongdoing. Support is greatly appreciate!

Sincere,
Webmaster

I'm a little bothered by the "wrongdoing" part; I'm not sure what that means. So, I call my friend who bought a ranch with all the money she earned in this investment. I ask her if I should consider cashing out and she tells me the SEC is just being super uptight, as they've been known to be. Besides, I don't want to be – *"that"* – person–you know, the one who cuts and runs when things get tough? Nope. I'm going to stay in for the long haul.

I'm not counting my chickens before they hatch or anything, but buying furniture for my new ranch house is sure gonna feel good!

It's Not About The Money:

I'll take care of the chickens I have and not count the ones that haven't hatched.

August 18

OUT, DARN SPOT!

"Humbly asked God to remove all our defects of character." – DA Step #7

For most of my life, I didn't think I was the problem. I thought money was. As in, the lack of it was my problem. And the only solution was more. If I could get my hands on additional greenbacks, I would be an exceptionally generous, thoughtful, crafty, giving, and loving person.

Once I got that cash, I'd be the person I was meant to be. *I knew* I needed relief. I knew the anxiety and fear I had around money wasn't normal. What I *didn't* know was I had a thinking problem that had a spiritual nature. Until I was willing to acknowledge true relief could only come from a spiritual solution, I couldn't address the behaviors that were making my life miserable.

Working the Program and Steps of DA allowed me to see what I was doing and the payoff I was getting. The defects of character that caused me to debt – anger, fear, impatience, greed, ego, pride, and self-sufficiency – didn't just disappear on their own after a few meetings. It took a lot of work. I had to act differently even when it didn't feel good. Yes, I changed my behaviors, but ultimately God had to remove my defects of character in His time. And although I'm sure it's hard to believe, I'm not yet perfect – I still have a few defects of character, even if they are less intense and pervasive than they used to be.

If I could have removed my defects on my own without God's help and the help of DA, I would have, because I like to think I'm capable of fixing anything. But then again, I also used to think money was the solution to all of my problems.

It's Not About The Money:

I might not always be the problem but God is always the solution.

August 19

TIME DRUNK

"I'm a time drunk, which means I have the tendency to compulsively devalue my time," the DA speaker began. "Time drunks don't care about what we're doing or where we're going..."

So, it's like drinking too much, only you don't even get high, you just waste time? I thought. *Boy, some of these DA people are kooky!*

"Rather than pursuing constructive goals," the speaker continued, "time drunks fritter away their hours in useless activities."

Poor guy, frittering his sad, pitiful life away watching reruns of CSI: Miami. *Which reminds me, did I set my DVR to record the latest episode of* Snapped*?* I made a mental note to check on the machine before I went to bed.

"It's like you're asleep, dreaming that you're awake," the speaker said.

No kidding, pal. That's like half the population!

"Time drunks often complete things based on what other people tell them to do, without knowing what's best for them," he said, shaking his head. "Others completely devalue what they accomplish. They'll climb Mt. Everest and forget they've done it a week later. Not only will they forget it, if reminded of it, they'd demean it."

I hope this guy's not going to talk much longer. I don't see what this time-drunk malarkey has to do with me being broke or in debt. I mean, I'm pretty good about time. How to spend it, what to do with it. I make good use of it. Too bad this guy can't.

"Will you excuse me?" I said to the woman seated next to me as I climbed over her and tiptoed out of the meeting.

I just remembered–I start the new job tomorrow morning and I promised my friend I'd take her dog for walk before work. I'll have to get across town in less than ten minutes in rush hour. It's doable. Probably. I guess I'll be a late for work. I'm sure they'll understand, seeing as it's my first day and all. Too bad I spent the last hour at this ridiculous meeting. Talk about a waste time!

It's Not About The Money:

If I'm devaluing my time or anyone else's, I am debting.

August 20

CREATIONS

"News flash," my DA sponsor said. "There is a God, and it is not you."

"Well, of course, I know that," I replied. "But I did read an article recently that said human beings create life anew every day, and we have the ability to take charge of our destiny."

"And how's that working out for you?" he queried.

"So far, not so good. It turns out I don't know what I'm doing, or even what I really want," I admitted.

"You know, I was under the impression I was God for the first forty years of my life," he said. "When I realized I wasn't, I was pissed off. In time I was relieved. I'm way too lazy to play God."

I'm not going to tell my sponsor this, but once I get my debt cleared up and a good chunk of cash in my savings account, I'll have a better handle on how to run my life. And it's not like I'm fooling myself into thinking I'm God, or like I think I'll be in *total* control of things, but I can appreciate the concept of being in charge of my destiny. And I'm fairly certain that being the captain of my own ship, if you will is an admirable goal. In time, with the right support system, a nicer home, and a clear career path, I'm fairly certain I'll have the life I want. There'll be no problematic relationships, no pesky coworkers, no stress, sadness, or grief. I'll do away with things like tornados and death and illness. I'll be the creator of great and wonderful things, kind of like the article stated.

I'm still working on the list of all the great and wonderful things I'll create once I'm back on top. Which isn't to say I've deluded myself into thinking I'm God. Because of course I'll ask God for help, when and if I need it.

It's Not About The Money:

Am I'm still playing God?

August 21

DISTRACTED

Debtors, compulsive spenders, and underearners tend to be…distracted. For many reasons–most of them fear-based–we debtors spend a lot of time pondering the past and worrying about the future. Ergo, we're rarely engaged in the present. For instance, right now, I'm wondering why I'm not further along with this meditation book, preoccupied with where I'll be living next year, and speculating about why I didn't treat my best friend Toddy better in the fourth grade.

There's nothing that creates more misery than being distracted or resisting the situation we're in. Okay, there *are* things that can create more misery, but for the purpose of this meditation, let's go with being distracted.

When we wish we were somewhere else, doing something else or with someone else, or refuse to accept where we are *right now,* we don't value our experience. When we divert ourselves from the present by living in the future or rehashing the past, we discredit who we are and we dishonor our relationships.

It takes a commitment to working the Twelve Steps, prayer, and calls to my DA buddies to keep me in the moment. When I ask for God's guidance and quietly settle into what I'm doing *right now,* the distraction of what could be happening, or has already occurred, eventually lessens.

Yes, there are things that might create more misery than denying or distracting myself from what's in front of me, but I can't think of even one of them right now. Because I'm too busy enjoying this moment.

It's Not About The Money:

God, help me stay in today and out of tomorrow.

August 22

WORKING SMART

I used to work hard. So hard that I would exhaust myself. And if the people around me didn't work equally hard, or share my maniacal dedication to a project, I would declare them unprofessional and lazy. I placed a lot of pressure on the people I employed.

The beautiful part of recovery is, I can acknowledge the unhealthy aspects of my past and take responsibility, without beating myself up and wallowing in self-pity. I'm learning to do things better and yet, I can also admit my flaws.

These days, when I sense I'm getting overzealous about work and turn down offers to go out to dinner with great friends so I can spend my Saturday night working, I know how to say to myself, "Hey, take it easy. Go have some fun!"

While I can comprehend that there are business owners who earnestly believe their employees need to be driven to the brink of exhaustion to prove they're worthwhile, I no longer work for them. Recovery has taught me how to get more done by being organized and detailed and taking things one step at a time. When I remain calm and relaxed, I don't work excessively, or act overly busy so I look like I'm getting more done. Today I work smart, not hard. Not too hard, though. I mean I work hard, but I don't *overwork* to look good.

Some folks just like to overwork. I can't do much about that except say, "Hey, take it easy. Go have some fun!" and allow them to look at me like I'm nuts. Not everyone appreciates my new, relaxed approach to work.

It's Not About The Money:
If I'm calm and relaxed, there's no need to overwork.

August 23

DON'T DO IT!

Despite what Nike says, "Just do it" is not good advice for debtors. "Just doing" anything can be a slippery slope, and when I start making financial decisions without getting feedback or direction from my Higher Power, my sponsor, or a pressure relief group, things go downhill fast.

I decided to write a letter to the executives at Nike, to see if they might consider changing their campaign slogan to something more thoughtful like "Don't just do it," or "Just do it, but wait twenty-four hours first." Even better, "Just do it, but consider the consequences."

In the meantime, I've put a Post-it note with the word "don't" over the picture of the buffed Nike tennis star that's taped on my refrigerator. It reminds me to stop and think before I just quit my job without having another one lined up, just buy an undeveloped acre of swampland in Florida, or just move to a new state to get a "fresh start."

I've not heard back from the executives at Nike but feel confident I will. Perhaps I'll see the new ad next month in my favorite magazine.

That's what I love about recovery. Even a major advertiser can have a positive influence on my life!

It's Not About The Money:

Today, I won't just do it!

August 24

SELF-RESPECT

There's a famous song called *"Respect Yourself,"* that suggests that if we don't respect ourselves, no one else will, either. In fact, they won't give a "good cahoot" about you. And, there's nothing worse than not being given a good cahoot. Believe me, I know. I used to expect respect from others simply because I was on the planet. But you can't demand respect. And if you don't have self-respect, it's almost impossible to get it from others.

Self-respect, for me, began in recovery. I had to begin to do things I respected. Lying, cheating on my taxes, paying my bills late, downloading movies for free, and spending compulsively did not feel respectable. I had to change my behaviors in every area of my life. That meant not expecting to be rescued, acting with dignity, keeping track of my finances and daily spending, and most importantly, turning my will and my debt over to a Higher Power. For several years, it was just trudge, trudge, trudge, and repeat. It felt like the closest thing to a living hell with no exit because change is hard work and long-lasting results don't come easily.

When I began to *act* respectably, I began to truly respect myself and others. I discovered that having self-respect is more fulfilling than trying desperately to get it from nameless others.

The best part is, now that I have self-respect, I get a lot more respect. I also give a lot of it. I also give a good cahoot to others and let me tell you, the only thing getting better than getting a good cahoot Is giving a good cahoot.

It's Not About The Money:

Today I wish you a good cahoot!

August 25

MISWANTING

I spent a great deal of my adult life holding out. If I was offered something good, I'd hold out for something better, whether it be a relationship, a job, opportunities, even shoes. Why settle for good when I could hold out for fantastic?

On the rare occasions when I got exactly what I wanted, I was immediately dissatisfied and unhappy.

While I could cite studies about how academic types from superior East Coast universities have proven that getting what we say we want never leads to happiness, and that we may have high hopes but the expectations never match up to the experience, I won't. Yes, humans have always mistakenly forsaken long-term happiness for short-term pleasures based on shallow, futile pursuits. Yes, it's normal for me to overestimate how great my life will be when I get that new Mercedes-Benz or twenty-percent raise.

For a debtor like me, scientific studies do nothing for my serenity when they prove how "normal" it is for me to be dissatisfied when I get what I want. The only solution is a relationship with God, staying out of debt, and being grateful for what I have. I've been much happier and more fun to be around since I stopped waiting for something better to come along.

This might seem to some like a compromise, and maybe it is. Then again, maybe it isn't. But I know for sure that holding out for more has rarely led to *getting* more. I don't need a scientific study to confirm that.

It's Not About The Money:
Today I'll take contentment over holding out.

August 26

SPLIT-SECONDS

In every Hollywood action film I've seen, there's a moment when the hero, in his moment of crisis, has to make a split-second decision–usually one that challenges his existing belief system–that will forever alter the destiny of mankind, the world, or at the very least, his immediate family.

That hero *always* makes the right decision.

Getting out of a dangerous spot at the last moment depends on the hero choosing to reverse the direction of his or her life in a matter of seconds.

When I make impulsive decisions, the consequences are mostly painful. Real life doesn't turn on a dime, and making a life-altering decision in a moment of crisis has never worked out well for me. Whenever I've done it, I've ended up broke, wearing shoes that were too small, or owning a bunch of useless penny stocks. Too many of those split-second decisions is what brought me into the rooms of DA.

Since my life is not a movie, I've decided not to take my cue from those action films. Until I can prove otherwise, I'll assume that action movies endorse split-second decisions because they sell tickets. But impulsive decisions for debtors like me lead to a lot of remorse and regrets.

The next time I'm facing a big decision, especially if it has the potential to affect the destiny of mankind, I'll do research, pray for guidance from my Higher Power, and seek counsel before making any decisions. And if the urge to make a split-second decision doesn't subside, I'll just go see an action flick.

It's Not About The Money:

Feeling the urge to make an impulsive decision? Me, neither.

August 27

WHACK!

"Banks are like pushers," said the fully tattooed hipster seated in front of me at the DA meeting. "Banks don't care about us! They want to keep us high on their junk. Smack, crack, banks are whack!"

The people in the room let out a collective giggle, as if to say, *Right on, dude*!

But I wasn't laughing. I'd had enough time in recovery to know how much debtors love to feel sorry for themselves. It isn't our fault we're struggling. If debtors ran things–the government, corporations, the postal system–the world would be a fair, gentler place to live. Everyone on the planet would have a lifetime membership to Netflix and a Mac computer. At the very least, the manufacturing and sale of foldout couches would be regulated, and the FICO system would be eliminated.

The reality is, a world run by debtors would be pandemonium.

Resenting or blaming anyone else for the disasters caused by debting is futile. I was the one who signed the loans, who made the bad decisions. I was the one who didn't pay my bills on time, who overspent, and at other times, refused to earn.

The banks didn't make me a debtor, neither did the credit card companies. The problem was me. And the solution was, too. As long as I maintain a daily connection to God, refuse to debt one day at a time, and keep track of my spending, I can maintain serenity and sanity.

When the meeting was over, I went over to Tattooed Guy to offer him some of my hard-won wisdom, but then decided not to. Instead, I welcomed him with a big hug and a smile and said a silent prayer for him. If there's one thing recovery has taught me, it's that trying to tell another debtor what to do is *whack*.

It's Not About The Money:

Being in debt without a Higher Power is whack!

August 28

HISTORY

"Made a list of all persons we had harmed and became willing to make amends to them all."
– DA Step #8

When it came time for me to do Step #8 in DA, I was nervous about making amends to my former employers. Yes, I lied on my resume, but, who doesn't?

"Rewrite your resume," my sponsor said, "and we'll go over it together to make sure it's accurate."

"I can't do that," I whined. "I've fudged so much and had so many jobs, I don't know what's accurate."

"I guess you have some work to do, then," he said, unflinching.

"What if I don't remember what was true and what was a lie, and when I make amends, I didn't do the thing I thought I'd done?"

"If you want recovery, you have to stop being dishonest."

I thought that was a pretty rude thing to say. I'm not dishonest. I'm not some lying-liar type of person. I'm just an exaggerator, one who appreciates hyperbole. Saying I have a problem with honesty is not funny, nor is it true.

Even though I didn't agree with my sponsor, I took his advice, because I knew where self-will and self-reliance got me. I made amends to the people I had harmed and rewrote my resume. If I couldn't find or recall the dates I'd worked for a company, I didn't put it on my resume. The funny thing is, the new career I found didn't require a resume, or rather, my resume didn't apply.

Maybe God helped me out because I was willing to make amends and stop lying. Or maybe it was because today I know the truth and I tell it. Most of the time. The only exception is when a little fudging is required, which is rare for an honest person like me.

It's Not About The Money:

Am I willing to make amends and tell the truth in all areas of my life?

August 29

NO CARP DIEM

Today some people are honoring National No Complaints Day, which is when we are asked to take stock of how often we nag, gripe, or object to what's happening in our lives.

For the next twenty-four hours, your job is to decrease your negativity and force yourself *not* to complain to *anyone* about *anything*.

If you find yourself complaining aloud or focusing on the negative, you must stop and place a dollar in a jar. The size of the grievance doesn't matter; big or small, the effect is the same.

If you're anything like me, you'll probably be saying, "Gosh, I'm a negative Nelly who does a lot of carping," before you've even gotten out of bed. By midmorning, you'll be ready to crawl out of your skin, what with all your sniveling and whining. But please take on the commitment to stay positive. Keep track of the negative comments and when you get home, take all the money you've collected and do whatever you want with it. I'm not going to tell you the money has to go to a charity or to start a pet adoption clinic – I'm a debtor, I get it – just don't shove it back in your wallet. Use it to start a savings account, or to treat yourself to dinner. The purpose is to become more conscious about your attitude, and to remind yourself that negativity robs you of joy and financial freedom.

So, off you go, and stop your grumbling, because today is No Complaints Day, or what I like to refer to as No Carp Diem Day.

It's Not About The Money:

For today, no carping, no complaining.

August 30

CHANGE

Before DA, I spent a lot of time trying to improve myself. I wanted to do better and thought if I concentrated and worked harder, I could change myself.

I decided to create a performance review of my behavior and ask friends to fill it out, anonymously, of course. The plan was to get their feedback on the areas where I was lacking.

After my friends all stopped laughing at my idea, they agreed to do it because they're good people. When I read what they wrote, I figured I could just do some behavior changes and BOOM! I'd be better. It didn't happen.

Then I got into DA and I started to figure out my problem wasn't that I needed to improve myself. Besides, even if I wanted to, I couldn't change myself. I am not God. Change is not up to me. I can act better, but I can't change without the help of my Higher Power. Change happens when God says it happens, but when I stay close to Him and work DA's Steps and Tools, it will happen.

The interesting thing about this whole story is, the more I tried to change, the less I did, and the less I tried to change, the more I did.

Don't give any of this too much thought, or you run the risk of getting weird about it.

It's Not About The Money:
Change comes when it comes.

August 31

KNUCKLES

I forgot there were thirty-one days in August so I have nothing prepared for today's meditation.

I used the knuckle method to count the days in the year, you know, the one where you clench your fist and count the months? January is the index finger knuckle, February is the space between the knuckle, March is the middle finger knuckle, and so on until you get to December. For some reason, I got thrown off and calculated August as having thirty days.

What I'd planned to do was sleep in and relax today. I wasn't going to do anything spiritual or recovery centered. I'd planned to ignore my DA sponsees and avoid making outreach calls. I was going to play hooky from work and go shopping. Maybe even spend time feeling sorry for myself.

It was, according to my knuckles, the first day of September and I deserved a break. Except that it's August 31 and the month is not over yet.

Instead of writing ditto here and refer you to yesterday's meditation, or repeat one I've already written, I'll write a new one.

My DA program demands that I practice rigorous honesty. I've got to stay the course, conquer my resistance, and break through the blocks. While it may be the end of the month, that's no excuse for me to let my recovery go. I still have to do my part, especially because no one else has shown up to write this meditation for me.

I feel good when I'm being authentic. Even when it means I have to admit to doing ridiculous things like using my knuckles instead of a calendar. But my authenticity makes up for my lack of intelligence, n

It's Not About The Money:

Don't give up, stay the course. Practice rigorous honesty.

September 1

PREDICTION

While it's not something I do regularly, today I'm willing to put my entire reputation on the line with the following prediction: Within our lifetime, a debtor will win the lottery.

Friends, I've received word today from ancient, yet highly reliable sources that it is possible for a dyed-in-the-wool debtor to earn millions in a lottery. Yes, some say it would be best if it were the result of them keeping their numbers, doing twelve-step work, and staying out of debt, but what is best is not always what happens.

According to my sources, which have made over two hundred accurate historical predictions, this incident will occur somewhere between 2017 and 2030, when said debtor purchases the winning Powerball ticket at a convenience store in Hackensack, New Jersey. It's not clear what the debtor will do with the proceeds, but sources say chances are the money will be gone within one year.

My sources predict that this occurrence will coincide with the collapse of the Indo-Australian tectonic plate, as well as a major shoplifting scandal within the royal family of Sweden.

It's Not About The Money:

Sometimes I'm better off trusting God over other "trusted sources."

September 2

CRAFTY

It's peculiar and crafty, my brain. It tells me everyone is having an amazing life. Everyone except me. It also hints that all my friends are planning an enormous, grand party and will purposefully not invite me.

When it comes to my money and finances, my brain tells me I'm the only person who has a hard time keeping a spending plan and reconciling her checkbook. That is, the times I've attempted to do it.

It says I'm the only one who has to work hard for everything while everyone else gets things handed to them. I must struggle, strive, overwork, underearn, and be in debt because when good luck was being passed out, I was passed over.

Even in DA, there are times when I'm certain I'm the one person who's not going to "get" recovery or have a fantastic life. I figure everyone else will get the Program's Promises, but not me.

I'm a slow learner. But today, I've decided not to trust what my brain suggests. Instead, I'll trust God, because at times it feels like my brain might be colluding with my fair-weather friends and planning parties without me.

It's Not About The Money:

God, help me remember I don't always have to listen to my brain.

September 3

MASTERY

Mastery is defined as a "comprehensive knowledge or skill in a subject or an accomplishment." To become a master, people often must go through an apprenticeship, which requires hundreds of hours of labor and training, but the result is a profound knowledge and expertise in a certain craft.

Like many debtors, I suffered from boredom, so it was difficult for me to master anything. I didn't have the patience or persistence to be an apprentice. I didn't see the need to waste years of my life learning, nor did I have any desire to squander my talent. My destiny wasn't to be someone's protégée; it was to be the expert. As a result, I was a dilettante and master of very few things.

I didn't have much patience for recovery, either. I didn't want to go through the agony of being a vulnerable, awkward newcomer, but there was no other way. I had to ask for a lot of help, look silly, be embarrassed and admit I was powerless over my debting. I hated every minute of it.

I certainly had no desire to become a master at recovery.

Finally, there came a point when I was no longer the one needing all the help. I was the one reaching out, comforting the newcomers. I became the one friends could call on when they needed help or encouragement. And that feeling brought me joy like I'd never experienced before.

There are few things that compare to how I feel when I'm of service to another debtor. I'm not saying I'm a master at DA or anything, but I feel a sense of accomplishment from the effort I've put into recovery. It's nice to know that my experience, strength, and hope can help others. And if it isn't, I can always pass the newcomer on to someone who knows more than me. Which happens to be a lot of people.

It's Not About The Money:

I may not ever be a master, but I've got something to give.

September 4

SMILEY FACES

This morning I received two e-mails about smiling. One said that people who smile a lot get more accomplished in a day. The second e-mail said human beings rely on faces to determine other peoples' moods and level of approachability. The more a person smiles, the more approachable they seem.

I wondered if this was a sign from my Higher Power that my job today was to pass on the message of the power of a smiling face? After a great deal of contemplation, I decided that, yes, it was a sign.

So, here is your message: Smiles are powerful.

Please make an effort to smile today. Even if–especially if–you don't feel like smiling. Say, for example, you receive a bill from the your accountant. Why not try smiling at the bill? Or, you're in line at the grocery store and the person in the ten item only express lane ahead of you has twenty items. Maybe you could try smiling at them? Or, perhaps you have a difficult phone call to make today. Try smiling throughout the entire call just to see how it goes.

Whenever you can today, whomever you're with, whatever you do today, try doing it with a smile because it will make you feel better. And, although I can't "technically" guarantee that by smiling you'll receive wealth and financial success, I guarantee that the odds of you being more prosperous will improve. And I know that because I just got another e-mail, which said, "people who smile more buy lower and sell higher."

It's Not About The Money:

Don't give me that face, unless it's a smile!

September 5

SELFY-LOVE

I've come to the conclusion that prosperity and self-love are interrelated. Not in a I-love-myself-and-screw-the-rest-of-the-world way, but as in, if I don't love myself, how on earth will I ever allow abundance into my life?

Being gentle and loving with myself is not easy, as I tend to think the best way to make progress is by beating myself into submission. But I've started to believe that being respectable and compassionate with myself might have better results. Perhaps if I were to treat myself like someone I loved and appreciated, I might experience more prosperity.

I'm considering the notion that the more willing I am to love and take care of myself, the more fulfilled I'll be. And it might be okay to ignore the thoughts of self-hatred or my the tendency to pummel myself into perfection.

I know, let's try this together! Let's start by saying:

"Hi there (Insert your name here),

You're doing just fine today. Just fine. I love you, and I mean that. I think you're as brilliant as you can be at everything you're doing right now!"

Just to show that you love yourself, maybe you could send yourself some flowers today. Or, you could send flowers to me. Either way, know that wherever you are right now, I am sending you loving thoughts and metaphorical flowers because you deserve them. And because you're brilliant!

It's Not About The Money:

Today's the perfect day to buy yourself some flowers, real or metaphorical.

September 6

WORDS

"Lord, give us the wisdom to utter words that are gentle and tender, for tomorrow we may have to eat them." – Mo Udall

I was so inspired after reading this prayer, I vowed never to utter another word unless it was gentle or tender or kind.

Within ten minutes, I regretted making that promise. Because I had to call my bank and deal with an outstanding credit issue, and it still takes effort on my part to be gentle and tender with the customer service agents who work for my bank. If forced to eat my words, they'd taste like a liver sausage and Spam milkshake.

Recovery has taught me to think before I speak, that I have to be hyperaware because my words can hurt others. I still need God's help to remind me to be kind. *Especially* when I'm dealing with banks and credit card companies. Sometimes my thinking is, *Listen, Mr. Customer Service Rep, the corporation you work for has ruined my life, and while I know you don't literally represent the evil monolith you work for and you probably have no power, I expect you to solve my problem RIGHT DAMN NOW!*

Yes, I have been known to act like a jerk when calling banks and for that, I am sorry. I'm a work in progress, as they say.

Conversations like the one above are rare for me. These days I'm careful about offering my unedited opinion about how a bank or institution might improve its company, that is, unless I'm being asked to participate in one of those bothersome phone surveys. For the most part, I keep my unsolicited remarks to myself, because I have to think about those words coming back to me. Since I can't be sure they're going to be sweet, it's best to keep them short.

It's Not About The Money:

Your words may come back to you so keep 'em sweet.

September 7

BOOTSTRAPS

I was a bootstrapper. I took pride in my ability to extract myself from bad situations by pulling myself out of the mire without help.

Why don't these debtors and underearners lift themselves up by their bootstraps, like I've done? I wondered while listening to people share at my first DA meeting. For my part, there was a bit too much "God" and "spiritual" reliance, so I left the meeting determined to propel myself up and above the masses on my own.

Yes, my debt was bigger than it had ever been, but I was confident I could fix it like I had in the past–with a yank and a swift tug of my bootstraps. With enough huffing and puffing I'd be laughing as I floated above the chimney tops like Mary Poppins, hovering over my greedy creditors and those mean-spirited banks that closed my checking accounts, or the insurance company that had the *audacity* to raise my monthly rates.

So I did it, all on my own. I cleaned up my act, got my accounts in order and raised that FICO score. From the outside, I looked dandy. But in time, I began to feel a disconnection from my Higher Power and my fellowship, and I couldn't escape from the feelings of scarcity. The air was thin where I was and I was lonely. Very lonely.

I finally went back to DA, and learned how *not* to bootstrap it. Today I have a loving God to guide me and Tools to keep me organized and financially grounded. The best part is, I have a fellowship that understands my tendency to "go it alone," so they stay in touch and remind me that it's not about the money, it's about my relationship to life.

These days, when I feel myself endeavoring to pull a Mary Poppins and sail above the rooftops, I pick up the phone and call a friend in DA for some perspective. And before I do anything, even if it's merely flying a kite, I ask my Higher Power to come along with me. Chim chim cher-ee and all that.

It's Not About The Money:

I'm so glad I don't have to bootstrap it anymore.

September 8

INSATIABLE

Sung to the tune of "Unforgettable":

Insatiable, that's what I are
Insatiable, though near or far
Like an AmEx card that sings to me
How the thought of new does things to me
Never before have I wanted more.
Insatiable, in every way
And forevermore, that's how I'll stay
That's why everything's exchangeable
Because I'm so damn persuadable
If one is on sale, then why not buy two?
Insatiable, in every way
And forevermore, that's how I'll stay
I'll keep my accounts untraceable
Because I am so insatiable
And all my friends, well, they are insatiable, too.

I know, but have you tried rewriting a classic lately?

It's Not About The Money:

When I'm insatiable, I might also be unforgettable. And, not in a good way.

September 9

NEEDS

You've finally done it, I thought on the flight home, after I'd been let go from a gig. *You've gone and completely ruined everything.*

I'd been given no explanation and sent home with pay. I stayed in bed and cried for three days. I truly had no idea what I'd done wrong.

My sponsor suggested I do an inventory, but I didn't think I'd played a part in the situation. All I was did at work was try to have a great attitude and be helpful, but there was so much confusion and disorganization. When I looked a little deeper, I discovered more. I'd asked repeatedly for basic information but the boss continually brushed me off. I recalled giving a colleague an eye roll and saying something negative about our boss's organizational skills, but who doesn't do that every so often?!

So, I did have a part in my being let go, including gossiping and thinking I knew better than the boss. Another aspect was my inability to admit I don't do well in fly-by-the-seat-of-your-pants situations. When I was told thirteen-hour days were part of the gig, I figured I could handle it. *I would* handle it, because I "needed the money."

What I've discovered is that while things aren't always right for me, it doesn't give me the right to be outwardly hostile or resentful of my superiors. I can ask for what I need; I can't force cooperation from another person, and if I don't get it, it might be time to move on. Of course, I ask God for guidance and get support from people in recovery, but ultimately it's my life. I must do what's right for me.

If things aren't working, I'm better off leaving a situation, no matter how much I "need the money." Unless they're offering like a million dollars, then you can bet your you-know-what I'm stickin' around and keeping my mouth shut. I'm slow, not stupid.

It's Not About The Money:

I've got to know when to hold 'em, and know when to fold 'em.

September 10

'THORITY

"I fight authority, authority always wins." – John Mellencamp

Even at an early age I had a problem with authority.

It's kind of a long story, but suffice it to say the adults in my life weren't particularly gifted when it came to child rearing. And since I was the most responsible person I knew growing up, I didn't have a lot of experience transferring authority.

As a result, I was often in conflict with people in control, whether they be bosses, instructors, or group leaders. A part of me wanted their approval but another part despised them. And so, when any opportunity to rail against the powers that be arose, I was all over it. My railing wasn't *always* obvious. Sometimes it showed itself as gossip, or passive aggression, or even ignoring authority completely. But, at other times I was outright hostile.

Even though questioning authority can be vital to world progress–there's the Tiananmen Square guy who blocked the tanks, the little British boy who rolled his eyes and refused to sit on Saddam Hussein's lap, the female journalist who threw off her chador while interviewing Ayatollah Khomeini–it has, more often than not, kept me from progressing in life.

Most of the time when I fight authority, I'm being driven by fear, self-righteousness, or even vengeance, disguised as principles. My issues with authority aren't generally motivated by the desire to change the course of history or save a nation, or anything that matters in the grand scheme. It's usually just because I'm under the illusion that my needs are more important than what is going on around me.

The time *may* come when it's necessary for me to take a stand for something that will affect the course of history. If that day ever does come, I'll be ready. Because I've had a lot of practice.

It's Not About The Money:

I'll say "no" to fighting anyone today.

September 11

CONSIOUS?

There's a popular New Age philosophy that says every time you utter the phrase, "I never want to be broke again," your subconscious latches on to the word "broke." According to this theory, the human brain is a magnificent organ capable of complex tasks, like managing involuntary muscle movement and respiratory functions, but it is not so good at decoding full sentences.

Apparently it only latches onto adjectives. And negative ones at that.

So, when I say, "I never want to be broke again," my subconscious tells the universe to fulfill my wish to be broke by putting me right back in the unemployment line or another underearning job. And so it goes, my subconscious mind is in a constant battle with my conscious brain.

Now, I'm no neuroscientist, but for today I say, "To heck with theories that don't work for me."

Sometimes I need to talk about my fears, and if I can't because I'm afraid that admitting I have it will create more of it, then I'm doomed to stay in denial. At the very least, I'd be massively confused.

My DA meetings give me a place to share my fears and get the support I need so that I can find solutions and move on. Unless I can share openly, growth is nearly impossible.

Yes, I'll continue to affirm that new house in the mountains and that fabulous job, but change can't happen if I turn a blind eye to where I am. I can think happy thoughts, but staying silent because I'm afraid of telling the truth about how I really feel doesn't work.

I don't have to trick myself or my subconscious. I can trust that God is in charge. He can hear me, He understands what I *really* mean and what I need. In fact, I think I'll try saying *that* aloud today, as often as I can. Please feel free to join me.

It's Not About The Money:

Hi, God, thanks for helping in spite of my overworked subconscious.

September 12

INNER KID

It was early in my recovery. I was finally earning consistently, but was still struggling emotionally. My friend looked at me squarely and said, "Your inner child is keeping you broke."

"Oh, God, not the inner-child thing," I said sarcastically. "I told that brat to pipe down in the '90s after I read those John Bradshaw books.

"That was kind of hostile, for someone whose inner child just needs a big hug," my friend replied.

I love my friend, who's a bit of an armchair psychologist, and I tried to shrug off his comments, but part of me knew he was right. I'm a debtor and an underearner. When it comes to money and work, an eight-year-old has been running the show for most of my life. And although I've never seen the show, I have a feeling it's in a foreign language.

Enough of the metaphor mixing. When I'm not earning enough, or I'm overspending and avoiding financial commitments, it's because I've allowed the younger part of myself to take over.

The solution for me is to ask God for clarity about what I'm feeling and write about it. Am I lonely? Afraid? Angry? Insecure? When I write about my feelings, I can acknowledge and feel them, spend time in meditation and prayer, and let them pass.

Sometimes I say to myself: "You can do this. You can reconcile your checkbook." If I need more support, I call a friend to help me through it. Then I turn my emotions over to my Higher Power and go on with my day. While it's helpful to understand how I'm feeling, at some point I need to take contrary action.

The feelings may return, but with help from God and the Tools of the program, I'll get through it. And, no matter how frustrated I am, I've learned it's never wise to tell my inner child to "pipe down." I won't go into details, but let's just say it's frightening to wake up in the middle of the night and discover your inner child trying to smother you.

It's Not About The Money:

I can feel my feelings and still have a good day.

September 13

URGENT

Before I found recovery, I was a Type A+ personality. Intense. Everything had to be done immediately. With urgency and a side of French fries.

In DA I learned this approach was based on fear that I wasn't safe in the world. My response to that fear was control. When I finally surrendered to my Higher Power and began working the Twelve Steps, I saw how powerless I was over my Type A+ tendencies. Although those tendencies were, no doubt, highly charming, they created a lot of stress.

I had to give up the need to control and allow life to happen organically. I also had to accept the idea that no amount of money would bring the freedom that a relationship with God could give me.

My new approach includes things like: keeping track of my numbers, turning my will and life over to my Higher Power, staying solvent, not incurring unsecured debt one day at a time, and being of service to others. There are many other things that my life includes, but as a recovering Type A+ personality, I'll stop there. Why get myself all worked up over another list?

I've lightened up and have a go-with-the-flow approach to things. Most things. Most of the time. A lot of the time. And, I've gone from being Type A+ to Type A-. One might even say a B+ on an exceptional day. That is, if the people I come in contact with aren't moving too slowly, or standing in my way.

It's Not About The Money:
Thanks, God. Life isn't so urgent anymore.

September 14

LIKES

I knew I had a problem when I found myself crouched on the floor, pressing a drinking glass against the wall so I could hear *everything* my conniving power-mongering colleagues at my hypercompetitive job for an entertainment company *were* saying about me in the office next door.

After I'd had an earful–I wasn't paranoid; they surely were conspiring against me–I pulled myself together and devised to make a plan. My main goals from that point forward became: managing my reputation and proving those clowns wrong. I vowed to be the smartest person on every project, and if I wasn't I'd shoot for the nicest, or the most fun. I knew if I worked hard enough, I'd get my officemates to change their minds about me. This was crazy because I had an intense job, the requirements of which didn't include being the "most likeable."

After that incident, I devoted most of my day to doing "spin control" on my reputation. I couldn't allow *anyone* to say *anything* negative about me, and if they did, I'd spend hours planning what I'd need to do to change their opinion of me.

It took time in DA to admit and accept that not everyone I like will like me back, no matter what I do. Of course, if I've done something wrong or harmed someone, it's up to me to take responsibility and make amends for it. But once I've done so, I have to allow people think what they want about me. I can't control how others feel, and their opinions of me are none of my business.

I've learned be polite and kind, but I don't have to devote my time and energy to getting people to like, or love me. I've also learned not to bring drinking glasses into my office at work. I simply don't need the temptation.

It's Not About The Money:

What other people think of me is none of my business.

September 15

RESISTANCE

"Whatever you resist, persists. When you allow it, it will disappear."

– *Anonymous*

I've seen this phrase written seven ways to Sunday and it still doesn't make any sense. It seems quite ridiculous to accept something I *really* don't want in order to make it leave. Whatever happened to resisting things or pushing against them until they give up and go away?!

Allowing a situation to exist without analyzing it, or nudging it along seems counterintuitive. And as for allowing things I don't like to...be? That's just plain weird. If I don't rail against my problems, or gather votes in my favor about how horrible things are, then how on earth will they ever disappear?

Even though I'm in recovery, I cannot, with one hundred percent confidence, sell myself on the idea that allowing things to just *be*, especially when I don't approve of them, will cause them to go away, but I'll give it some thought.

Okay, so I've given it some thought and I've decided that I will give the whole allowing-things-to-be-until-they-go-away approach a try. I'll begin by *not* resisting the dirty dishes anymore. Instead, I'm going to *allow* my dishwasher to stay full. Until it isn't anymore. That seems like the perfect place to start.

Where will you start?

It's Not About The Money:

I'll allow whatever is to be. No nudging.

September 16

SUPPLY & DEMAND

When I came into DA, after having lost it all, I vowed to change my ways. Instead of the demanding, entitled snob I once was, I decided to start saying "yes" to any work I could get. Unless it was illegal or immoral. Or had anything to do with cats.

The upside of that experience was I gained humility and compassion for others. The downside was, I became scattered. I had three part-time jobs for the first few years, and I'd drive up to sixty miles a day for work that paid next to nothing. I wanted to show I was willing but I wasn't discerning. I felt like I was selling my soul for minimum wage.

Eventually I slowed down, but only from sheer physical exhaustion. And that was when I learned the spiritual meaning of "supply and demand." As I became less available for underearning jobs, the demand for my services in higher paying positions increased. I wish I could say it was by design of some genius master plan but I'd be lying. It just happened that way and I made the connection. When I stopped being available for dead-end, low-paying jobs, better opportunities appeared. When I said "no" to cheapskates, a higher quality of employers started pursuing me.

Who knew?

Now I'm able to graciously say, "No, thank you" to job prospects that don't serve me. It frees me up for better opportunities. And as the demand for my skills continues to increase, so do my fees. It's so much more fun to say "yes" to well paying work I enjoy than to lowly paying work I hate. And I say that without even a hint of entitlement or snobbiness.

It's Not About The Money:
It's fun to be well paid for work you love.

September 17

OUT

I've heard some say religion is "about keeping people out of hell, and recovery is for people who've already been there."

Even thought I'd attended church and had faith in God, when I got to DA, I'd stopped connecting to the God of my youth. I'd tried everything to fix the pain–possessions, success, traveling, existential exploring, etc. I was still depressed. Too much had happened to me–financial losses, relationship stresses, death–and I felt justified in having an attitude. Life hadn't worked out as I had planned, and I was certain God had something, if not everything, to do with it. My hell was the daily feeling of being overwhelmed by life, my fears about not being "normal," and the shame I felt about needing help.

Recovery gave me the courage to tell the truth. I was angry at God and embarrassed about not knowing how to do life or relationships. And when it came to finances, I had no idea how to manage the very basic things, much less how to save money or handle a checking account.

In DA, I met other people who'd been through their own version of hell. Instead of shaming me or giving me trite advice, they listened, hugged me, and accepted me despite my confusion, anger and sadness. They told me I didn't have to figure out my relationship with God, and they didn't preach to me about what I needed to do to get out of the financial mess I was in. They just asked me to keep coming back.

In time, I renewed my relationship God and it's better now than it ever was. DA was fundamental in showing back to the God who led me out of the hell I was in. Believe me, I spent a lot of time there and I'm glad I never have to go back again.

It's Not About The Money:
Thanks, God, for showing me the way out.

September 18

MIRACLES

I still remember the day. I'd just began the DA Program and was doing laundry when I discovered a five-dollar bill in my jeans. I started to cry because it meant I had enough money to buy a treat for myself!

When I was living under the weight of crushing debt, there was no amount of money that I couldn't account for. I didn't have "around 30 bucks" in my account. I had $27.97. I lived in constant terror, thinking in exact numbers, because I needed to know if using my debit card for a pound of bananas and a loaf of bread would put my account into overdraft. A minor slipup could mean the difference between another 99-cent taco or a salad for dinner. I was living to pay my debts first. Whatever was left over was mine, and it was certainly not enough for me to live well. A frappuccino was a major treat, one I could only afford once a month.

My life had gotten very small.

Things didn't change immediately. It took a while before I could believe that things like loose change or an unexpected check for in the mail was a sign that God was taking care of me. But there were times when there was no denying the fact I was the recipient of miracles. Like when I was completely out of food and a friend would call from out of the blue and treat me to dinner. Or the barista at the coffee shop would offer me a free latte for no reason at all.

The interesting part is, the more grateful I was for the pint-sized miracles, the more of them I received.

Now that I'm solvent and can afford a latte anytime I want one, I look back on those days with fondness. Sometimes I even miss those lean days. Okay, "miss" might be extreme, but there are days when I'm wistful about how grateful I was for having the basics. Although, I admit, I much prefer higher-quality things.

It's Not About The Money:

I'll show some love for little miracles today.

September 19

PERFECT

I'm a perfectionist. I have a hard time starting things and an even harder time finishing them, because I always want to put my best foot forward. I have high standards and my passion for excellence drives me to run the extra mile, never stopping, never relenting.

And when I don't achieve the results I want, I get snippy. My insistence on dotting every i and crossing every t breeds disorder, causes delays, stress overloads, and a lot of broken things: promises, friendships, dishes.

The truth is, the real world doesn't reward a perfectionist. It rewards people who get things done, and the only way to get things done is to be *imperfect* ninety-nine percent of the time. Only by trudging through mistakes and mishaps do I ever experience the momentary bliss of excellence. I make a decision to take actions and learn from the outcome in every area of my life. It ain't perfect and it ain't often pretty.

When I'm feeling the weight of my imperfection, I do what works best for me: take a walk outside, ride my bike, clean my kitchen, anything that will change my chemistry. Or make an outreach call to someone who's kind and supportive.

DA teaches me I won't do much perfectly but I keep trying, because it's how I get better. Daring to do something badly and resisting the need to be perfect can be fun. In fact, I'm enjoying writing today's meditation because I'm in total acceptance that it might suck. And I wrote that despite the fact my inner perfectionist says I should never use the word "suck" in a sentence because it's tacky.

It's Not About The Money:

God, help me do whatever I need to do today imperfectly.

September 20

GOOD DEALS

I recently returned to school and, debtor that I am, selected the cheapest school in order to save money. Within a month it was clear to me that not only was the school questionable in its business and health practices, the "rules" and expectations of the students were constantly changing. The instructors were harsh and would scream at students if they weren't "getting it." I hated every second I was there but I didn't want to be a quitter.

Five weeks away from my graduation day, I quit.

"Good for you," my DA sponsor said when I told him.

"What? You aren't going to call me a quitter?" I asked. "It'll cost me $1,800 to transfer to another school, and I'll graduate late."

"Well, you chose that school because it was cheap," he said.

"And I got what I paid for."

"I'm proud of you. What you did is not quitting. It's called self-care. The instructors at that school were abusive, and you kept pushing yourself to stay because you had paid the money. I'm glad you finally realized that happiness and serenity cannot be bought."

There have been times when I walked away too soon–when things weren't going my way and I was too immature to deal with them–but DA has taught me there are times when quitting is not only okay, it's critical to my serenity. There is such a thing as an unacceptable situation. If it's a no-win situation, walking away can be a sign of recovery, as long as I do so with dignity and grace.

I transferred to another school and graduated. I called my sponsor.

"You were right. I can't put a price tag on my serenity."

"Yup," he said. "Never trade your sanity for a 'good deal.'"

I'll never trade my sanity for a good deal again. Unless it's an *insanely* good deal. Like a brand new convertible Tesla for twenty dollars or something like that.

It's Not About The Money:

I can't put a price tag on my serenity.

September 21

RISKY BUSINESS

I was having dinner with my friend and film producer, Sam, at our favorite Mexican restaurant.

"You know the script I've been working on?" I started, dipping delicately into the salsa bowl.

"The one about...women?" he said, yawning.

"Yes. I've decided I'm going to produce it myself."

"What'll you use for money?" he asked nervously.

"Well, I have some savings. I can raise the rest, you know, venture-capital type stuff. There are tons of tech geeks who'd love to invest in a film!"

"Please tell me you're kidding," Sam said, pounding his head on the table. "Normal people don't use their life savings to make a movie."

I glared at him. "I thought you were my friend."

He was right—normal people don't do that. But unrecovered debtors operating on self-will do.

I made the film and ended up in some deep you-know-what. About-half-a-million-dollars-and-an-investor-in-federal-prison deep. The signs were there all along, I just didn't want to see them. It took a lot of soul searching for me to figure out I had a debting problem.

Debtors Anonymous has taught me new ways of doing things. I don't take risks with my money on "creative ventures" unless I do plenty of meditating, praying, and planning. I don't make financial decisions or purchases without the support of trusted friends and respected fellows in DA to give me valuable and thoughtful feedback.

I've also discovered that, if a friend ever looks at me again and says I'm not normal, it might be better for me to pause before kicking them and walking away.

It's Not About The Money:

Am I getting feedback about my "creative ventures" before moving forward?

September 22

HELP!

There was a point in my life when I remember making the conscious decision to earn so much money, I'd never be vulnerable again.

People I cared about had betrayed me, family members–many of them–had died prematurely, and I'd lost everything–my home, my job, my car, and my relationship in a matter of months. Life was messy and unpredictable and money would bring me security. At the very least, it would cushion further curveballs life might throw me.

So, I went out and made a lot of money. And I didn't feel better. Or more secure. Life wasn't less unpredictable, either.

When I crawled into the rooms of DA, broke as all get out again, I had to admit money wasn't going to keep me from the agony of being human.

"I need help!," I said, as I burst into tears at my first DA meeting. I knew I couldn't do life alone anymore. I needed a village of people who understood me, folks who could show me how to do things differently. I also needed a place to sleep, a car, shoes, and a job.

I needed a spiritual awakening, the basis of which was a relationship with a Higher Power. At first, that connection to God came from the kindness of others in program, because I couldn't get past the old, punitive God of my youth. It took many sleepless nights and plenty of screaming matches (me at God) before I was able to trust Him and turn my life over.

What I did not need was a bunch of money.

Now I love hearing people in DA say the words, "I need help," because it's the beginning of surrender and that's where the healing begins.

Know what words I don't love hearing? "Sorry, we're closed," but that's another story for another day.

It's Not About The Money:

Thank goodness God's doors are never closed.

September 23

TRYING

There are times when I worry that my praying doesn't qualify as praying, that I'm not doing it the "right" way and God might not be paying attention.

The fear comes as a result of an excruciating experience from my youth. I was being interviewed for my first professional job after college, by my "dream" company. I told the interviewer, and one of the company's top executives that I'd try to be his best employee ever. He picked up his expensive Cross pen and threw it on the floor.

"*Try* to pick that pen up off the floor," he said.

I quickly picked it up the pen and put it on his desk. He threw it back on the ground. "There is no such thing as 'try,'" he said, in the way short men with too much power do.

Despite that life-altering, traumatic incident and the resulting emotional scars it caused, there's a part of me that still believes it's worth trying something, no matter how poorly I do it.

I think it's the same way with prayer. As long as I keep trying, it doesn't matter where I am or how I'm sitting or what I say when I pray. Trying to pray is praying.

As I look back on the Cross-pen incident, I'm glad I didn't get that job. I'd have hated working for that company and would have fantasized about trying to place that pen you-know-where every time I saw my short, power-hungry boss. Alas, I did not have the gift of recovery back in those days.

It's Not About The Money:

I'm not gonna try, I'm just gonna talk to God today.

September 24

GEOGRAPHIC

For my first three years in DA, I was convinced that moving to another state was the solution to my problems.

"So, you're considering a 'geographic'?" my DA sponsor asked when I brought the idea up of moving for the hundredth time.

"This city just isn't working for me. It's crowded, the people are rude. And it's hard on my skin and nails."

"How would things be better in a new state?" he asked.

"Well…"

"A state where you have no job, no home, or friends?"

That was *precisely* my point. If I could just get away from the people I knew, especially the ones I owed money to, I might *finally* have a shot at a decent life.

"I need a fresh start," I whimpered.

"You need a meeting and some perspective. Rearranging the chairs on the deck of the *Titanic*..."

"Okay, you might be right," I relented. "Maybe I just need a haircut."

"Maybe," he said gently. "In the meantime, why don't we have dinner and go to a meeting together?"

At dinner, he reminded me that a "geographic"–moving from one place to another to escape my problems–was pointless, because I take me–and the behaviors that created my debting problems–with me. He suggested I pray before making decisions about going *anywhere*.

The odd thing is after dinner with my sponsor and an inspirational DA meeting, the urge to move subsided. I did get a haircut the very next day and it was way too short, so I hated it for a long time. I am, however, glad I didn't move.

It's Not About The Money:

Rearranging chairs on the deck of the Titanic rarely changes the outcome.

September 25

NON-EXUBERANCE

I used to panic when things were going really well in my life, because I figured it was only a matter of time before things would completely fall apart.

Call it the calm before the storm or waiting for the other shoe to drop–I wasn't entirely comfortable being happy. There was a part of me that thought, *Who am I to have a wonderful life or earn a lot of money when people are starving, losing their homes, or getting divorced?*

As a result, when I'd had more than a few exceedingly good days in a row, I would start cranking my exuberance down. And if I happened to be having a good run and encountered people who were having a bad time, I would downplay my joy and excitement.

I'm no shrink, but I *think* that's kind of screwed up.

In DA I learned to be responsible for my feelings. I don't have to hide my joy or assume I must be in denial just because I'm having an awesome day. And likewise, just because I'm having a stellar run doesn't mean I don't care about others.

I don't do the world or the people I love any good if I hide my joy, and I certainly don't need to feel guilty about having a wonderful time.

Today, even when things aren't going well, I can still be happy. I have a relationship with a God of my understanding and I know things are exactly as they should be, even if they aren't going my way. Likewise, when they are going well, I can show my enthusiasm without worrying I'm being disloyal to those who are having a difficult time.

I'm reminded of my sponsor who often says, in that perfectly composed, obsequious tone, "You get to choose happiness." When I get past the initial annoyance, I usually come to the conclusion that he's right. I *can* choose to have an awesome day, even an awesome life.

It's Not About The Money:

There's nothing to panic about. I'm gonna choose exuberance today.

September 26

HUH?!

One of my Step #9 amends in DA was to a former boss. When I worked for his company I was a total wreck. I was petulant; a difficult employee, at best.

Some days I assumed I was a great talent and the place would fall apart without me. On other days, I would hide in my office, afraid that he'd discover what a loser I was and fire me on the spot. Beneath all of that weird behavior was pain: I thought I was worthless.

I started the meeting by telling him I was working a Twelve-Step program.

"You're a drunk?" he exclaimed, shocked.

"No, I'm a debtor," I said slowly.

"What, you have a gambling problem?"

"No gambling. No drugs," I said, "Just a complicated relationship with money."

"What the hell does that mean?"

Suddenly, I was embarrassed. I couldn't explain DA, and more specifically, I couldn't blame a substance for my kooky behavior. While I learned in DA that this is typical behavior of a debtor–superiority and inferiority ideations, creating chaos when things are calm, and self-sabotage–I knew I had to take responsibility if I wanted recovery. The source of my problem was my reaction to life, which manifested itself in my relationship with money. I acknowledged that my actions had impacted my work and other people and I asked him if I could make restitution for it.

When my meeting with my former boss was finished, it occurred to me that he might always think I was just a jerk who blamed my problems on money. It also occurred to me that he still had no idea what a debtor was. It's okay, sometimes I don't, either.

It's Not About The Money:

I don't have to explain nothin' to nobody, I just gotta do what's right!

September 27

CERTAINLY

I used to crave certainty. I couldn't even define the word but I knew it had something to do with money and material possessions. I figured I'd know it when I had it.

Oddly enough, the most creative times of my life have been when I was unsure about the future. Some of my happiest moments occurred when I had no idea what the next day held for me.

There is a gap between knowing and not knowing, between certainty and uncertainty. That gap is called "faith," and it's where beautiful things can happen. In faith, I allow God in and I feel calm and safe, even though I'm might not have the certainty I crave. The times I've acted impulsively and gotten in over my head have usually occurred because I simply couldn't handle uncertainty.

Yes, having faith is hard, but having no faith is even harder, because when I try to control the outcome, I do rash things.

I still love certainty (aka "control"), but when I find the presence of mind to put my will in the care of my God and allow uncertainty to wash over me, I get pretty creative. Today I'm feeling kind of creative. In fact, I'm going to go out and bask in all of the uncertainty I'm experiencing right now.

Are you with me?

It's Not About The Money:

I'm certain I can trust God today.

September 28

FAB

When I first came into DA, I was fairly aggravated, because I'd had dreams of doing some fabulous things, and so, every time I heard someone talk about turning their will over to a Higher Power and working a spiritual program, I grew more irritated. I wanted out of debt, and turning my will over to God meant one thing: giving up my dreams of a fabulous life.

I had a distorted view of what a fabulous life was. I mean, I knew it was having the kind of job where all I had to do was show up and shuffle a stack of papers, say something clever, and once in a blue moon give a presentation that people loved so much I'd get a standing ovation when I walked through the hallways. I knew having a lot of money and millions of people the worldover admiring me would be fabulous. I knew being thinner would be fabulous.

A fabulous life did not include things like being loving, sharing my gifts with others, or putting anyone else ahead of myself. It did not include being humble or spiritual.

As I began to work the program and Tools, I saw people with fabulous lives and they were not the wealthiest people. They were people who had full lives. People who were good friends and loving partners–they were the folks who made other people smile. They were active in their community, sponsoring and being of service to others. They were the givers, not takers. And they changed my perspective on what a truly fabulous life means.

I don't need a lot of money, an entourage, or a limousine. For me, it's staying open and willing to be of service to others. It's knowing that God has a plan for my life and I can trust it's going to be fabulous enough.

It's Not About The Money:

Fabulous isn't better when it comes to my spiritual growth.

September 29

DUNG

There's a story about a little girl whose father drives her out into the country and stops off at a farm on her eighth birthday. When the little girl opens the door to the barn, the entire place is covered in horse dung.

The little girl jumps up and down, squealing with joy and delight.

"What are you so excited about, honey?" her father asks.

"Because, Daddy, with this poop all over the place, I just know there must be a pony in here!"

I'm a bit like that little girl. My true nature sees the wonderful possibilities in a less-than-stellar situation and thinks it might include a new pony. Ultimately, though, my adult brain takes over and convinces me everything's gone to crap.

My head and my heart are constantly at war. Is my life a bunch of horse manure, or am I about to find the pony? Do I believe that my Higher Power has something marvelous and exciting waiting for me behind the next barn door? Not always.

Still, no matter how I'm feeling, or what's going on around me, I can remain hopeful, just like that little girl (who did, by the way, get a pony!). I like to think of DA as God's reminder for me to keep my focus on the pony instead of the manure.

It's Not About The Money:

My true nature always trusts there's a pony.

September 30

30 DAYS

I'm just about done with DA. I've gone to at least two meetings a week for the last month and I think I've got a solid grasp on this debting stuff.

I've also been listening to CDs from that perky blonde financial guru–the one with the Midwestern accent–and I'm feeling much better about my future. I now think I have The Courage to be Rich. It's a feeling I didn't use to have, but I'm suddenly feeling like I'm ready to to Unleash the Billionaire Within me.

And I'm not being haughty. I just think I'm finally empowered to be the Rich Person I Already Am!

I've started making plans for what I'll do once I finish this DA stuff and get focused on making some real money. Maybe I'll start a charity for poorly dressed children, or something or other about saving spotted whales. I'll definitely give it some thought. I'll have a lot of free time because The 20-Minute Workweek seminar I just registered for requires only twenty minutes of work per month.

I don't really want to quit DA, but I'm not sure I'll be able to fit in these meetings anymore, because I'll be so busy with all my plans.

Seriously, my debting problems are pretty much resolved.

I get it. There are those people who really, really need a program to keep them spiritually centered and out of self-will and ego. I have a tremendous amount of compassion for those folks. I do. I'm exceptionally sensitive in that way.

It's Not About The Money:

There aren't any shortcuts to spiritual freedom.

October 1

PRIMERO CELEBRACIÓON

Hola! Feliz primero de octubre! The next thirty-one days are going to be the best ever, because the entire month of October will be dedicated to celebrating *you* and your uniqueness.

There is, and never will be, another you in the history of the world. Sure, there are many–perhaps millions–of folks who might claim to be better than you, but I know for sure they are wrong. And I can say that without having even met you.

I know, you're probably thinking, *Why are you celebrating me? What gives?*

Look, my little chickens, this isn't simply *me* celebrating *you*. It's also about *you* celebrating *yourself*. It's about you honoring how cool you are. So, for the entire month de Octubre, you are going to take a moment each day to remind yourself that you're perfect exactly as you are right now. Even if you never change a single thing about yourself.

Okay, let's get started.

Think of three things that you really like about yourself and write them down on a piece of paper. Carry that paper and read it aloud at least three times throughout the day. Three times a day for the next thirty-one days.

Naturally, as the month goes on, you'll forget to celebrate yourself, so I'll be here to remind you. (I'll say something like, "Go back to the meditation on October 1st.")

So start celebrating right now, because there is and never will be another you. Can I get a whoo-whoo from you?!

It's Not About The Money:

I can think of so many things to love about you!

October 2

EXTRA, EXTRA

It used to be that any extra money I received had to be spent right away. For example, when I received a big check from the IRS for my tax return, I was so ecstatic that within days of getting that return, I'd be close to broke again.

I was so accustomed to my bank account hovering near zero that it felt weird to have a chunk of money weighing me down. I'd think, *This money's burning a hole in my pocket. I have to get the things I want now! Soon enough the money will be gone anyway and I'll have nothing to show for it.* The movers would deliver a roomful of brand new furniture and a spiffy new computer. Then I'd head out to the shopping mall to look for the most luxurious, overpriced, scented candles I could find. Always lots of scented candles.

I had to spend the money before it disappeared.

It never occurred to me that I might want to save that refund check for future bills that would inevitably come, or for unplanned situations that might happen. It's almost as if having the money precluded normal things from happening, like I was frozen in time and there was some invisible force field sheltering me from having to pay for things like gas or groceries.

DA has taught me to handle the discomfort of having a lot of money in my bank account, and not just only right after tax season. It feels incredible to know I have a slush fund. It's not too heavy or burdensome; it just feels good.

I will admit, no matter how much I have in that slush fund, I'm always tempted by luxurious, overpriced scented candles, especially if they smell like pumpkin pie.

It's Not About The Money:

It feels good to have a slush fund.

October 3

TOUCHY

One of the biggest gifts of DA was the opportunity to sponsor other debtors and help them through the Twelve Steps.

"I love my new sponsee. I just wish she wasn't such a pain in the ass," I told my sponsor while having dinner one night. "I can't give her any feedback without an argument. She's so touchy, you know what I mean?"

My sponsor nodded.

"Always feeling she's being put upon and constantly demanding that life treat her better?" I said, sipping my iced tea.

"Uh-huh," he said.

"Before saying yes to anything, always wanting to know what's in it for her."

"Yup."

"Sooo glad I wasn't like that when I came into program."

He smiled.

"What?"

"The beauty of sponsorship is that I'm constantly learning about my own behavior," he stated. "I often see aspects of myself in my sponsees."

"Okay. So, I was demanding and defensive. But I don't remember being *that* bad. Was I that bad?"

"You're great," he said, patting me on the hand.

Then he said something profound about the gift of sponsorship, but I don't remember one word. I was thinking about just how obnoxious I must have been when I first met him. I'm not fixated on it or anything, but I'm definitely going to ask him to be more specific about it the next time I see him.

It's Not About The Money:

God loves me no matter how touchy I may be at times.

October 4

EASY

I've noticed that when it comes to decisions about money or business, people want answers *right away*. And while they rarely say the words "hurry up," I feel pressure to act quickly. I used to find it impossible to delay making decisions, especially if the "offer" had a time limit on it. Whether it was a job or a product or a service, I could not say, "I need some time to think about this." As a result, I made impulsive decisions without considering the consequences because I didn't want to offend anyone, and because I was afraid to lose a good deal. Greed, fear, and anxiety caused me to rush into decisions that got me into some uncomfortable situations.

Thank goodness my friends in DA remind me I have the right to pause before making a decision. I can even take the time to get to know a person before doing business with them! I don't have to say "yes" to every offer. When I began to slow down, I was less affected or intimidated by the people I was negotiating with.

When I learned to step back and turn my decisions over to God instead of rushing them, I got clarity about what I wanted. I was much calmer, and as a result, things usually turned out well. I didn't see the other person as the enemy and started seeking win-win solutions.

Today, when an opportunity is presented to me, I say, "That sounds like an interesting idea. Let me put some thought into it and I'll get back to you." Then I give the other person a time frame for my decision and I stick to it.

Instead of losing opportunities, I've gotten more, because as it turns out, the best way to negotiate is to know what *I* want and need. Success comes when things are right for *me*. Imagine that. I don't have to rush.

It's Not About The Money:
Take it easy today, 'lil pardner.

October 5

WHAT IFS?

Once upon a time, there was a princess whose favorite pastime was sitting on her throne in her castle and pondering the question, What if?

What if she never got another great job?

What if she died broke?

What if she couldn't pay all her debts back?

What if there was an earthquake and she hadn't stockpiled enough canned goods or gold coins?

One day, the princess decided to write down all of her what-ifs on a piece of paper. It took her six months to finish the list. Afterward, she took a very, very, very long nap.

When she woke, weeks later, she looked at the list and had a big, hearty laugh. Because she realized that most of the what-ifs that were causing her great sorrow were entirely out of her control and would probably never happen.

The princess immediately put the list into a box. She said a prayer of surrender and turned all of the worries in the box over to God. The princess hasn't opened the box since.

Of course it's only been a day, but the princess feels fairly certain she won't open the box again. Not today, anyway.

It's Not About The Money:
What if I forgot I even had a list of what-ifs?

October 6

FEEEEEEEEELINGS!

"I feel like I'm having an anxiety attack!" my sponsee cried over the phone. "I can't pay my rent *and* buy groceries this month!"

"Here's what I recommend," I said. "Every morning, before you do anything else, get on your knees pray or meditate. Spend fifteen minutes giving thanks for the things you have."

"I don't have time for that," she snapped.

"But you're not working," I reminded her.

"I don't feel I can spend a whole fifteen minutes being thankful."

"Okay, then do it for half an hour," I said.

"I can't!"

"It doesn't make sense right now, but acceptance and gratitude are the solution to many of your problems. It has nothing to do with how you feel." I did sound very wise, if I say so myself.

"The answer to *my* problems is money," she muttered and clicked off the phone. She called me an hour later to tell me I was too militant about recovery and she needed to find another sponsor.

I understood. When I came into DA, I was on the verge of suicide most of the time. It was only because I was so broken that I was willing to try something new and listen to a sponsor.

Willingness is a action, not a feeling.

My sponsee never returned to DA. Not everyone gets recovery in the same way or at the same time. But one thing is certain–if I want to stay solvent and debt free, I have to be willing to go to any length required of me, and most of the time that means being uncomfortable. The beautiful thing is, I always have a choice.

It's Not About The Money:

I'll do what I need to do, regardless of how I feel.

October 7

PROMPTLY

Step #10 in DA says, "We continued to take inventory and when we were wrong, promptly admitted it." In my DA home group, we call it "making a promptly," which means we promptly admit we're wrong and make amends. We don't hold off until we can "get around to it."

That being said, there's a huge difference between knowing I need to make a promptly and actually doing it. They're two different things entirely.

It's not that I don't *want* to make an amends. I just think it's important to reflect on things before taking full responsibility, and if the other person agrees to meet me in the middle and establish an equal level of wrongdoing, I'm more inclined to make my promptlies, promptly. No reason to be hasty.

Ironically, my DA sponsor doesn't agree with my approach to promptlies. According to him, I need to be willing to take full responsibility for my part. Period. It has nothing to do with the other person's part or whether or not they acknowledge any wrongdoing.

While he may have a point, I'm not sure I follow the logic. *Why would I want to take full responsibility when someone else's part may well be greater?*

Alas, my life improves drastically when I make my promptlies promptly, even if my part is miniscule. I feel lighter, knowing I've done the right thing, even when the other person allows me to take the blame and refuses to take responsibility for their role in the situation. In that sense, I have a lot of maturity.

It's Not About The Money:

I'll make my promptlies promptly. At least, before I give it too much thought.

October 8

PLEASANTVILLE

I recently read a survey that confirmed the people who live in the city I wanted to move to are the happiest human beings on the planet.

According to the study, this city, which is experiencing a period of immense economic growth, also got high marks for safety. The subways are pristine and on time, and the police are seen as helpful and friendly.

The survey suggests that residents of all ages feel positive and at the peak of their potential. They all have enduring relationships, great health, and complete freedom to choose from the best that life has to offer. They're the most productive humans on Earth, their median income is the highest in the world, and they are the best citizens–not one person in the entire city has a police record or has received anything more than a parking ticket.

Residents can snow and waterski all year round, surf and sail, attend free museums, festivals, and outdoor theatre. Shopping, cafes, and restaurants are plentiful and the service there is the best in the world. Prices are also extremely reasonable.

As if that isn't enough, the weather is 72 degrees every single day. Each house and apartment in the city offers a simultaneous view of both the sea and the mountains, as well as free and easy access to all parks, forests, and lakes. The streets are so clean people have been seen eating off the ground.

"This place is basically utopia, everyone I know is completely fulfilled, and I don't recall ever hearing of someone having a bad day," one local woman was overheard saying, "It's too bad we no longer allow anyone to relocate here."

October 9

MYSTERIES

It never once occurred to me that the end of my debting career would begin the day I sat down in a damp church basement, with a group of folks I surmised couldn't get enough money together to afford a stale slice of pizza from a 7-11.

Every single time I stepped into that meeting I'd start crying. I was terrified I'd never get work again and convinced I was useless. I was often hungry and miserable, and just when I'd start thinking things couldn't get worse, I'd hit another emotional "bottom."

In truth, that depressing, bleak little basement held the solution to all my debting problems. I got a sponsor and worked the Steps, and even though I didn't understand how, I was restored to sanity.

Even today, I can't explain how my life turned around. I can't pinpoint the day, or where I was but eventually I began to change. And for no compelling, specific or logical reason, there would be days when I would feel gratitude or hope. And my outsides started to change: Unexpected gestures of sweetness from others, coincidences and opportunities that appeared from out of the blue, little miracles I couldn't explain. I started to...believe.

It's still a mystery how I came to believe, but I do know this: I keep working it and it keeps working, so I'll simply accept that mysteries are just that.

*Remember, it's Celebrate You Month! Review October 1st meditation.

It's Not About The Money:

It's a mystery, but DA works for me.

October 10

ON PURPOSE

I was online and came across an executive at a TED conference giving a speech called "Finding Your Life's Purpose in 5 Minutes."

Wow! I thought. *I've spent decades on self-introspection baloney and I could've figured it out in five minutes?*

The guy's talk was so absurd, it reminded me of a Monty Python sketch called "How To Do It." It opens up on a set with Alan (John Cleese), a nerdy guy in a bulky sweater, and Jackie (Eric Idle), a man wearing a dress and wig seated next to him.

ALAN (JOHN CLEESE): Hello, children, and welcome to "How To Do It." Last week, we showed you how to split an atom. This week, we'll show you how to play the flute and construct box-girder bridges. But first, Jackie will tell you how to rid the word of all known diseases.

JACKIE: (ERIC IDLE in a dress) Hello, children. First of all, to rid the world of diseases, you must become a doctor, and discover a marvelous cure for something. Then, when the medical profession starts to take notice of you, you can jolly well tell them what to do. Make sure they get everything right, so they'll never be diseases ever again. And that's it.

ALAN: Thanks, Jackie, that was fantastic. Next week we'll be showing you how all people can live together in peace and harmony, and how to irrigate the Sahara desert. 'til next week then, cheerio."

JACKIE: Cheerio, children!

It takes time to figure things out, and people who are absolutely certain of their life's purpose are rare. I may *never* know my life's purpose, but I don't think it guarantees that all my dreams will come true, or I'll always be fulfilled and I doubt my purpose will be revealed to me in a five-minute presentation.

The best part about the "Finding Your Life's Purpose in 5 Minutes" speech? It was fifteen minutes long.

It's Not About The Money:

Today I'll give God ten minutes and ask Him what He's got for me to do.

October 11

FRIEND

Dear Friend,

There are times when I wonder if you're listening to the things I'm writing. I mean, I don't know anything about anything. I don't have this money or recovery stuff down. I'm just figuring it out as I go.

One day at a time and all that.

Sometimes I worry that I might freak you out by telling you the truth about how freaked out I get around money. Maybe you'll think DA doesn't work, because if it did, then I wouldn't be so screwed up, right?

It's hard not being able to talk to you or hear back from you, not connecting "one on one" as they say. I hope you're doing okay and not discouraged.

Going to meetings and working on recovery from debt and compulsive spending is exhausting, and I worry about you. Do you have people in your life to laugh with? Are you resting enough? Are you working the Tools and staying solvent? Are you connecting with your Higher Power on a daily, if not moment-by-moment, basis? Are you getting enough Vitamin C? Are you wearing sunscreen? And by that I mean, every day? UVB rays can kill. Seriously.

Okay, that's enough. No pressure. I just wanted to check in to make sure you were okay. If not, please e-mail me at misti@mistibwrites. We can talk about whatever you like. But, for your sake, if you reach out to me, you'd better have that sunscreen issue resolved.

Sincerely,

Me

It's Not About The Money:

Remember, it's Celebrate-You month, so review meditation from October 1.

October 12

PLAYING SMALL

It used to be that when I was working on a creative project, I would let go of my vision of what I wanted for fear of being called "difficult" or "demanding." I was often afraid to ask the people I'd hired to do their jobs because I wanted to be "nice," and didn't want to offend.

Whenever I play small in an effort to make someone else feel better instead of requesting what I really desire, I always regret it.

"What does this have to do with debting?" you may ask.

"A great deal," I'll answer.

When we deny our needs because we fear upstaging or upsetting someone else, or give up our dreams and deny our desires for the approval of others, we're in danger of self-debting. The fallout includes resentment, passive-aggressive behavior, anger, and misery. The record-keeping goes, we skip meetings, start overspending or making impulsive purchases, or just straight out blow money indescriminately.

The line between asking for what I want and demanding it, especially when it involves money, can be blurry and I still have difficulty with it. But now I have a DA community who understands that, for whatever the sundry oddball reasons, "asking" doesn't come naturally to me.

Playing "nice" comes naturally to me, but I have to step out of that zone as often as I can. That isn't to justify being demanding or rude, it simply means I ask for what I want and need in a firm manner. It also includes saying "no" to things I don't want. Especially when it's a creative project and my reputation is on the line. I don't have to be cranky about, but I also don't have to always be "nice," which is okay by me. Well, it's not *always* okay. But today, it feels okay.

It's Not About The Money:

Am I "playing nice" and building resentments?

October 13

LOUIS, LOUIS

When I came into DA, I didn't give a second thought to paying three thousand dollars for a Louis XV chaise lounge with a credit card, then borrow money from my cousin to pay my rent.

I didn't consider that my actions–not the mean-spirited pushers of the plastic equivalent of crack cocaine–were what was ruining my life. If the banks didn't charge such high interest rates and I didn't have to use those cards for the lunches I was forced to go out to, I could've gotten caught up. Besides, why were they charging *me* so much when *they* were making billions of dollars? Why didn't they just take the money from their millionaire investors, or partners, or even their rich customers?!

Solvency required that I stop doing stupid things and grow up.

And yet, when I first came into DA and stopped doing stupid things, I felt crazier than before! How could it be that not doing stupid things made me feel so insane?

I was told that if I turned my will over to a Higher Power, changed my behavior, and kept my side of the street clean, I would feel uncomfortable at first but eventually I'd experience sanity and peace. I had to trust my fellows in Program, who gently showed me saner behavior. Then I began to trust a Higher Power. In time, I found I could trust myself as well.

Taking contrary action, i.e. behaving sanely, felt insane to me for quite a long time, but ultimately it led to solvency, and solvency led to sanity.

Today, solvency and sanity feel incredible and so very comfortable to me. Even more comfortable than a three-thousand-dollar Louis XV chaise lounge. Or at least as much as.

It's Not About The Money:

Sanity is definitely more comfortable than an expensive sofa.

October 14

RIGHT ON!

"Would you rather be happy or would you rather be right?" my sponsor asked me while I was complaining about my last relationship.

Can I get back to you? I wanted to say. Because I'm pretty damn happy when I'm right.

"Happy, of course," I responded with what seemed like the perfect combination of sincerity and humility. I didn't feel like getting into it.

Being right can be addictive. I read an article that said that human beings get "high" from being right. There's a neurochemical component to it; neurotransmitters are distributed through the body when it's "winning." It's what helps an athlete crush his competitor and the businessman win the big deal. People feel invincible when they're dominating.

Eventually, people can get addicted to being right. The long-term effects of being right all the time–aside from becoming a total wanker–can include isolation, loneliness, joblessness, and general misery. It stands to reason that if someone feels superior due to a perception of being right, then the person being dominated could be feeling, well, not so great.

Thankfully, recovery has taught me that the pleasure I get from being right doesn't last long and it definitely doesn't keep me warm at night. Even more importantly, I've learned that the love hormone "oxytocin," which is distributed throughout the body when we connect with people who care about us, is as powerful as the chemical that's activated when we win. And the high from oxytocin lasts longer than the one we get from being right.

Oh, and oxytocin increases our ability to trust.

Suffice it to say that being happy and feeling loved can feel darn good. So, then, the answer to the question "Would you rather be happy or would you rather be right?" can unequivocally be "I'd prefer to be loved."

It's Not About The Money:

God, help me practice not being right today.

October 15

KEYS

Recently, I got a fortune cookie that read: THE KEY TO YOUR PROBLEM IS THE IGNITION KEY.

Standing still when a problem came up in my life was like nailing a tablespoon of peanut butter to the wall. Next to impossible, and very messy.

When problems of the financial type arose, my first question was, "Where is the exit door?" I believed my problems and concerns were bigger and more powerful than I was, and I'd convince myself that I was mentally challenged when it came to numbers. At the hint of a financial discussion, my car keys were the first things I would grab.

Now that I'm in recovery, I can stay–somewhat–calm when conflicts or concerns about money and finances come up. I'm able to sift through the information I receive and ask for help from people I trust. Then I turn the rest over to God. I try to leave it there, but sometimes I take it back a few more times until I've exhausted myself. Then I really turn it over and move on.

I now know I'm more powerful than my problems. And sometimes it's better to gently walk away and turn my problem over to God, or at least give things time to settle before I try to figure out what I should do. There are times when I've found that going for a long walk or having a bite of Chinese food works, too.

It's Not About The Money:
Find problem and you will also find key, grasshopper.

October 16

NOTES

I was doing a morning check-in call with my DA action partner. I'd been griping about how the days all seemed to run together, with my doing the same ol' things: send out resumes, follow up on job leads, make outreach calls...

"Why doesn't God just tell me what to do?" I sighed. "Leave me a note or something."

"Because if God told you what to do, you wouldn't listen." She giggled. "What do you want to do?"

"To go back to bed," I said.

There's a part of me that doesn't trust myself so I immediately reject my first instincts. I'm afraid I'll do things the wrong way. It's hard to follow your heart and pursue your dreams when you're constantly judging yourself. I mean, even the greats had to start somewhere. Imagine if someone was standing over Michelangelo, critiquing his every brushstroke as he was mapping out *The Creation of Adam*. Or if a group of people were standing at the base of Mt. Rushmore, mocking Gutzon Borglum because George Washington's head was too big?

Part of my recovery from debting has been about learning to trust that God will lead me. I don't have to figure everything out today. I can take the time to explore what I might enjoy, and change course if it doesn't pan out. Additionally, I don't have to rely on someone else to tell me what to do. Or not do. No one else has the answers. It's up to me. The answers come quietly, and seldom in the manner I expect them.

There are times when it would be easier if God would just leave me a note and tell me what to do. But my friend's right. If I ever got a note from God–or anyone, for that matter–I'd probably crumple it up and throw it away.

Then tell that person to mind their own business.

It's Not About The Money:

God can lead me without telling me what to do.

October 17

NICK OF TIME

I often fear I'll run out of time. Like a chubby, hairy old dude with a young model girlfriend, or the housewife who dates her personal trainer, I fear my own mortality.

I fear I'll end up like that woman who lay dead on the floor of her apartment for three years before a London police officer found her. No exaggeration–I saw a documentary about it on BBC.

I worry I'm not going to be able to fit everything in before I die. I'm concerned my Higher Power has forgotten all about me and I'm the only person who won't recover, that the world is coming apart at the seams and I'll die broke and alone, which is why I refuse to own a cat, no matter how depressed or full of self-pity I am.

There are times when I give up before I've even begun.

But not today, friends, because, you and I, we have a recovery program, and at this moment, we have all that we need. Or, as my sponsor says, "Look, kid, if ya got food in your gut and a place to sleep, ya ain't got nuttin' ta worry about."

No, my sponsor doesn't speak like Tony Soprano; it's just more dramatic when it's written that way. For today, I'll stop watching the clock and worrying about a future I cannot control. Wanna join me?

It's Not About The Money:

I'm not really crazy. I just write myself that way.

October 18

THE "D" WORD

"I'm not sure I want to call myself a debtor," my neurotic new sponsee said. "It's so negative, like saying I kick puppies or something."

"Then don't," I responded, trying to think of a clever follow-up line.

"Good. I refuse to go through life calling myself the D word, because It feels like a life sentence, and I don't think I'll *always* be a debtor."

When I was new, I wanted to be over the whole money problem thing, too, and didn't want to be branded a "debtor." In fact, I knew plenty of people in meetings who used every word *but* the D word when referring to themselves.

"I take that back. *You* are a debtor. But instead of fearing it, why don't you honor it? Take it out of the corner and embrace it?" I said, trying to lighten the mood. "Dress it up and braid its hair. Rejoice in it. You're creative; do something creative. Don't make it a life sentence."

This woman looked at me like I was nuts.

The thing is, I'm constantly looking for a way out of admitting I'm a debtor. I'm a shape shifter, and I can quickly convince myself that debt won't bring me to my knees and make me want to throw myself off a ledge. But coming up with clever names for something doesn't change what it is. My debting mind wants to take me down.

So I say, Bring it on, debting mind! I have resources now and it doesn't include calling you by a cooler name.

It's Not About The Money:

Debting is what it is, no matter what I call it.

October 19

BIG IDEA

One of the ways compulsive debting manifested itself in my life was in the form of the Big Idea. The perfect life was awaiting me, if only I could come up with the one idea that would skyrocket me to fame and fortune.

I spent years contemplating and concocting schemes I thought would lead me to the big time: pitching Hollywood producers and agents, taking classes, attending seminars, writing spec scripts. I spent a lot of precious time pursuing potential projects with Hollywood "players," but I refused to do the day-to-day things (e.g., financial tracking, staying consistently employed, making marketing calls for new business) that would lead to success and long-term solvency. It was hard for a person with as much talent as I to take on tedious tasks like holding down a job or paying the bills on time. I was constantly dissatisfied.

When I came into DA, I figured I'd let the dust settle until I could put together my next Big Idea and then I'd move on.

Years later, I'm still in DA. The work I do now isn't glamorous, and I wasn't "discovered" by anyone–except a Higher Power. Yet I'm happier now than I have ever been and I don't even know why. I just continue to show up to my meetings, take the next indicated step, stay in touch with my sponsor, work with others in program, and start my day saying to God, "Who would you have me be today?"

That's pretty much it. No Big Idea, just a series of small ideas to keep me serene. And while my ideas are not all that big, some of them are kind of clever. At least I think they are.

It's Not About The Money:
It's the small ideas that keep me in recovery.

October 20

THE NEGOTIATOR

I was new to DA, still in terror and panic over my finances, and I hadn't booked a gig in two years. I went to meet a potential client after having sent her a detailed proposal for my marketing services.

"I noticed there were no numbers on your proposal. How much do you charge for your services?" she asked.

"Um…five?" I said. "Five what?"

"Per hour?" I asked.

Her eyes widened. "Five hundred per hour?"

"Five thousand and a two-thousand-dollar deposit."

"I have no idea what you are talking about. Can you just give me a rate?" She was becoming exasperated.

"Yes, five thousand," I stuttered.

"For what?" She eyeballed me suspiciously.

"For you. For whatever you want. Just pay me five thousand and we'll go from there. If you want to."

She shook her head in seeming disbelief.

I'd done it again. I'd choked because I'd lost all my confidence and was afraid of talking about my fees. I tried to collect myself.

"Well, my hourly rate is $150 an hour, or at least it used to be." Most professionals would have charged her $200 an hour for the project.

She drummed her fingers on the desk.

"Whatever you have is fine," I said, trying to redeem myself.

She stared at me, slack-jawed. "What?"

"Okay, I want $12.50 an hour. And a Starbucks gift card," I said, slamming my hand on the table for dramatic impact. "But that's my final offer!"

It's Not About The Money:

It's hard to know what you're worth when you don't know your worth.

October 21

DONE

"*You're* still *going to those DA meetings? You've got a great job now and you paid off your credit card debt. Aren't you finished with that stuff yet?"*

The first time someone said that, I paused. Was I done with DA? I'd done some twelve-step work, I was going to meetings, and had more peace around money than I'd ever had in my life. I even felt hopeful about the future.

Maybe I am finished with the program, I mused. *Maybe I don't need it anymore.*

The next morning I had to stop by the bank before I went to work. I got a little irritated, thinking about the fact *they* charge me to keep *my* money, so I flipped off the ATM machine. Later, I offered to treat some friends to dinner, but I started to sweat when they ordered because I was terrified the meal would cost too much. Instead of enjoying their company, I was panicked the whole time.

And I remembered the reason I still went to "those Debtors Anonymous meetings."

I'm not totally incompetent, but there are times when I get "hunches," which consist of ideas like quitting my job and opening up a sustainable sandal company. Or moving to Costa Rica to work on a banana plantation. At other times, it's a tiny voice that says, "Life would be sooo much better if you had more money. You wouldn't have to deal with another annoying person the rest of your life."

You see what I mean?

In DA, I've learned that my thinking is my problem, not the money. And my reactions to those thoughts are what create the majority of my problems. That, and the hunches I sometimes get.

It's Not About The Money:

I'm not done, and don't know if I ever will be. How 'bout you?

October 22

THERAPEUTIC

I'd spent years in and out of therapy and had no clue I had a debting problem.

I sat for hours on various couches talking about the reasons for my self-loathing and shame. We dug up a lot of old stuff, including my nagging fear that there was never enough of *anything* for me. I related stories and processed a lot. I got in touch with my anger, resentment, and fear but never found a spiritual solution. And after I'd paid off the therapists–always on a sliding scale, of course; debtors rarely pay full price for therapy–I still had no clue what to do. I did, however, have a lot of knowledge, which made my head full.

Money had always been an "issue," a source of discomfort in all my relationships, and a bone of contention with and between every person in my family. And when it came to banks, corporations, and financial institutions, I was out and out unpleasant.

Not one of those therapists ever suggested I had a problem with the almighty dollar. I don't blame the therapists, because they were just doing their jobs, but it seems odd to me now, this obvious maladjustment in the way I related to the world in terms of money.

It may or may not be important to understand the reasons why I debt, but no matter the cause, I'm still powerless to change it without God, a program of recovery, and a Twelve-Step program to keep me on track.

I may or may not still need a shrink. That depends on who you ask.

It's Not About The Money:

I'll get off the couch and take the right actions today.

October 23

JOYOUS

Nothing has kept abundance and joy from my life as much as fear. Fear of rejection, fear of failure, fear I'm not good enough, or fear that I'm stupid and the world's ready to nail me for it.

When I'm afraid, I get small, or do the opposite: I get cocky and arrogant. I push people away and focus on how different I am from everyone else. I can't see the beauty of life.

I stop asking questions and shut down.

The antidote to fear, "they" say, is love. I think they might be right. Love being, for me, in the form of a Higher Power. When I ask for help from God, I remember that I'm not alone or in charge and I have nothing to prove. I just have to show up, do my best work, be of service, and try to stay grateful.

When I choose to move out of the fear and step out of myself, the joy begins to show up again. Suddenly, abundance is all around me. Maybe it's an invitation to dinner or a free movie ticket.

Or even a cup of coffee and a few laughs with a friend. Yeah, laughter. That's my favorite one.

*Remember, it's Celebrate You Month! Review October 1st meditation.

It's Not About The Money:
Come on, get happy!

October 24

TRIGGERS

When I first came into recovery, I purposely avoided triggers: department stores where I'd be tempted to spend my entire paycheck on soy-based candles, five-hundred-dollar fruit juicers, or wood-fired pizza ovens. I'd take the long route home to avoid wealthy neighborhoods, and I unsubscribed from the expensive online catalogues I'd been getting for years. I also monitored my time with people who triggered my jealousy and envy.

While these were honest efforts to stay out of debt, their success depended on my willpower. Changing behaviors is important to recovery, but willpower cannot solve the problem of debting and compulsive spending. Once I start down that path of believing the solution to life is having more money, possessions, security, or alternatively, hoarding money, willpower is the last thing I should rely on.

I can avoid triggers and manage my behavior, but the only long-term solutions include working a spiritual program that includes being of service to others and staying out of debt one day at a time. When I do those things, I don't have to take the longer route home or be insecure around people who have more than me.

Life is easier when there aren't so many triggers to worry about. Although I did read an article that suggested sleeping with a dim light reduces the amount of melatonin necessary to regulate moods. Too much light in a bedroom can trigger side effects like high blood pressure and brain-related problems. But those are different kinds of triggers and a conversation for another day.

It's Not About The Money:

Willpower is not the answer to my triggers. God's power is.

October 25

FIFTY PERCENT

My philosophy in life was always: If I can't do something a hundred percent then I won't do it at all. Since I could never handle my finances well, I chose to not do it.

When someone in DA suggested I create a spending plan and offered to show me how to put it together, I was so excited. I bought pens and paper, a stapler, yellow and red file folders, and organized my desk. I was gonna make my spending plan and I was gonna do it right!

Then I started to panic. I'd never be able to stick to a spending plan perfectly. Panic turned to despair, so of course I threw out the multi-colored pens and used the file folders as makeshift dustpans.

It took me a year and a half in DA before I was able to create my own spending plan, and only with the help of my fellows. After I created the plan, I sat on it for two years and never looked at it again. But there came a time when I was recovered enough to review that spending plan and start implementing it. I don't follow the plan with complete consistency, but I keep trying. I struggle with the fact that I'm not doing it at a hundred percent but I'm learning to be okay with that.

Now I say, when it comes to my recovery from debting, even if I'm only fifty-percent successful at something, it's worth doing, which makes me glad I'm not an air-traffic controller or a heart surgeon. A fifty-percent success rate in those situations probably wouldn't bode well for a long-term career.

It's Not About The Money:
In recovery, even fifty percent is fine!

October 26

WINNING!

When I came to DA, I followed the advice of people who said, "Hang out with the winners." I wanted to be a winner. I mean, why fool around with the losers?

The winners, as I saw it, were slick and successful, folks who talked a big game and seemed to have all the answers. I went to meetings where people were doing "deals," where the "movers and shakers" convened.

People who were struggling to find spiritual health, the ones who were less showy, didn't appeal to me. *Sure, I could learn something from the quiet, wise people, I thought, but learning patience and wisdom aren't at the top of my list. I need to get my life back and make some money.*

My first DA sponsor was hip, slick and showy and, suffice it to say, one day I discovered it was all show with absolutely no substance. Then I began working with another sponsor who was wise and strong, but not showy. He wasn't interested in helping me "get back on top." His only interest was in leading me back to a loving Higher Power. You might say he's like the guy in *The Karate Kid,* only not as short, and he's Irish. He doesn't ride a motorcycle, either.

This person has taught me that "winning" has nothing to do with what I earn or how cool my job is. He reflects myself back to me: a woman who is learning to be authentic, without relying on the world to make her feel worthy. He shows me how to be kinder to myself, and in turn, to do the same for others. He's taught me that being more "other-involved" and less "self-involved" might be the signs of a winner.

I don't need to go to showy meetings to get recovery. And I don't have to "hang out with the winners," unless I include hanging out with myself, because now I kind of feel like a winner.

It's Not About The Money:

As long as God's at the center, I am winning.

October 27

C.O.N.T.R.A.C.T.

I was receiving a PRG from two friends in DA about a new project I was pitching.

"Get everything in writing before you start the project, and make sure the contract…something…something…something" was all I heard after that. My mind went blank.

Just hearing the word "contract" spooks me out. Even if someone walked up to me on the street and said, "Here's a million dollars. Just sign this contract. No obligation, no commitment whatsoever," I wouldn't sign it. Okay, maybe I would, but I wouldn't want to. It's odd, this disdain I have of contracts, because I love words and contracts contain a lot of them. I love words, except when they're strung together and combined with numbers in such a way that makes them a contract. And also when they contain deadlines or the potential for anyone to someday say, "I'll see you in court." The only things I hate more than contracts are courtrooms, even when they're on TV and I know the guy holding the gavel isn't really a judge and the woman in the suit yelling at the jury isn't really a lawyer. I have issues with lawyers, too, but you probably have already guessed that.

So, why all this fear around simple, sweet little words when they make my life better, clearer, less stressful? When they can bring an opportunity to complete things and improve my relationship with the world? When they are important to my serenity in the long run?

I still don't know, so I ask for help from others who don't have that fear. The beauty of recovery is being able to ask for hand and not feel ashamed. I may never have a love affair with contracts, but then, again, there's always hope. And I mean that in a non-binding way, of course.

It's Not About The Money:

I may never love them, but I appreciate the clarity that contracts bring.

October 28

TERMINAL

I first heard the term "terminal vagueness" in DA, and it means: "a systematic avoidance of monitoring finances, including avoiding communication with creditors, leading to an overestimation or underestimation of account balances."

Before recovery I was shrouded in vagueness. From the moment I got out of bed to the time I retired at night, I was disorganized. I was constantly late for plans and appointments, and unclear about anything having to do with my finances, whether it be keeping track of my cash flow or reconciling my checking account. I rarely checked the mailbox, and paid all of my bills late, even when I had the money.

Terminal vagueness was my constant state for most of my life. I was vague about everything, and this made me anxious. When I wasn't anxious, I was just plain exhausted.

I discovered the antidote to terminal vagueness is clarity. Clarity for me means being aware of my checking account balances, keeping all of my commitments, and showing up on time.

I don't know exactly why, but the only way to overcome vagueness is to take constant, conscious contrary action. Yes, it's hard work and goes against what I'm often feeling, but it's not excruciating or anything.

I mean, there are plenty worse things than having to recover from terminal vagueness. Like going to prison. Or being kicked to death by rabbits.

It's Not About The Money:

Am I missing something, or is that my terminal vagueness rearing its head?

October 29

BESTEST

Today I hit the overwhelm button on those demanding, I-know-better-than-you self-help articles. You know, "10 Things You Must Do to Have a Better Life," or "Ways to Be More Productive," or "Three Ways to Build More Muscle," or "Get Smarter Faster."

These "bestest" articles as I like to refer to them, used to appeal to me, before I was in recovery. When I thought the solution was in making more money or getting what I wanted, I devoured those simplistic ideas like they were ice cream sundaes covered in caramel and topped with marzipan cherries.

I'm a human being who struggles. I'm often in conflict about money and love and relationships, and I act it out in many ways. Ten thousand articles will not change me; figuring out how to be the "best" will not take away the pain of living. The only remedy for a human being in recovery is spirituality, which I find in the rooms of DA, in my Higher Power, and in relating to other debtors. What works for me is taking each day as it comes, trying to be kinder and appreciating what I do have.

When I try to motivate myself to be better, best, bestest in "10 Ridiculously Simple Ways," I am "4 Ways Closer to Landing in a Ditch" and "2 Steps Away from Totally Freaking Myself Out."

It's Not About The Money:

I don't know better than anyone, and no one else knows what's best for me.

October 30

ENTHUSIASM

Enthusiasm—n. (*Greek* enthousiasmos) *inspiration or possession by a divine impulse, or by the presence of God.*

I was abundantly enthusiastic as a kid. I had many passions, which included swimming, buttercup flowers, and comic books.

I was also obsessed with sketch comedy TV. In eighth grade, when the A+ students went on a trip to Disneyland, the rest of us were left for a seven-hour study hall. Because I had some talent for writing skits, I talked my teacher into letting me write and direct a live show, starring my fellow less-than-stellar classmates.

While everyone else hadto sit in study hall, the students in my live show got to spend the morning rehearsing. At the end of the day we'd perform for the entire school. My job was less about being creative and more about herding kids like cats, but I loved the challenge of trying to get performances from kids who were truly horrible at comedy.

Whenever I think about that time, that's what I remember: my passion for writing skits, playing with friends. Swimming. Buttercup flowers.

When we come into DA, our enthusiasm has often been beaten out of us. But the beautiful thing is, as we recover, our passions return. Wherever you are on your journey, you still have a spark of passion. It doesn't mean you have to try to make money from it, it just means that no matter how bad things are, there's a pure part of you that can be enthused.

Right now, think about one thing that excited you as a kid, and spend ten minutes today doing some form of it. Maybe it's jumping rope, maybe it's looking at puppies, maybe it's sitting in a park.

No matter how broke or broken you feel, take ten minutes to do something you once loved. When your enthusiasm is reignited, even if only for ten minutes, so is your heart. Come on now, admit it, simply thinking about reviving some of your passion makes you feel a little better, doesn't it? I thought so.

It's Not About The Money:

Are you as enthused about your day as I am?

October 31

IMAGES

I'm not really sure what an image management consultant does day in and day out, but when the gigantic retail chain in the midst of a major PR disaster hired one, it sounded like something I'd be interested in. I like images, I like consulting, and I definitely like managing things.

In fact, before recovery, I was my own image consultant, highly skilled at making things look considerably better than they were. My ego was committed to looking good no matter how horrible I felt.

I even tried to look good when I was unemployed and sleeping in my friend's garage. Spiritually and emotionally I was drained, juggling one credit card to pay the other, vague about what I had, dealing with the constant anxiety of being unable to manage life.

I continued to manage my image, though.

It took some time in DA before I was able to tell the truth about how bad things were, how anxious and depressed I was, and how I feared I'd never be "normal" again.

It was only when I stopped trying to manage my image that my life became manageable.

I don't spend much time worrying about "looking good" anymore, although I do think I'd make a great image consultant. Because I like images, I like consulting, and I definitely like managing things. And, even when I'm really down, I still make the effort to color coordinate my outfits, because who knows – there may be a major PR disaster around the corner. It never hurts to be prepared.

*Remember, it's Celebrate You Month! Review October 1st meditation.

It's Not About The Money:

I don't need to manage nothin' for no one no more.

November 1

DARK THOUGHTS

I woke up this morning discouraged because I realized that, despite all my hard work, I'll never get ahead, and there's probably no point in trying anymore.

I didn't even bother getting out of bed to write today's meditation.

I mean, what's the point? The big fortunes have already been made, and the Bill Gates and Mark Zuckerberg's of the world won't be leaving their vast fortunes to me. No, those types will more than likely leave their money to the Spotted Whale Foundation or some other ridiculous charity.

And the chances of me finding a high-paying creative job are about as likely as me winning the Powerball lottery I never play. Companies don't hire genuinely creative people. History has shown that the brilliant artists of the world usually die penniless before the age of fifty. From tooth decay or hammertoes.

Aside from being staggeringly brilliant, my mind can be a dangerous place, overrun by very dark thoughts. Thoughts that tell me there's no point in getting out of bed or bothering to show up for work.

While it might be in my nature to fall into the dark hole of despair, I know how to help myself out of it because of DA. I can pick up the phone and call someone who'll remind me I'm not alone. I can turn my day over to God and ask for help with managing my dark emotions. Instead of staying in bed, I make the decision to get into action and try to be of service to someone else.

Without fail, I feel better when I refuse to listen to those dark thoughts. While I may never make a billion dollars, my teeth are in excellent shape. And although I do have a hammertoe, my life is good. Very good, indeed.

It's Not About The Money:

Hey, dark thoughts, you can pipe down. I'm trusting in my Higher Power today.

November 2

MY WAY

"Everything's wrong. I hate my life," I said to my sponsor.

"Things aren't necessarily going wrong just because they're not going your way," he replied.

I normally appreciated my sponsor's thoughtful, gentle wisdom, but not on this particular day.

"Well, I know what I like, and I'm fairly certain it isn't the life I'm living."

I hung up the phone, threw myself onto my bed dramatically, and began to sob. I was deluged with a flood of memories, a torrential downpour of a life of debt, chaos, and misery.

Then I called a friend in program. "DA's not working for me," I cried.

"I *think* your life is working pretty well. When I met you, you had sixty dollars, no car or a place to live. Now you're working, you're in school, you went to the lake for a few days. But I get it. You just want your way–"

"No, that's not it!"

"Instead of trusting God and being grateful for what you have–"

"I AM grateful!" I yelled. "I just know what I like and it isn't this!"

I think I want spiritual maturity but the truth is, I want my way. My way seems reasonable, well thought out, and considerate of others. God's way includes a myriad of outcomes, and some might be good, some not. It's hard for me to judge unless I'm getting exactly what I want.

I'm reminded of third grade, when I was petrified to go to school because of a school bully, so, I told my mom I was dropping out of school. The very next week the bully moved and I didn't have to quit school. I had a fantastic school year!

Things are okay. They may even be going well. I can't tell yet. Which is why it's best I trust God that today things are as they should be, even if they aren't going my way. That doesn't mean, however, that I won't do still do some whining and complaining.

It's Not About The Money:

Today, even though it's hard, I'll try to trust God instead of my way.

November 3

JUST 'CAUSE

I remember the first time I bought three reams of paper because it was on sale–three for the price of one. Although I needed the paper and could afford it, I was nervous about buying so much at one time. I was new to DA and only beginning to understand my discomfort about having more than "just enough."

When I was in deprivation mode, I'd buy only what I needed and no more. If I saw laundry detergent on sale for two dollars off, I wouldn't buy it because I might need those two dollars. I'd pass up a great deal on laundry detergent because I wasn't out of detergent yet. I'd wait until it was completely gone and pay whatever price–usually a higher one–the store was charging that day. Buying ahead of time to save money? That seemed crazy!

Recovery has shown me how to plan ahead for things–from health insurance to vacations to new clothes–instead of waiting until everything's broken down and I'm desperate. Today, I look at the cost per ounce of an item and if it makes sense, I buy ahead of time instead of waiting and paying a higher price.

I'll probably never buy in bulk or carouse in those colossal membership stores, dining on honey baked ham and egg roll samples, but I no longer overpay for things simply because I fear having more than "just enough."

It's Not About The Money:

I can have a little more than just enough if it calls for it.

November 4

HORRIBLE BOSSES

It took me a few years in DA before I came to the conclusion that I didn't have to do business with mean people who lied.

Like many debtors, I thought I had to take *any* job to show I was willing to earn, even if it meant working for unkind, unethical people. And every time I did so, it ended badly. I'd take jobs with horrible bosses and promise to keep my mouth shut, but it was impossible, because I thought I knew a lot and I had a big mouth.

So, I'd monitor myself for a while, and put up with way too much, until one day, "out of the blue," I'd flip out and tell said unkind horrible bosses *exactly* what I thought of them.

But after a few years in recovery and a few more of those experiences, I said the following prayer:

"God, can you help me out here? I know I'm not perfect and I have a tendency to be a know-it-all, but I don't want to do business anymore with unethical people. I think I'd rather work with decent, thoughtful people. Amen."

Then I went on with my day. My jobless day.

I haven't given it a whole lot of thought until right now when I realized I haven't worked for a lying, horrible boss in a long time. One might say this reflects something about me. Maybe I've changed and become a better employee.

I suppose that could be true, as I have been known to do some thoughtless things in the past, but I've never been called unethical or mean spirited. Because mean people suck. And even though I've said before I despise the work "suck," it's the only one that makes my point here.

It's Not About The Money:

Thank you, God, because I rarely run into mean people anymore.

November 5

PASSED

My version of the past is not, nor has it ever been, accurate. For instance, I have the tendency to romanticize former relationships, locations, and jobs.

The past seems wonderful in hindsight.

It's easier to look back on the past and feel sentimental because I know things turned out okay. But when I was living in those moments, I had no idea what I was doing.

For me, finding a Higher Power keeps it all in perspective: the past, my present, and my future. When I stay grounded in today and remember that my Higher Power has a plan for my life, I don't have to make up stories about the past. I can let go of it, knowing it wasn't better "way back when."

While the present can be difficult at times, I have Tools for living and I know that my feelings aren't facts. I don't have to fantasize about how great the past was or agonize what might happen in the future.

In fact, I feel kind of good about the future; I believe it holds incredible things for me. I know this because in the past I wore sunscreen and avoided chewing tobacco and so for it has worked for me.

Now it's your turn: List three things that have turned out well for you recently.

It's Not About The Money:

The past is passed and the future is looking good.

November 6

CRITICS

"You wouldn't worry so much about what others think of you if you realized how seldom they do." – *Eleanor Roosevelt*

The problem for me was always that I cared about everything everyone thought of me. Even when I didn't think much of them. How whack is that?

Negative feedback has always been difficult for me.

I once received a bad review about a film I'd written and directed. The caustic critic said the film showed a "lack or thought or talent." That comment bothered me for years. Years! I had writer's block for three years because of that review. Never mind the good reviews; I focused on the bad one. Ones. Okay, there were two bad reviews, but there were many good ones as well. I don't remember what they said, though, I was too focused on the bad ones.

In DA, I've come to learn that the opinion I have of myself is more important than the opinions of others. When I'm doing my best and feeling connected to God, others peoples' opinions don't matter as much.

When I feel good about my contributions to the world, no matter how small they are, I feel okay. However, if I start looking outside myself for approval, I'm in trouble. The solution here seems fairly straightforward, does it not?

My opinion of myself matters more than anyone else's opinion of me. Besides, most people aren't thinking that much about me, anyway. In fact, I'll bet that jerk critic doesn't even remember writing the horrible review that ruined three years of my precious life.

That's okay. I have forgiven him.

It's Not About The Money:

God, help me remember my opinion of myself matters.

November 7

PROGRESSIVE

I thought it was kind of endearing when my best friend in college gave me a license-plate holder that read, HOW CAN I BE BROKE WHEN I STILL HAVE CHECKS? It was a nod to Reese Witherspoon's character in *Legally Blonde*, although I was long out of college by the time that movie debuted,. There weren't many adorable, airheaded yet smartfemale role models in the '90s.

I digress. The license-plate holder felt like a sign that I had good taste and was destined to live a life of luxury. In truth, it was a sign that I was on my way to a debting problem.

When I was sent to DA by a credit counselor after college, I didn't think it was a big deal. How could I be a debtor when I had no money? Yes, I had impeccable taste, but I wasn't raised with a silver spoon. Major debt was a rich person's problem since they were the only ones who could get big loans. I went to two meetings and never went back.

When I returned to DA many years, and a ton of debt later, I was desperate. My debting had gotten out of control and DA was the "last house on the block" for me. And I'm not talking proverbially; it was literally the last house. As in, I was homeless. I finally understood what "they" meant when they said debting was "progressive" and if left untreated, it only gets worse with time.

This second time around in DA, I stayed because I was ready to change. I worked the Steps, used the Tools, and took the direction I was given. Today my life is more fulfilling than it's ever been. My relationship with God and others continues to grow and improve all the time.

Now my license-plate holder reads, I'D RATHER BE SKIING, because it's true. And when I go on those ski trips around the country, I always pay for them with cash. Now, how progressive is that?

It's Not About The Money:

I'm progressing to a better life, one day at a time.

November 8

MENTORS

I always dreamt of having a mentor. Someone who'd discover my talent, take me under his or her wing, and show me how to become super successful. Someone who'd show me how to get everything I wanted in the easiest, quickest way possible. I figured a mentor would speed the process up, and I had no problem riding someone else's coattails.

Most of my mentors have been of the spiritual sort, not superstar business executives or celebrities. My mentors have been the people who couldn't stand me, people who appeared to be selfish, arrogant, and egotistical.

Folks who held the mirror up to me, reflecting aspects of myself I didn't like.

At the risk of sounding overly spiritual or trite, my mentors are everywhere. And they're usually there to remind me of things like staying "right-sized" –no better than or less than anyone else–and being kind and helpful. I've yet to meet a mentor who was interested in showing me how to earn millions from my charming personality, or tell me I was perfect and hand me the keys to a new Porsche and an oceanfront mansion.

The mentors who've taught me the most are the ones I would never in a million years have chosen. And they probably wouldn't have chosen me, either. I say probably, though, because I'm basically a delightful person who's a lot of fun to be around. The mentors who didn't choose me are the ones who missed out.

It's Not About The Money:

Would you be, could you be, won't you be my mentor?

November 9

WILLING

Sometimes I seem willing to try new behaviors, but it's not true. I say I'm open, but I'm not. I was going to continue writing this whole meditation in the first person so as not to offend, but let's face it: you're a debtor. You debt, therefore you owe. By definition, you're not willing. And at this point in the book, I think we've built up enough good faith for me to call a spade a spade.

Sure, you might be willing–if you know you'll get something at the end of the engagement or the job or the relationship. But you aren't always as willing if it means acknowledging your selfishness and impatience. And, be honest, if there's nothing to be had from whatever it is you're doing, wouldn't you rather skip it and go see a movie? I'm with you. Go the extra mile? Not unless there's some guarantee involved. I can relate.

The Twelve Steps teach us to be willing. When we turn our will and our lives over to a god of our understanding, we increase our ability to grow. Willingness gives us the courage to take contrary action and show up for others. In recovery, we learn to do for others without asking for anything in return, because that makes our lives better.

I have to ask for willingness twenty to fifty times a day. Even then, I don't always have it. Or sometimes I get it and then lose it.

Nevertheless, I continue to ask for willingness because it opens the door to joy and recovery. I also keep asking for a goldendoodle puppy but I haven't gotten that yet, either. I'm still willing.

It's Not About The Money:

God, help me to remain willing, even when there are no cash prizes.

November 10

TWO FERS

"Our Public Relations Policy is based on attraction rather than promotion."
– DA Tradition #11

Debtors Anonymous doesn't promote or advertise its recovery outside the rooms of the program. This is why you will never see a sign outside a meeting room that says Fifty percent off recovery, this week only! or 2 for 1 Discount, or Bring a Friend, Get Better Faster. (I like that last one, though, because I know *exactly* whom I'd bring with me.)

No promotions, no discounts, no special offers. I don't have to sell or promote the Program of DA. Besides, when I tell most people I'm in Debtors Anonymous, they have no idea what it means. They usually assume I'm a kleptomaniac.

The thing I love most about the fellowship of DA is that, just by showing up to a meeting, I immediately feel understood and more connected to my Higher Power. This in and of itself is a huge load off, because I don't want to be forced to take part of any special offer, or become part of someone's "marketing downline" to participate in DA. Where else in the world is it fine for me to just be my neurotic self who is kooky around money, time, the future, the past, and the present? Where else can I go and tell the truth about my oddball responses to life and not have to worry I'm not doing it right? That's right. Nowhere.

It's Not About The Money:

There's no discount for recovery, but you can still bring a friend.

November 11

FRAUD

Before I started recovering from debt, I felt like an impostor, like I should've come equipped with a fraud alert – you know, the kind that can be put on credit cards? I feared being exposed as the fake I was. A Phony. Potential Asperger's Patient. ADD. ADHD. Mentally Challenged. Person Who Will Inevitably Screw Everything Good Up.

It was very strong, this internal fear that someday, someone would pull the covers off me and the world would see I was a big, fat charlatan.

Then I read a survey that said that ninety percent of the respondents feared they were faking their way through life, living in dread they'd be found out as imposters at any moment.

In recovery I learned that the only way for me to get past the fraud alert angst was to get busy and stay busy: seeking a connection to God, asking for directions, and doing whatever was next on my to-do list.

The trepidation may never go away, but it gets quieter when I spend time in service to others. Nowadays I seldom feel like a fraud, except when I'm wearing exceptionally high heels or talking to a stockbroker or a mathematician. Or scientist. Or professional athlete. Or neurosurgeon.

It's Not About The Money:
You really have nothing to hide.

November 12

GIVER

I wasn't that big on giving without expecting something back, at the very least a public "thank you" or a lifetime of total allegiance. I would've preferred a float in the Rose Parade but that never happened.

The truth is, I wasn't receiving a ton of "thanks" because I didn't give that freely. Sure, I'd help out the homeless–though not if it included the option for them to use my shower–and I'd do favors for friends but not if it would put me out. I reasoned it away: *I have so little, what can I offer others?* I gave only if it served me by making me look better or feel okay about myself.

When I started working the Twelve Steps of DA and got feedback from friends I trusted, I began to see I was less of a giver and more of a taker. I took peoples' time, borrowed their resources, and felt fairly entitled to the things I got. Seeing that in myself, as uncomfortable as it was, allowed me to come clean.

The DA Promise #12: "*We will recognize a Power greater than ourselves as the source of our abundance...*" encouraged me to be generous and share my resources, because my Higher Power is the source of my abundance, and the size of the gift doesn't matter. It can be spending time with a friend, using my creativity, or simply giving a compliment to someone at the grocery store.

I no longer force myself to do things so I'll be worthy of a parade, nor do I withhold my generosity because I've determined that what I have isn't enough. I guess what I'm saying is, I've become a bit of a giver. And you know what? The more I give, the more I receive, so in that sense, in my giving it's almost like I'm taking!

It's Not About The Money:
God, show me how to give more than I take.

November 13

FEELING GOOD

"The only way to do great work is to love what you do. If you haven't found it yet, keep looking. Don't settle." – *Steve Jobs*

Even with something as inspiring and fun as writing this meditation book, there comes a moment when it becomes a job. And that's when the love starts to fade.

For me, the loving feelings began to wane when things like math or contracts came into it, or things got boring. Or when I'm expected to deliver it to someone on a deadline. Clocking in and out is also a no-go. Heavy lifting? No, thanks.

I've decided not to follow the saying "Love what you do" because firstly, there are too many sayings being thrown around without regards to their meaning, and secondly, it's a setup for disappointment, especially for debtors, who expect everything to be handed to us on a silver platter, and who want something for nothing.

Instead I will say to myself, "I'll do work I enjoy, which is pretty much a lot of things." Then I'll tell myself that even cool gigs become routine, and although I may start out doing something I love, there'll be days when I won't enjoy it, because some days I'm just difficult and not that happy.

DA has taught me that I'm bigger than my feelings of boredom and monotony and even enjoyment. I don't have to be in a chronic state of euphoria or excitement. I can just do normal. Besides, *nothing* feels good all the time. Mostly *all* things don't feel good all the time.

Even when things I love get dull and humdrum, I remind myself that my mood always improves when I show up and finish the work I've committed to do that day.

It's Not About The Money:

Finish one thing you love today.

November 14

INNER CRITIC

I used to have a harsh inner critic. I was pretty severe when it came to judging my own actions.

No matter what I accomplished, my inner critic was always lurking around, waiting to nail me. And she was relentless. She was never happy so I had to tread lightly. I couldn't slap her on the arm and say, "Lighten up, mate. You're way to serious!" because I knew it would make things worse. Besides, my inner critic was a part of me, a human with feelings, so if I yelled at her I'd be yelling at myself.

One day I started a dialogue with my inner critic and what she told me was, "I say what I say because I just don't want you to make a fool of yourself or waste your life pursuing pointless dreams." I wanted to say, "Well, it's too late for that, my friend," but I didn't, because I knew she was doing her best to make me a better person, the kind who paid her bills on time and didn't overspend. She didn't know it wasn't her job to fix me, and that even if it was, she wouldn't accomplish that by being bitchy.

When I got into DA, my inner critic pitched a fit. She kicked and screamed and got really loud. At first I felt bad for her, but ultimately I had to tell her it was time to pipe down because I wanted to recover.

"I'll listen to you as long as you're civil. If you're going to be mean, I'll tell you good night and walk out of the room!"

We're working things out, my inner critic and I, and our relationship is much better since I started standing my ground. I know she's doing her best, but as those in therapeutic settings tend to say, I must "set some boundaries." And every so often, I do. There are times, though, when I can get my inner critic to shut up by buying her a frozen yogurt.

It's Not About The Money:

I don't have to yell at myself. Neither does anyone else.

November 15

PROMISES

When designing the cover for this book, I was tempted to fill it with images of prosperity: an expensive car, designer clothes, a yacht, and a lot of diamonds, because people told me it's what sells books, especially a book about money.

I was advised to use a title like "Grow Super Rich and Extra Spiritual," or "Make Millions by Doing Nothing," or "Attract More Prosperity This Afternoon" –anything that promised success and wealth. I was tempted to do it because I know it works. They're the kinds of books I used to buy.

I should have called this book, *Forget About the Money, Folks, This Is About Turning Your Will Over and Having a Spiritual Experience.*

Recovery doesn't promise us anything. Living a spiritual life and working a Twelve-Step program doesn't assure me a better job, a nicer home, or higher-quality…anything.

While in recovery, I've had money and I've been miserable. I've also been broke and miserable. I've had no money and been happy, and I've had a lot of money and been happy. I've also been to Austin while I was in recovery and I loved it. I've been to Chicago and I wasn't all that fond of the weather. But that was before recovery, so I might give it another chance because I loved the people.

What I'm saying is, money and prosperity aren't guaranteed, but contentment and peace are. Of all the things I've owned and experienced, so far my DA recovery, while challenging, has brought me the deepest satisfaction.

Now I don't have a yacht or an expensive car or a massive home, but I finally have a kind and loving Higher Power and serenity. As corny as it sounds, I feel wealthy inside. I know, that last sentence won't help sell as many books as – *"This Book Will Show You How to Get Stinkin' Rich Overnight"* – but it's the truth. And it's a promise.

It's Not About The Money:

I promise, it really isn't about the money.

November 16

MAGIC

Sometimes I get so inspired by what I've learned in DA, I'd like to scream, "Wake up, people! You don't need money to create or experience an amazing life!" I want to do it from a mountaintop with a megaphone so everyone can hear it. At least, anyone who happens to be nearby. Actually, I have a pretty loud voice so I wouldn't even need a megaphone.

I just feel the need to remind people that when we're caught up in pursuing the dollar, we stop noticing the small miracles. We stop being curious about the simple pleasures and don't spend time indulging in nature or enjoying the freedom of doing nothing.

Money may bring choices, but it certainly can't substitute for a relationship with a Higher Power, or the sense of awe you get when you're living in the moment. When we're forced to rely on God to provide the next thing we need, our level of trust grows.

Can I say that learning to live from moment to moment is a lot of fun? No. Can I say that life is calmer when I have money? Yes, because it gives me more options. But money can't compare to my ability to create, nor can it match the power of my mind when it's engaged and learning. Money will never take the place of physical health, or the sweetness of a good friend, or the joy I feel when I'm exploring nature.

Okay, I'll put the megaphone down now.

It's Not About The Money:

I'm gonna shout it to myself today: It's not about the money!

November 17

NO! YES!

I just read an article that suggests the harder I try to change, the more I will find people who want me to stay the same. According to the theory, our brains are afraid of change, especially when it's good, because change might not be safe and our brains crave safety.

Strange, no?

Odd that my brain wants safety more than anything else, and that change, even if it's good, is so risky that my brain and the people around me don't like it. The study notes that even new people I meet will challenge my new behavior.

Sometimes I get mad at my brain. Why would it be so unkind to me when I'm just trying to improve myself? Why can't my brain just give me a break? Isn't life challenging enough?

I don't know why my brain is the way it is.

I don't necessarily like the fact my cerebellum is actively working against me so I've decided to say no to that part of my brain. It's not easy, but it's what I must do, say "no" to the part of my brain that wants me to regress, and to the people who want me to stay stuck.

So I give myself a nice little pat on the head and remind my brain that it can trust me. Then, I yell out "yes" to the change, and "no" to the staying stuck, until my brain gets so confused that it can't remember how to keep me from changing.

It's Not About The Money:
No to the stuck and yes to the changes!

November 18

'LOOMIES

"You can just f--k off!" the woman screamed at me.

It was Thanksgiving and I'd been working at a retail store we'll call 'Loomingdale's. People were being given fifteen-dollar gift cards for every hundred dollars they spent.

This particular woman hadn't spent enough to get a second gift card, so I explained to her she'd need to spend more money to get an additional card.

"Why don't you just give it to me, for goodness sakes. I'm only five dollars short of another hundred dollars!" she demanded in a shrill British accent.

When I told her I wasn't authorized to do that, and she'd have to purchase something else totaling five dollars or more, she flipped out, hurling a string of expletives at me. I'd never heard a Brit scream like that before. It was kind of cute but also...offensive.

What a jerk, I thought as she continued to shriek, demanding that I consider changing the store's gift card policy on her behalf. Actually, I thought of something much harsher, but I'm trying to impart a spiritual message so I'll leave it at that.

I started to spin out about what an entitled, greedy cow she was–until I remembered all the times I'd been rude because I was afraid I wasn't getting my "fair share," or I wasn't going to get what I thought was my fair share.

I imagined how much fear she must have been in to behave that way, and said a prayer for her. And then I imagined what Her Royal Highness would look like as she fell down the escalator with those damn gift cards in hand.

It's Not About The Money:
Thank God it's progress, not perfection.

November 19

CONSCIOUS CONTACT

"Sought through prayer and meditation to improve our conscious contact with God…" – *DA Step # 11*

The meditation part of this step used to make my heart leap because I was not the meditative type.

Spending time getting to know my mind and myself better was not hugely interesting to me. I'd had a glimpse of what was going on inside and delving deeper into that mess wasn't a comforting thought.

I agonized for a long time about Step #11, about how I should learn to be that person who meditated. Then, one day a friend of mine shared in a meeting that meditation had changed his life. I asked him how long it took him to get comfortable with meditating.

"About fifteen years," he said.

I'd never done *anything* in my life for fifteen years.

I haven't started meditating, but I do pray. Sometimes it's formal, like reading one of the prayers I'd memorized as a child. At other times it's a casual talk with God, you know like, "Hey, God, it's me, just checking in. I don't have any of this figured out yet but I'm doing my best. Could you help me today with whatever I have to do and show me how to be the person you want me to be? Thank you."

Meditation still stresses me out, so instead I go for a run or sit in silence under the stars at night. At other times, I'll go for a hike or listen to classical music, anything that's meditative and soothing to me. I've learned to do what feels natural to me; it doesn't have to be formal or prescribed to me by other people. As long as it's improving my conscious contact, it's good enough.

It's Not About The Money:

Am I improving my conscious contact? Then it's enough.

November 20

ASAP

I need a plan so I can recover. Now.

What? Five years?

I don't have five years. I need results now. I could be dead in five years! I might be on the streets with a knotted beard, drinking Nyquil from a brown bag. There are a whole host of things that could happen in five years.

Two years?

Well, that's a bit of an insult when I'm standing here, right now, wanting to change today. Look, whatever you're saying it's going to take is too long. I need help today. I need changes to happen now. ASAP.

A year?

Are you kidding me? I don't have a year. In a year I could lose my fingers in a boating accident. No, I don't have a boat, but that really isn't the point here. My life is a mess and it's only getting worse. The longer we stand here debating this, the worse it gets. I may not have twelve months left.

Six months?

262,974 minutes? Way too long.

A month?

That's thirty days or thirty-one. Even that's kind of pushing it when you're starting where I am. For goodness sakes, I've seen people lose everything overnight.

Forget it. I don't have time for recovery. Sorry. I need something to happen now. I don't even think I have time to finish this sente–

It's Not About The Money:
It's okay, we've got plenty of time.

November 21

SIGNS

I'm not really sure exactly what my DA sponsor said, but what I heard was, "Stop acting like a victim. The world isn't conspiring against you."

At first I thought, *What does he mean by that? Has he been talking to my boss or listening in on my phone calls? Checking my e-mails?*

The truth is, I was being singled out, for a lifetime of misery and financial failure. While I won't go so far as to call it a conspiracy, there had been recent incidents involving a parking attendant and the way the teller at my bank behaved the last time I went in. The barista at my favorite Starbucks had given me pause. The people in my DA home group weren't being very nice, either. As for God, we hadn't connected in weeks.

Yes, I believe there might have been some sort of "meeting of the minds" of certain people conspiring to take me down.

I'm not some weirdo doomsday prepper with a bunker stockpiled with dehydrated peas and ammunition, but there are times when I wonder if the people who love me and the people who can't stand me are actively planning my demise.

And just because I don't have proof doesn't mean it's not happening. The signs are all around me. I'm a debtor and we are experts at analyzing this stuff.

It's Not About The Money:

The signs are all around me.

November 22

NO COMPRENDO

Despite my desire for this not to be true, DA has taught me that comprehending the past rarely does much to help me create the future.

Working a program of recovery allows me to identify my patterns, and that allows me to accept what I've done and why I've done it and forgive myself, but that alone doesn't change my behavior.

I have to decide to change, work with others in program, and release the past. It's only by looking forward–not backward–that I will ever change my patterns and do things differently.

Yes, it's a bummer because I love wallowing. It's familiar to sink into feelings of depression over how bad my life is, how hard my life used to be, and how much I've had to overcome. At times I even get dramatic about it and throw myself on the bed like Jan Brady screaming, "I hate my life!" But inevitably, I come up for air and call another debtor in recovery.

No matter who picks up the phone, I'm always reminded that the past holds nothing for me. It's only in choosing to think and act differently that I can create a new life.

You know, even though I often hate the person on the other end of the phone when I hear words like "contrary action" or "being of service," but I'm always humbled by the truth when I hear it, especially when I hear the phrase "it works if you work it." Truly, it does.

Don't try to comprehend, just have the best day you can today.

It's Not About The Money:
They don't call it the present for nothing.

November 23

MORALITY TALE

A woman was off to meet friends for dinner and had promised herself she'd go only if she had the cash. After a thorough ramsacking of her house resulted in not even an extra dollar, she remembered her daughter's adorable Little Pony Princess handbag that contained a hundred dollars in cash and a few marshmallows. She'd borrow some of the money from her daughter and return it when she got her next paycheck.

Two days later, the woman needed more money, so she decided to take the remainder of the cash from the handbag and pay it back in one lump sum. The following day, she crept back into her daughter's stash and pillaged the remaining loose change. As she was taking the last bit of change, her daughter discovered her in the closet.

"What are you doing, Mommy?" the little girl asked.

"Just making sure you have all your marshmallows," the woman whispered as she handed over the Little Pony handbag.

"The marshmallows are here but all my money's gone," the girl muttered.

"I invested it, honey, but I promise I'll give it back to you in no time, with interest."

The little girl didn't forget and continued to ask about her money. Weeks later, the mother replaced the money but forgot about the interest.

The next day her daughter approached her. "Mommy, I'm just a kid, so I'm not mad at you for not including the 5.8% interest I should've earned on this loan. But it's clear you don't know what you're doing when it comes to investing, so from here on out, I'll be handling these things. And, Mommy, you shouldn't lie to your daughter."

It's Not About The Money:

God, show me where I could be more honest.

November 24

HEAR, HERE

Recovery in DA requires that I expose myself–in the appropriate manner–to others in program. That includes being transparent about what I'm struggling with, where I've blown it, and where I need help and support.

When I think about some of the actions I've taken, or things I've said while under the influence of debting, I feel pretty foolish. And when I repeat them aloud to others, sometimes I feel even worse.

But I can't recover if I don't tell the truth. I need to be free to be real with others without judgment and with complete anonymity.

Anonymity is critical to recovery, which is why DA meetings say things like "what we hear here, stays here." When I know what I'm sharing is private and will never be shared with anyone else outside of a meeting, I can share honestly and feel totally safe.

Anonymity allows me to experience safety. And openness. And ultimately, healing.

From there, who knows what else is possible? World peace, a softening of the polar caps–or would that be hardening? All I'm saying is expose yourself–in the appropriate manner–a little. Give authenticity a chance. And give peace a chance while you're at it.

It's Not About The Money:

Give authenticity and full exposure chance today.

November 25

BLESSINGS

Most of the time I do not want what I have. Counting my blessings is something I forget to do because I'm often busy counting the things I don't have.

In recovery, I discovered the antidote for my insatiable greed lies in remembering my blessings. Whether the things I have in abundance are love, kindness, or time, the only way to increase them is by giving those very things away to others. When I get out of my head and search for ways to give to others, I feel abundant and am reminded of how blessed I am.

I don't do these things because I'm noble. It's because I have learned in recovery that the want-what-you-already-have mentality works when I do it. It's the only thing that leads to serenity. When I take time to list the good things I have, my state of mind and my mood change. I lighten up, and even if things don't change immediately, I always feel better.

Sometimes I have to start small, like making the commitment to not yell at other drivers. Sometimes I can only commit to smiling at three people I don't know. Other times, it's doing something nice for someone else and not telling anyone I did it.

Even if my contributions are small, it gets easier to do more as the day goes on. Mostly. There are times when it gets harder to be nice and loving as the day goes on, but not often. On average, I would say I have a 98% success rate at my day improving when I decide to want what I have and share my blessings with others. That's a fairly good percentage, I'm sure you would agree?

It's Not About The Money:

Today I will want what I have.

November 26

DEBTORS PUMPKIN PIE RECIPE

This one's been in my family for years. Enjoy!

1 freezer-burned piecrust, leftover from last year
8 cups festering anger at health insurance company
1 oz. stop at a Payday Loan to buy these ingredients
1 lb. of pumpkin to go in what, I don't know; do I look like I know how to make a pie from scratch?
1 dollop of superiority

Place pumpkin and sugar in a bowl. Offer a ten-minute monologue about how you'd've been on time, but your car was repossessed and you *wanted* to retrieve your valuables–the credit cards that would allow you to catch up on rent–but it was gonna cost whatever the repo guy felt like charging. Since he only accepted cash, you had to stop by Payday Loans.

Wonder aloud how the world's gotten to the point where banks can do whatever they like. Mention the story of the old lady who fell for a check fraud scam. When her bank told her they were going to take her Social Security check to cover the overdraft fees, she closed the account and went to another bank, but was blacklisted and unable to open an account anywhere

Toss in a comment about how all this economic instability makes it hard for you to remember things like what goes into a stupid pumpkin pie. Storm into the bathroom and refuse to come out until someone turns down the damn TV and asks you how therapy is going.

Return to the kitchen to finish layering the pumpkin mixture into a mostly frozen piecrust. Crank the oven to 650°, and wait until your aunt and her boyfriend arrive to show off their identical neck tattoos.

Before dinner's halfway over, begin clearing the table, complaining about what a scam it is that banks can charge fees to cash checks written by their own customers. Smile and tell everyone you hope they've enjoyed the pumpkin pie you made from scratch.

It's Not About The Money:

Nothing like spending Thanksgiving with a debtor!

November 27

THE BIRD

I recall being so angry about having to pay rent and utilities that I'd pay them late, even when I had enough money.

That damn mortgage company has a heck of a lot more money than I do, I remember thinking. *Why should I pay the loan on time?* I would get especially angry if the payment involved the government or a large institution. So I'd pay late and feel completely justified.

In other words, I was a deadbeat. A deadbeat who was flipping the bird to a universe that had screwed me over. At least that's what my reptilian brain was telling me. I never once considered this approach to life might not be normal.

My natural reaction is victimization in its finest form. Unless I have a spiritual practice, my lower brain will be running the show and that victim-like attitude will seep into every area of my life. I'll start noticing things like how little people care for me, how underappreciated I am at work, how life isn't fair.

For me, debting is not as much about owing money or how I do or don't spend it, as it is about my attitude and my level of willingness. Debting is not so much about the amount of money I owe as it is about the anger I have toward having to do life like "normal" people. It's the feeling there's just never enough–in my life, my heart, and my bank account.

It goes on and on from there, unless I get on my knees and ask for my Higher Power's help.

The thing is, I can flip the bird to the universe and to my creditors, but ultimately that bird is gonna get flipped back at me. I imagine a flipped bird is an unhappy bird, and I'm scared of unhappy birds. I once had a friend whose ostrich got so mad at her that it tried to peck her to death. It hurt just to hear about it.

It's Not About The Money:

I'm not flipping anyone off today, thanks to my Higher Power's help.

November 28

EYES

Every time I heard "He had an eye toward the future..." I always wondered, What about that second eye? Wouldn't it be better to have both eyes set on the future?

When I consider my future, I want both my eyes on it. Heck, I want my eyes, ears, nose, fingers, and feet all pointed toward the future, while I'm at it.

In DA I've learned it's important not to do anything half-arsed. Or half-eyed, in this case.

So, as we trudge the path to happy destiny together, I say we do it with both eyes and both feet planted firmly in the here and now, all while focusing on the future–which is asking a lot for commitmentphobes and perpetual juveniles, as debtors are known to be.

And, in the event that you can only commit to lending one eye toward the future, I will be with you in spirit my fellow debtor. Because that's just what we do for each other. Should do for each other. At least, it's what I think we should do for each other.

It's Not About The Money:

Go on, you can have both eyes towards your future.

November 29

PUMP OR STOMP

Today is either Stomp Out Pessimism Day or Practice Optimism Day, whichever you prefer.

If you're a pessimist by nature, you'll probably go with Stomp Out Pessimism, whereas if you lean toward optimism, you'll choose Practice Optimism. Alas, there is no right or wrong!

In optimism there is magic. In pessimism there is nothing. In optimism, there is joy and hope. In pessimism there is lacking and crankiness.

It's pretty simple–you either want the prime rib filet from a top-notch steak house, or you're gonna settle for a quarter-pound "burger" made from connective tissue and plant materials from a fast-food joint.

I'm not preachin'; I'm just reporting. But I think you're with me now, yes?

What you're going to do today, my little chickens, is cultivate a lack of pessimism or an increase in optimism. As confusing as that might sound, it's quite easy. The point is not to lie to yourself about things being great if they aren't, or to deny what is missing from your life. The point is to get your focus on what is decent right now!

Today, there will be several things required of you. First, write down one thing that makes you happy and keep the note handy. Second, talk to two new people today. And three, smile at five people. I know, your internal pessimist is saying, "How the heck can this help?" but your little optimist is saying, "This is going to be such fun!"

My internal optimist thinks you're going to have a exceptional day!

It's Not About The Money:

Pump it up or stomp it out!

November 30

MATURE

"To be mature you have to realize what you value most. It is extraordinary to discover that comparatively few people reach this level of maturity. They seem never to have paused to consider what has value for them. They spend great effort and sometimes make great sacrifices for values that, fundamentally, meet no real needs of their own. Perhaps they have imbibed the values of their particular profession or job, of their community or their neighbors, of their parents or family..."

– Eleanor Roosevelt

The quote goes on to say that not having a clear understanding of your values is a real waste, and if you've allowed that to happen to you, you've missed the point of life. That seems to be a slightly negative note to end on, so I've decided to add a bit to Mrs. Roosevelt's thought.

Even if you have allowed other people to define your values up until this moment, your life is not a waste. You can decide now to change. Even if you haven't taken time to pause and consider what you value, you can do so today. Just because someone else tells you something is important doesn't mean you have to agree with that person.

Get on your knees and ask your Higher Power to show you where and how you should be spending your time and energy. Find out what you value and start moving toward it, no matter how tiny the movement. It's never too late to clarify what you value and take action. That's a much sweeter note to end on, don't you agree?

It's Not About The Money:

Today, I will pause to consider what I value.

December 1

RESULTS

"Having had a spiritual awakening as the result of these steps, we tried to carry this message to compulsive debtors and practice these principles in all our affairs."
– DA Step #12

Note that one word. The. Not a result, but the result. It's not,"Hey, it could happen," but "it will happen." It's a promise that when we work the program, we are guaranteed a spiritual awakening as the result.

That promise meant very little to me when I came to DA. I wasn't looking for a religious experience. I had no desire to seek out the deeper mysteries of the universe, I wasn't in pursuit of some kind of existential joy. I just wanted to be able to pay the rent and get those pesky credit card companies off my back.

But I started to read the twelve steps and I kept gravitating back to the promise in Step #12 because it meant something to me. I wanted a bigger life, one filled with purpose and meaning. As I continued on the DA path, I began to desire spiritual connection more and more, and there came a day when that promise meant the world to me. I was so grateful for the hope and help DA had given me, I wanted to share it with others, if they wanted it.

It's funny–I didn't hit the big time, I didn't start earning a huge income, and yet I feel like, because of what I've learned in recovery, I have more to offer now than in my entire life. More than when I made a ton of money and had a better home and car.

Don't get me wrong, I'm no Ghandi, but the results of the hard work I've put into the program are starting to show. And it's not like anyone should expect anything grand of me, because they'd be sorely let down. I'm just saying I think the recovery thing is starting to work.

It's Not About The Money:

Holy cow, the results of a spiritual program are starting to show!

December 2

GRATITUDE

I used to hate the word "gratitude." It was so nauseatingly spiritual, and the last thing on my mind when I got into DA was being spiritual.

Until I could say the word "grateful" aloud without feeling like a phony, I used the word "appreciative." It was my way of admitting I was grateful without saying it. God knows I didn't want to be throwing around cheesy clichés like the strange people I had met in DA.

Instead of being grateful, I decided to count the things I appreciated about my life. I started small, noting things like a pretty sunset or someone being nice to me. Or the fact that I had my health.Soon enough, I caught myself saying, "I'm so grateful," and really meaning it. At first it felt odd, hearing those words come out of my mouth, but in time it began to feel natural, even pleasant.

Without planning to be, I'd become Grateful Girl.

Now I enjoy being known as someone who is grateful, because I truly am. I'm grateful for how much better my life is. It might not be exactly the way I want it to be, but it is good. So, my sweet little chickens, if you're feeling uncomfortable about being the "grateful type," stick around. It will grow on you.

It's Not About The Money:
Stick around. You'll get grateful.

December 3

SCENES

In a lot of modern American films, there's a requisite scene that occurs when the filmmaker gets lazy, tired, or both.

It's the scene where the once wimpy main character finally stands up to her malicious, immoral boss and makes some fantastic speech about how he can't hold her back any longer. As she picks up her handbag and last paycheck and marches through a row of cubicles, her colleagues fall in line like dominos and applaud. The music swells as she delights in her newfound courage.

If the filmmaker is really lazy, the man of her dreams stops her in the middle of the aisle and gives her a big, juicy kiss.

I always thought I was playing the part of the heroine. Railing against The System, taking on causes that weren't mine to take on. Ironically, when I did those things, the people I thought I was liberating ignored or avoided me, even when they agreed with me. They cheered me on in private, but when the time came to step up, they were all about saving their own butts. They most definitely weren't about saving mine.

No one applauded or kissed *me* after I made my final, award-winning speech. They just sent me home with a box filled with all my belongings.

In recovery, I've learned that not everything has to be a scene. While I'm not in a movie or Showtime series–although I think that would be fun–I can disagree with others without making a federal case out of things. I do not represent "the people," so there's no need to make grandiose pronouncements to the powers that be. I'm a worker among workers. My work is to show up, do the best job possible, and serve God and others.

Since I've cut out those obligatory liberation scenes in my own life that usually go nowhere, work isn't nearly as dramatic as it used to be. But it sure is more interesting.

It's Not About The Money:

Life is not as dramatic as it used to be, but it's definitely interesting.

December 4

THE AVOIDER

I used to have this thing about being undervalued, especially when it came to work situations. I was always on high alert and worrying about being underpaid.

The truth is, I often *was* underpaid and undervalued, because I didn't value myself. As a result, I'd avoid salary negotiations and accept whatever was offered, or be so inflexible during contract negotiations that I'd come off as a money-grubber. Being the avoider was my more common approach. That's when I'd accept less than what I wanted but I'd pout about it. I reasoned that since I had settled for an underearning job, I was justified in doing a half-assed job or showing up late.

My DA inventory showed me that I had made the decision to take those opportunities, and I had to ask myself, Who was shortchanging whom? Me or them? Them or me? Eux ou moi?

I was told to let God be my employer, which scared me at first I didn't get the concept but I gave it a shot. Every morning before my job search, or before a project, I would pray:

"Okay, God, you're the boss, and although I don't know if I like that, I'll give it a try. I hope you don't relegate me to lousy jobs, or stiff me at the end of the pay period. Help me to be a good employee, whatever that means. Amen."

In time my perspective changed. I put my focus on doing my best work, and in turn I began to attract opportunities where I was well paid and worked with great people.

Nowadays, no one can undervalue me unless I allow it and I no longer avoid negotiations. But I'm less concerned about being shortchanged than doing my best for my New Boss Upstairs, because, trust me, you don't want to be known as a shoddy employee when you report to You-Know-Who.

It's Not About The Money:

Nowadays, there's not much to avoid.

December 5

HEART

"My heart's telling me to quit my crappy job," announced the woman I was giving a PRG to; the same woman who was on the verge of losing her home because of her debt.

"Tell me more about that," I said.

"I believe in following my heart, and it's telling me that things will work out, but I need to quit my job so I can pursue my dreams."

"And what is your brain saying?" the sole male member of the PRG asked."Uh...I haven't asked my brain what it thinks."

If there's one thing we debtors love doing, it's trying to convince ourselves that ignoring our responsibilities in favor of a reward that has practically no chance of happening is a good idea. Sure, we have bills to pay and food to buy, but what of our *dreams and visions?*

What debtors mean when we say we're following our heart is, we've decided to set aside reason, ignore the consequences, and trust that our emotionally charged guess will prove to be right. Only a debtor in danger of losing her house because she can't pay the mortgage will spend money on books or vision quests that are so expensive she could've used the money to pay off a her debt.

And most debtors don't even know what we mean when we say our "heart." Is it gut instinct? A supernatural urging? A result of not having had enough sleep the night before? In reality, the urges that tell us to do insane things almost always spring from our addiction to chaos.

"Your heart gets a voice but your brain gets the final word," I said, surprised by my own wisdom.

"There's nothing wrong with having a dream, but I suggest you findanother job before you quit your current one," my PRG partner stated.

In our fantasies, following our heart always pays off. In recovery, it's about the *worst* way to make a decision. Sometimes we need the support of others and some good old-fashioned logic. At other times, we need a slap upside the head. A gentle slap, of course.

It's Not About The Money:

God, show me where my heart might be misleading me.

December 6

SUSCEPTIBLE

I received an email from my neighbor this morning, which read:

Dear Friend, Madame:

I discover I have inherit my Kingdom of a Nigerian Village. When I arrived here I discovered funds equivalent to $350 thousand Canadian dollars. The fund is presently with the bank awaiting my disbursement as beneficiary to the funds. Recently, my Doctor told me I would not last a month due to plantar fasciitis problem. Upon your reply I shall give you the contact of bank, will issue letter of authorization to bank that will prove you the present beneficiary of the money. Please reply to my email address to receive your benefits.

Sincere,
Ted

Even after all this time in DA, I was tempted. But then I thought of my recovery and how I'd feel if I sold my soul for a few hundred thousand dollars, Canadian. This was my reply:

Dear Ted,

I got your e-mail. I think you're wise to choose me as your beneficiary because I'm reliable and agreeable. I'm happy to do whatever you want with the money, even if it means spending it all on myself. When you die I'll remember you as the best neighbor I never bothered getting to know. I don't have my bank information, as my account was frozen, but I'll get it to you so I can get my money. Or I'll give you my information, you can pass it on to the bank, and they can mail me the money. Does that sound good? I hope so, and take care of those feet!

Sincere-ly
Me

It's Not About The Money:

Is there any area of my life where I'm feeling susceptible?

December 7

PONZI, SCHMONZI

"Remember Anna, the massage therapist?" my friend Sandy says, as she finishes tacking up a painting of Mao Tse-tung on the wall of her art gallery. "She bought a condo with the interest she earned from latex gloves!"

Sandy's just remodeled her house and bought an SUV with the money she's made from her investment in a Chinese latex glove manufacturer.

"If you want to make big bucks, you've gotta get in now," she continues, "I don't want you to miss out on a sure thing."

Six weeks after I invest my life savings into gloves, the company is shut down by the government, and the owners are accused of operating a billion-dollar Ponzi scheme. When I tell Sandy all my money – that's being held in an account in Belize – has been frozen by the government, she throws a middle finger in the air.

"Ponzi, Schmonzi," she says, as she jumps into her new SUV, "to hell with the U.S. government, trying to keep the proletariat down. I'm going to China, where workers get healthcare and six weeks' paid vacation."

Before DA, I was always on the lookout for a quick fix. I relied on "hot tips" and people who seemed to know best about how to earn money – which rarely included working hard and saving consistently. DA taught me to slow down, ask for direction from my Higher Power and get feedback on from reliable friends in program before handing over my money.

In DA I've learned there is no *fix* that's *quick*, and the beest financial tips I've gotten include: 1.) keep track of the numbers, 2.) stay out of debt, and 3.) leave the results up to God.

Today I avoid asking for "hot tips" from friends, even when they sound like a sure thing. Because even though my house could benefit from a remodel, I'd prefer to do it without government officials being involved.

It's Not About The Money:

No quick fixes. Just sanity and serenity.

December 8

THE WORST

Sometimes–okay, most of the time–when I receive an e-mail from my boss, I assume the worst. I'm convinced it's going to read something like, "I've decided it was a mistake to have hired you. You're vastly overpaid and a bit dim. Anyway, no need to come back tomorrow..."

Even in program, if I'm doing an excessive amount of thinking, I'm going to end up assuming the worst of myself, others, institutions, and especially the government.

The one exception: dogs. I almost always assume the best of intentions from dogs. I never, ever think they're going to attack, even though I was bitten by a German shepherd when I was seven. Maybe it's a character defect, maybe it's just my "stinkin' thinkin'," but it seems I'm always preparing for the worst. No one will show up for the party. He doesn't love me anymore. I have no friends left. It's probably skin cancer.

I'm so thankful I have DA because it reminds me that the problem is seldom "out there," it's usually my warped perception. And when I get out of my head and stop assuming the worst, things get better, even if only a little.

In DA, I get love and understanding from other people who know how I think and where I'm coming from, especially when I say things like, "My life is the worst it's ever been. It's never going to get better." They get it. They've been there, too. They've just chosen not to stay there. At least not permanently.

It's Not About The Money:

God, help me remember it's rarely the worst, ever.

December 9

BAFFLING

"I think it's great you're getting your life on track," my friend began, "but do you really need a twelve-step program to fix your money problems? Why don't you just get a better job and save some money?"

I love it when people say this. It's like when I was working in the film business, trying to get movies made, and my family would say to me, "Why don't you drop your script off to someone at Disney?" For a long time it drove me nuts, but after years of hearing that, I started saying, "That's a fantastic idea. I'll give it a shot!"

Unless someone has been under the influence of debting and can understand how deep the negative emotions or the obsession that goes along with it, that person can't understand why it requires help of a spiritual kind.

"It's a mental obsession, a fear that there isn't enough, and it really has very little to do with money," I said. "It can't be cured by a book or a seminar or changing my attitude. It requires a spiritual solution."

"You know what I think?" my friend said, patting my arm. "I think you've lived in California too long. But if it works, I'm happy for you."

Debting, compulsive spending, and underearning are symptoms of a "dis-ease" that is cunning and baffling. It's not something that an occasional meeting or a desire to change can fix. The only thing that keeps me spiritually sound and solvent has been the program of DA.

Recovery is a daily practice, a choice I make to stay out of debt, turn my will over to God, and be of service in all areas of my life. There's no magic involved, but there's also no other way around it. If there were a shortcut, you can bet I would've taken it.

It's Not About The Money:

Recovery is baffling, but it works if I work it.

December 10

ADVENTURE DAY

When I was a kid, I rode my red Pixie bike to school, to the store, on highways, wherever I wanted. I set up ramps with pieces of plywood to jump from and got into fistfights with boys who tried to stop me from mastering a wheelie. I had Adventures.

As an adult, I told myself I didn't have time for that kind of nonsense. I had to work and I couldn't afford Adventures. So, I stopped having them.

Today, my little chickens, is Debtor Adventure Day, and the activity is whatever you think would be fun or different–roller skating, eating a new food, riding a Ferris Wheel. The only rule is, it can't involve work or debting, borrowing or stealing.

I understand, you're a debtor, so first response to Adventure Day is, *I don't have time for fun. I have to work, or worry about finding work, or making money, dang it!*

There is no point to Adventure Day. There's no goal, nothing to conquer or accomplish. It doesn't have to cost money or be a big deal. Maybe you'll go dancing or eat ice cream, maybe you'll go rollerblading–it's entirely up to you!

Just open your heart and your mind and have an Adventure today, no matter how big or small. It doesn't have to include popping a wheelie or getting into a fistfight, just something unfamiliar. And legal.

It's Not About The Money:
Happy Adventure Day.

December 11

NO!

When I'm stressed out about money, I have a hard time saying no to jobs and situations that may not be good for me. This rarely ends well.

When I'm all about the money, I miss out on things I love doing and I settle for good enough. When I take on projects with people I know are difficult, just for the money, I don't enjoy myself. The odd part is, I rarely end up getting ahead financially. Something *always* happens–unforeseen car repairs, an emergency or setback of some sort–the rewards just aren't there.

When I spend day after day doing work I dislike, with people I dislike, it costs more than money. It depletes my energy, my peace of mind, and my affects my serenity. Working and earning money is necessary, of course, but my emotional energy is important. I seek to use my skills and my time in a way that God can bless. When I'm all about the money, I may be earning but there is a cost to me. It costs me my precious energy, my passion, and my serenity.

Saying "yes" to work I don't want to do is a big, juicy setup to resenting the person I've said "yes" to. When I'm operating from that place, I rarely dazzle anyone with my hard work, and ultimately I disappoint myself. I also end up acting like a spoiled brat. That's not very empowering, is it? I agree. It's not.

I've come to believe that my Higher Power wants me to work for more than money and what I can get out of it. God wants me to be of service to others, to maintain my serenity, and to fulfill myself.

It's Not About The Money:

I can say no when it's just about the money.

December 12

AWAKENING

In the beginning, recovery for me was simply not accruing unsecured debt. Once I'd been able to do that for a period of time, I figured I'd solved the whole money problem. I started keeping track of my spending, paying bills on time, starting to pay back my debt, and saving, if ever so little. I felt like I was building a life, attracting better places to work and harmony where I lived. I was able to look the world in the eye without shame.

After a few years in recovery, I began to dream again about my future instead of fearing the misery it might bring. The world began to appear friendly and welcoming rather than the nightmare it once was. Debting, at that point, under any circumstance, was unthinkable.

As I continue to recover and work the Twelve Steps, there are moments when I truly feel as if I'm experiencing the oft-promised spiritual awakening. Instead of dreading the future, I know what it means to feel real joy, and it has nothing to do with what's in my pocketbook. I'm able to be my authentic self, and I have an intuition about who I am and what I was created to do.

Prosperity and abundance have begun to take on much broader, yet deeper meaning. Abundance is a spiritual experience and emotional in nature. It's not like I'm floating on a cloud or living in some state of existential bliss. I don't always feel abundant but I know how to feel prosperous, and it *always* begins with gratitude. Ironically, it never includes anything to do with money or possessions.

It's Not About The Money:

Abundance has nothing to do with what's in my pocketbook.

December 13

REGRET

There are people who say they live by the philosophy of "no regrets," and they are some of the most irritating people I've ever met. Because they are lying. We *all* regret *something.*

One of the most painful moments in recovery is when we come to that distressing realization that things went wrong for no other reason than us. No one else caused them. It was us. And while it's important to remember that everything has led us to where we are now, there are some of us who spend plenty of time pondering paths not taken, or thinking about how fantastic life would have been if only we'd done it "right."

When I'm in the harrowing spiral of regret about things I have done or things I have not done, it never involves feelings of pleasure or peace. Regret whispers in my ear, "You could have done more. You could have." Regret refuses a place for God, and it certainly leaves no consideration for miracles.

Embracing and accepting choices I've made that I find regrettable is not easy. It takes courage to accept that things are exactly as they should be. It requires that I put my hope and faith in a loving God, and keep moving forward even when things don't work out according to my plan. I have to believe that God's plan is the best plan for my life, and that my "mistakes" are also included in what is meant to be.

For today, I will try to steer clear of all regrets, especially the one that's starting to bubble up in my head about how much more I could and should have done with today's meditation.

It's Not About The Money:

I may have regrets, but God can still work His plan.

December 14

THESE THINGS

There's an old *Sesame Street* song called, "One of These Things (Is Not Like the Others)." It reminds me of how I used to view the terms "solvency" and "sanity" in the early days of my recovery. Not only were the two words not like the other, they didn't even belong in the same sentence.

Sanity for me was about landing a boatload of money and paying off my debts. Solvency was, well, pretty much the same thing. Okay, I retract the "not like the other" comment. Let me put it this way: In the beginning of recovery, I didn't understand much about either.

What I *did* know was that solvency and sanity didn't happen at the same time. Early on, solvency–the practice of not incurring unsecured debt one day at a time–did not feel sane. It felt more like a death sentence. My less-than-solvent behaviors–vagueness, underearning, compulsive spending, and feeling entitled–felt like sanity. For a long time, keeping my numbers and commitments, going to meetings, calling for help when I needed it, and praying seemed pretty unreasonable.

In order to recover from debting, I had to change my behaviors, and new habits never feel sane to me. Okay, I can't say never because I did reach a point when acting sanely felt magnificent, but it took a while. Eventually, sanity felt healthy and solvency became an integral part of my recovery.

Today, each of those things is like the other. Although they're two different words with two different meanings, in most ways they seem like they should go together.

It's Not About The Money:
Solvency and sanity are a lot like each other.

December 15

INSANE MEMBRANE

There are times when I outright reject the entire "insanity" aspect of the twelve steps, as I do not think I am insane. At least, not like some other people.

I mean, I've been to the county fair and the dentist's office and man, there are some wacky folks there. My head tells me, *You might be peculiar but you are not insane.*

Then my heart will say, *Well, if I'm not insane, then why isn't my life working?*

And then my head says, *Who says life isn't working, Heart? You're a hollow muscle in the middle of my body that pumps blood. You have no ability to diagnose a mental condition!*

My heart replies, *Look, no one is saying you are mentally unstable. Insanity and DA–or any other twelve-step program–is defined as a lack of sound mind as an elective peace and serenity. Insanity is just the lack of a sound mind, Brain. The reason your life isn't working is because you're so damn judgmental!*

Then my head says, *Okay, well, when you put it that way, I don't reject that outright.*

Around and around my heart and my head will go on for hours before they both settle down. It hurts, because I want my heart and my head to be aligned. And because that kind of stress cannot be good for either of them. I know it's bad for my skin, and that alone is reason enough for me to stop.

It's Not About The Money:

Today, I'll do my best to ask my heart and my mind to be nice to each other.

December 16

VISION

Hey, it's the holidays, and since there's no shortage of catalogs lying around, it's the perfect time to create a vision board! Maybe you aren't a vision-board type, but keep an open mind, here. Consider that most really successful people created a vision board at some point in their lives. So, put your favorite music on your mp3 or cassette player (in which case, it's way past time for a vision board) and prepare for a little creative session.

You'll need a poster board, a glue stick, magazines, catalogs, books, maybe some paper and pens...doesn't this already sound like fun?!

First, take time to get quiet and picture yourself living the life you want. It doesn't have to be about "things," it could reflect your ideal reality, whether it's a strong marriage, or a paid off mortgage. It may include a car, a dream wedding, a new job or a house. Maybe it's learning to play tennis!

Start by pulling photos from magazines, catalogs, or cards and images from books–whatever floats your boat. As you glue the images you've selected on the board, mentally commit to those goals. If it's an activity, start telling yourself you will do it. This is the first step toward making your dreams a reality.

The powerful part of a vision board is that it keeps your goals front and center. Hang it where you'll see it every day, or take a photo of it and make it the background for your laptop or phone. Choose one goal to focus on next year and find creative ways to save up for it. It could be a jar labeled with a goal where you keep your loose change, or place all your five-dollar bills, instead of spending them.

Not only can a vision board help you decide where your money could go, it can tap into your longing to achieve things that seem out of reach right now. Even if it's just a teensy amount, the important thing is that you acknowledge one goal and direct energy toward it on a regular basis.

C'mon, visions are important, and they can't happen without dreaming, so take a little time today to do some dreaming. I know I'm going to!

It's Not About The Money:

Dream a little dream today.

December 17

GIMME, GIMME

I read story about a seven year-old girl's Christmas List, which included: A thousand dollars, a new grill, an iPhone, a puppy, the Beanie Babies collection and "a thing that can turn something into anything else at any time."

That's my kind of girl, I thought. I want everything I can get, all the time! And, if it's free, I'll take a new grill, a puppy, and anything "that can turn something into anything else at any time," especially if the "anything else" involves money.

And I don't want to have to share it.

In the event that you're feeling charged by this holiday season and your inner spoiled brat is running riot, I urge you to remember this: You are not seven years old. Whatever you buy while under the influence of the holidays, you will eventually have to pay for.

Yes, I understand that you want to make up for past holidays, when you had little or the fact that you're unhappy with your partner, or you feel unattractive and lonely–my favorites–but buying a bunch of "stuff" is *not the solution!*

Get to a DA meeting, call a friend and ask your Higher Power for help. Put all purchases on hold for twenty-four hours, and do not succumb to the voice that says you'll feel better if you overspend. Unless you plan on hosting a telethon to reimburse yourself, you will not feel better if you overspend. You're not planning a telethon, are you? I didn't think so.

Only hugs and lots of love for you today, my sweet little debtor.

It's Not About The Money:

I won't make choices today that will cost me more later.

December 18

BIRTHDAY MARY

Today is Mary Todd Lincoln's birthday, and while ol' Honest Abe's wife was vivacious and interesting, she was also known to be quite the spendthrift.

The Imelda Marcos of her time, Mrs. Lincoln had her own version of emancipation, and it included buying gloves, ball gowns, cashmere, and diamonds. She repeatedly made trips to New York and Philadelphia to order damask, wallpaper, carpets, and curtain materials, most of which came from Europe. In 1864, a Washington merchant sent a bill for three hundred pairs of gloves ordered over a period of four months. She paid three thousand dollars for a pair of earrings and a brooch, and five thousand dollars for a shawl. In 1864!

One historian said that Mary Todd's spending was like a drug for her tortured nerves. Supposedly, Mary Todd got caught up in buying orgies, and she hoarded her belongings in trunks and boxes everywhere. The charge accounts for these items amounted to appalling sums. She also bought things she could never use, and definitely couldn't afford. Apparently the stress from death threats against her husband, war, and succession was too much for Miss Mary, so she sought relief in overspending. Eventually her debting, along with other issues, led her to an asylum.

There have been times when I've dealt with pain by overspending. The problem is, when you're a debtor, there are never enough clothes, shoes, or diamonds to make you feel content.

I'm not going to get all negative about Miss Mary. It is her birthday, after all, and she didn't have the benefit of DA. But if she did, I have no doubt she'd have been a dedicated member. At the very least, she'd have been one of the better-dressed women in the room.

It's Not About The Money:

I don't need to overspend to feel emancipated.

December 19

ACTS OF FAITH

"A savings plan is an act of self-love," I heard the DA speaker say. I smiled and nodded politely. It made sense, in the way that taking vitamins and getting enough sleep does, but that was it. Having a savings plan was probably prudent, but an act of self-love? That was a stretch.

I never considered a savings plan because I rarely thought about my future. Before I found DA, life was a struggle, something to get through. I didn't have time to plan. The present was spent moving from one financial crisis to another, trying to stay on top of the endless debts I had accrued and paying the minimum on my credit cards. In the back of my mind was the unexpressed thought, Screw the future! I'm here now. I'll take what I can get. Therefore, my bank account revolved around a balance of zero, even when I was making serious dough.

Of course, I made general plans for the future, but I didn't believe my dreams would materialize. When and if I completed a goal, or something fantastic occurred, I diminished it. Anything fortuitous that happened was a coincidence, or worse, a setup by God, who was waiting to give me a swift kick in the bum. And as we all know, flipping the bird at the Higher Power that has granted amazing things to you is not the ideal way to continue receiving.

It took a long time before I could plan for my future. I started small with baby steps, pennies, and dimes in a jar, a dollar here and there in my savings account. Humbling, but I did it.

Today, I get a thrill out of saving. It's fun to see my accounts grow. It's an act of faith. Saving is not only self-love, it's future love. As in, I love myself enough to hope for a future. A future where there might be something amazing waiting for me.

It's Not About The Money:

I love saving, and saving loves me.

December 20

SPIRITS

When I was eight, I wanted a new skateboard, but my mom couldn't afford to buy me one. So, I took a tin can, wrote the words CHRISTMAS DONATIONS on it, and went door to door, singing Christmas carols.

When my mom discovered what I'd done, she demanded I return the money. "We're not a charity. You give that money back!"

"But, Mom, they said I had a good voice!" I protested.

"Give it back. Besides, you can't sing Christmas carols in July!"

I stormed out the front door, crying. As I returned the money to the neighbors, I made a decision to never be broke again.

I was still determined to get a skateboard, so the next night, I organized a séance with friends to conjure up some cash. We danced in a circle around a stack of Monopoly money at the stroke of midnight, chanting, "The door is open, the circle unbroken, come to us tonight, spirit of prosperity and light."

Nothing happened, but when my mom found out she promptly took me to church. "You're headed down a dark path," she said as she dropped me off. There are some who might say I was a money-grubbing, opportunistic kid who was headed for trouble, but I'd like to think I was an entrepreneur who was too young to get a job and not smart enough to build a computer.

I'm not completely over my debting and money issues, or the discomfort some of my schemes to earn money have caused me. I still struggle with compulsive spending, workaholism, and worry about not having enough. If there's one lesson I've learned in DA, it's this: The wanting for more never ends.

When I start obsessing about what I want and how I'm going to get it, I know I'm on the path to insolvency. If I don't connect with God and keep going to meetings, it's a short jaunt from desire to gyrating and chanting around a bonfire, conjuring up spirits. Or to shaking down my neighbors with some dubious holiday money-making scheme.

It's Not About The Money:

No conjuring today. God is in charge of all my needs.

December 21

SUNNY SIDE UP

Holy, sunshine, Batman! It's Look On the Bright Side Day!

Today, looking on the bright side may be a bit difficult, as it is winter solstice and the shortest day of the year. No matter where you live, December days tend to be cloudy, and it's always a shock to the system when you leave work for the first time and it's pitch-dark outside. Yes, the first day of winter is always a bit traumatic. In spite of this heavy winter solstice talk, I have faith that you will succeed at being optimistic.

Look on the Bright Side Day calls for us to interpret whatever we're going through as being for the best, even if it doesn't appear that way.

Many of the most difficult times in my life have brought me positive outcomes and powerful lessons. And I'll admit, moany of those lessons weren't apparent to me until decades later and the funny thing is, I was in a place in my life when the problem didn't matter anymore. Isn't life funny? Or, as Alanis Morissette vehemently yet incorrectly claimed, isn't it ironic?

So, if yesterday was horrible, and even if today hasn't been so sunny, try looking on the positive side. Even if it's five o'clock in the evening and it's pitch-black outside, try giving the day it another go. Decide to start your day over and begin by looking on the bright side. C'mon, Sunshine, give it a try!

It's Not About The Money:

You can look on the bright side anytime you want to.

December 22

HOMELESS HOLIDAY

It was Christmas Eve and I was new to DA. I'd just left my low-wage retail job and taken a nap in my borrowed truck before changing my clothes and heading off to my waitressing job.

While this might seem heartbreaking and sad–I can only hope–a part of me felt superior about having to work so hard. I used to get a bizarre satisfaction from working during the holidays. Perhaps it's because I'm a martyr of epic proportions, but a great deal of my life I felt sorry for myself, because I worked so much.

I felt sorry for myself, so I did things that perpetuated the cycle of self-fulfilling disappointment. And there's nothing more disappointing than being homeless on a holiday. When I realized my life was definitely dramatic, but not in the way I wanted it to be, I had to make changes, starting with identifying attitudes and choices that contributed to the "poor me" complex. The cycle of disappointment was familiar and comfortable, but it's kind of a silly way to go about life. I wanted to change, I just didn't know how to.

Recovery showed me how me to stop playing the martyr. Well, it didn't show me, I had to figure that out myself, but over time I stopped it. Sure, it's dramatic to be homeless, but there's nothing theatrical about living it.

It's Not About The Money:

Things might not be great, but I don't have to feel sorry for myself.

December 23

GIFTS

It used to be that when I started earning a healthy salary or landed a hefty bonus, I'd go nuts and spend everything all at once. If it was during the holidays, I'd spend it all on gifts for my friends and family.

Did I do it because I remembered so distinctly all the times I wasn't able to afford gifts? Was I trying to make up for times when things were bad? Was I just spitting into the poverty wind, laughing in the face of my penniless past? Hey, take that, brokeness! I'm rollin' in the Benjamins now, pal, and I'm gonna make up for what I missed out on.

Overspending in the way that I did was unwise, mainly because:

1. I had no idea what a poverty wind was, and
2. brokeness can't feel my wrath, nor does it care what I think. It's also not a real word.

There were times when it felt good to finally be able to compensate for the lean times, but recovery in DA taught me how to be generous without going overboard. If I'm using gifts or money or things to prove my love, or to look good in the eyes of others, I'm on the road to insolvency. Giving until it hurts and overspending will ultimately lead me back into debt.

It's perfectly fine to give charitably whenever I can, but I don't need to give too much to make up for the losses I experienced in the past. It never serves me to rub my good fortune in the face of brokenness or spit into the poverty wind. Whatever a poverty wind is.

It's Not About The Money:

God, please help me remember I don't have to give 'til it hurts.

December 24

CORRECT

I used to argue a lot with my family. Some of it was about important things like politics, but mainly it was small stuff, like lyrics to old Michael Jackson songs or the names of '90s TV sitcom characters.

Some of my family members–namely, me–had a difficult time letting things go when they were right. I would lie in wait until the next time a particularly "important" subject came up again and I'd nonchalantly throw out, "By the way, just so you know, I was right about that song."

I wasn't consciously trying to be obnoxious; I just wanted people to know the "correct" answer. I thought it was my duty to let the people I loved know when they were wrong. Of course, when I was wrong about something, I'd let the subject go. What I didn't realize was that no one else cared who was right. They had completely forgotten about it.

Recovery has taught me I'm not doing the people I love any favors by correcting them or keeping track of when they're wrong. Recovery has also shown me that most people don't care how often I'm right. I'll never win enough "points" to earn love or happiness.

No one's keeping score.

I have to remind myself of that often, because this holiday season I'll inevitably see the relative to whom I'll feel the need to say, "Hey, remember last Christmas when we were arguing about the lyrics to that Van Halen song 'Jump'? Well, you were right. David Lee Roth is saying 'I got my back against the record machine,' not 'I got my rack against the wrecking machine.' I stand corrected."

Nope, I won't say it. I'll let it go. Unless that relative brings it up first.

It's Not About The Money:
My need to be right often makes me wrong.

December 25

MERRY, MERRY

I recall one Christmas when a family member of mine changed the date and location of our dinner, but didn't tell me until Christmas Eve we wouldn't be celebrating Christmas until the day after Christmas.

"Who the heck celebrates Christmas the day after Christmas?" I screamed at her over the phone.

This family member will go to her grave denying it happened that way. Yes, I'm a debtor, and yes, I tend to be a dramatic, but I'm not exaggerating when I say I was devastated. The change of plans ruined me. I didn't know where I'd go for Christmas, now that my family was celebrating the day after The Day.

I agonized over it and it was, well, pretty rough. I felt abandoned and was in a lot of self-pity, as might be expected. However, as the day went on, I began to realize this was a common pattern with my family, and those last-minute changes have always created a ton of anxiety for me. I guess I'm just weird in that way.

Anyway, it occurred to me close to the end of Christmas day that I didn't have to be miserable. I remembered I had some pretty cool friends in recovery I could go visit and share the rest of the holiday with.

Thankfully, I can count on my friends in recovery to celebrate a holiday on the day it was meant to be celebrated. Of course, they'd probably show up late but they'd never pretend it's a Tuesday when it's a Saturday.

It's Not About The Money:

I'm going to have a wonderful holiday, even if I have to change plans!

December 26

RE-GIFTING

Before I found DA, I used to take whatever came my way, especially when it came to gifts. If someone gave me a present, I told myself I should learn to like it, even if I didn't love it or could tell it was a re-gift. I thought it would be uncouth or selfish not to pretend I loved anything that was given to me.

In DA, I learned it's okay to want what I want. I don't have to like something because it's free (like those monochromatic carbohydrate breakfasts they serve at commuter hotels), or because my cousin got it online for a discount, or because it came in a package of four. I especially don't have to like something because someone else tells me I should like it, or because it's supposed to be good for me.

I might not get what I really want, but by golly, at least now I know what I want. Sometimes I'll even ask for it ahead of time, as in, "This year, for my birthday, I'd love to go out to dinner with you," or "For Christmas, I'd appreciate a gift card to Home Depot" (that'll be the day, but you get the idea). I'm learning to know what I want and ask for it. I've stopped pretending to love things I can't stand, like re-gifts.

I've also come up with a way to deal with people who are bad at re-gifting. When I get an obvious re-gift, I say thank you and write his or her name on the present. That way I know exactly what to give that person next Christmas.

Not really. I'm way too polite to do something that conspicuous.

It's Not About The Money:

I may not get what I want, but now I know how to ask for it.

December 27

HARMS

"There's someone missing on your amends list," my DA sponsor said when I finished reading my Step #8.

"Who?" I thought I'd been pretty thorough.

"You," he replied.

That's so 1990. I'm not making amends to myself, I thought.

"We harm ourselves when we debt in any way, like self-debting or denying your gifts. It's impossible to value others when you don't value yourself," he said.

Great, now I'll have to find a new sponsor, I thought, smiling.

"It takes courage to forgive yourself. It's not selfish; it's generous. You open yourself up, and it's risky. But forgiving yourself makes it easier to forgive others."

I can't really argue with that one.

"When you begin to take care of yourself, you stop demanding that others do it for you. This program is all about self-love."

Oh, brother! I thought I'd done an internal eye roll, but it must've shown on my face.

"Stop with the eye rolling and start writing down the ways you've harmed yourself. All I ask is that you be willing."

I wasn't. It took a year before I was able to make amends and actively forgive myself. One full year.

Much of our DA recovery is making restitution for the messes we've made and a lot of it has to do with other people. But I finally began to see that self-forgiveness is essential to freedom from fear and obsession.

"Self-love" however, is not a term I toss around lightly–mainly because it bugs the crap out of me–but I can say "self-forgiveness," because I can't really forgive others if I can't forgive myself.

Forgiving myself is the most difficult thing I've ever done. But I'm glad I did it because it's led to you-know-what. See? I didn't even have to use term "self-love" to get my point across.

It's Not About The Money:

All I need is love. Thanks, God.

December 28

BIG GIRL

I once heard someone say that recovery for debtors is about getting one's "inner adult" out of the trunk and into the driver's seat.

Is that true? Have I locked my Big Girl Self in the trunk? I started to worry. My trunk is cramped and very disorganized. It contains a leather dress I was going to have dry-cleaned in 2009, Christmas mugs I forgot to give away last year, a soggy pair of boxing gloves, a bike pump, biking shoes, a military-size American flag, a space heater, and a box of makeup I bought but never used.

I started to obsess about the possible punishment for locking an adult in a trunk, which I think should carry a kidnapping charge. But as I've learned in recovery, obsession is simply another way to keep myself from enjoying life. It's trying to control things, and it takes me away from what I'm doing right now.

Instead of obsessing about my tendency to obsess, I decided to start my morning meditations with a visual of myself removing my inner adult out of the trunk. I take her by the hand, lead her to the driver's side of the car and say, "There's the wheel, Big Girl. You get to drive."

For giggles, sometimes I'll say, "Hit it, Thelma!" to my Big Girl self, just like in the movie *Thelma and Louise,* minus the part where Thelma drives them into the Grand Canyon. In my visualization, we drive to a swanky hotel in South Beach, where a group of gorgeous cabana boys greet us with palm leaves and pina coladas.

It's easier now to allow my Big Girl Self to take over and make the decisions. Especially because, once I've clothed and fed her, I've discovered she's a blast to hang out with!

It's Not About The Money:

I'm going to allow the Big Girl to drive today!

December 29

TWISTED

I didn't grow up in an orphanage like Little Orphan Annie, but my childhood was rough, especially when it came to money. I recall my Dad sitting me down one day.

"Daughter," he said, "it's time for you to get a job."

"But I'm in second grade, Dad," I cried.

"True, but textile mills hire kids your age. They're called mule scavengers, and they crawl under the machines with a brush to pick up dirt and loose cotton."

"They outlawed that practice in 1934," I countered. "Besides, it's dangerous. If I got to close to a machine, I could lose my scalp."

"Well, start thinking about getting a job. Soon enough you'll be paying rent, and you'll need to know the value of a dollar," he said as he handed me a broom.

Okay, I'm embellishing, as I have a tendency to do. I didn't get my first job until I was fourteen, but I remember being pissed because I had to work for everything, including my clothes and my car, simply because my dad wanted me to graduate summa cum laude from the school of hard knocks.

"Life isn't fair," he'd say every so often. "You may as well learn that now."

I carried a lot of anger and resentment about that, until I started working the steps in DA and saw that holding on to that resentment was affecting my peace of mind. The past was over. It was one hundred percent up to me to release it and decide what kind of future I wanted. I could continue to be angry, or I could take what I'd learned–albeit harshly–and use it to make life better.

I choose each day how I'll be, no matter what happened "back then." Living fully today means turning my will and my life over to God. I learned a lot from my tough-love father, and I can say to this day I've always known the value of a dollar. I will admit, however, I never have been and never will be big on sweeping floors. That's what I hire the orphans to do.

It's Not About The Money:

The sun can come out today. I'll let God handle tomorrow.

December 30

PLANS

Today is the eve before the eve when we human beings start making plans, which lead to goals, and then to New Year's resolutions. At the risk of seeming like a wet blanket, I'd like to recommend we lower the expectations a smidgen this year.

There's something to be said for having low, to no expectations, when it comes to money and possessions. I'll also note that people who have little to no expectations are happier, calmer, and have a lot of friends, even if they are imaginary. I also offer up the fact that people with low standards are invited to more parties than those of us with exceptionally high standards. Why? Because they rarely say "no," and unlike those of us who need to read the guest list and confirm the caterers before we commit to going, they're just happy to be invited.

You can never be let down when you expect nothing.

As for myself, I'm giving serious consideration to this year's resolutions. Despite my earnest attempts at making resolutions, e.g. I'm gonna lose ten pounds or I'm going to be a better person, I've never lost those pounds and I'm not a better person. It's not for lack of trying; I wrote my resolutions down and spent time visualizing myself thinner and nicer. But I came to the realization that not only was I vague about my resolutions and didn't set time frames to achieve them, I was mostly making just another list of things to beat myself up about when I failed to achieve them.

I've decided that this year I'm throwing off the shackles of *always trying to turn myself into someone I'm not*. I'm in acceptance of who I am. For today. I can always change my mind tomorrow. I don't think I will. I just know that today I'm keeping my standards low. Lower. Lower than they've ever been.

It's Not About The Money:

Today I'm going to keep those expectations in check.

December 31

ACTUALLY

New Year's Eve can be more stressful than fun for debtors like me, because we have ideas about how things *should* go. As if that's not enough, many of us spend the day watching the romantic classic, *Love Actually*.

One of the stories features Jamie (Colin Firth), a writer who, after his girlfriend cheats on him, runs off to a French chateau to write a novel – on a typewriter next to a pond, no less. Jamie's gorgeous Portuguese housekeeper, Aurélia, speaks no English, and although they can't say a single word to each other, soon they're both smitten, each talking out loud about their feelings of love, knowing the other won't understand.

When Aurélia gives Jamie a ride to the airport –he's off to London for Christmas without his novel – it was lost when Aurélia let it blow into the pond, and she gives him a goodbye kiss, Jamie realizes he's in love with her. He returns to France, and shows up on Aurélia's father's door step, yelling at him in horrible Portuguese. He's like, "I'm here to ask your foot for my daughter in marriage!" At first the father's confused, because he thinks Jamie's proposing to his other, unattractive daughter, but they figure it out in time to get to the restaurant before Aurélia's shift ends.

When Jamie and the local villagers (who, oddly only speak Portuguese) arrive at the restaurant, Jamie asks Aurélia to marry him. She responds with a gleeful, "yes," because she's learned English! The fact that they've not spent one day speaking the same language is of no concern. The fact that it'll be years before they'll ever have a complete conversation is also of no concern.

The point is, love, actually. They've found the courage to say "I love you," so life's difficulties are over. They get to go straight to happily-ever-after. Which really *is* the way life should be for everyone, shouldn't it?

Easy to see why New Year's Eve might be a little anxiety-provoking, right?

So, this year, I've decided to say the following: "Hey, New Year's Eve, you don't have the power to ruin my life with your outlandish expectations. While I appreciate and even love you, actually, you're really just another day.

It's not about the money:

With God's help, my expectations will be managable today.

Misti B. writes humorous books about life in recovery, mainly because no one else is writing them–at least from a witty point of view. Her pre-recovery writing included a successful career in the entertainment industry, having written and directed a feature film, numerous stage plays, screenplays and live events for TV. These experiences, combined with her highly dysfunctional upbringing provide the fodder for her humorous, yet inspiring recovery stories. Her first book is entitled, "If You Leave Me, Can I Come With You? Daily Meditations for Codependents With a Sense of Humor."

You can learn more about Misti by visiting www.MistiBWrites.com or follow her on Twitter: @MistiBWrites.

Made in the USA
Charleston, SC
19 February 2015